Lecture Notes in Computer Science 3344

Commenced Publication in 1973
Founding and Former Series Editors:
Gerhard Goos, Juris Hartmanis, and Jan van Leeuwen

Jacques Malenfant   Bjarte M. Østvold (Eds.)

Object-Oriented Technology

ECOOP 2004 Workshop Reader

ECOOP 2004 Workshops
Oslo, Norway, June 14-18, 2004
Final Reports

 Springer

Volume Editors

Jacques Malenfant
LIP6, Université Pierre et Marie Curis and CNRS
8 rue du Capitaine Scott, 75015 Paris, France
E-mail: Jacques.Malenfant@lip6.fr

Bjarte M. Østvold
Norwegian Computing Center
PO Box 114 Blindern, 0314 Oslo, Norway
E-mail: bjarte@nr.no

Library of Congress Control Number: 2004117083

CR Subject Classification (1998): D.1-3, H.2, F.3, C.2, K.4, J.1

ISSN 0302-9743
ISBN 3-540-23988-X Springer Berlin Heidelberg New York

Springer is a part of Springer Science+Business Media

springeronline.com

© Springer-Verlag Berlin Heidelberg 2004
Printed in Germany

Typesetting: Camera-ready by author, data conversion by Scientific Publishing Services, Chennai, India
Printed on acid-free paper   SPIN: 11363484   06/3142   5 4 3 2 1 0

Preface

This year, for the eighth time, the European Conference on Object-Oriented Programming (ECOOP) series, in cooperation with Springer, is glad to offer the object-oriented research community the ECOOP 2004 Workshop Reader, a compendium of workshop reports pertaining to the ECOOP 2004 conference, held in Oslo from June 15 to 19, 2004.

ECOOP 2004 hosted 19 high-quality workshops covering a large spectrum of hot research topics. These workshops were chosen through a tight peer review process following a specific call for proposals ending on November 30, 2003. We are very grateful to the members of the Workshop Selection Committee for their careful reviews and hard work to put together the excellent workshop program. We also want to thank all submitters, accepted or not, to whom the workshop program equally owes its quality. This selection process was then followed by a selection of workshop participants, done by each team of organizers based on an open call for position papers. This participant selection process ensured that we gathered the most active researchers in each workshop research area, and therefore a fruitful working meeting.

Following the tradition of the ECOOP Workshop Reader, we strove for high-quality, value-adding and open-ended workshop reports. The result, as you can judge from the following pages, is a thought-provoking snapshot of the current research in object-orientation, full of pointers for further exploration of the covered topics. We want to thank our workshop organizers who, despite the additional burden, did a great job in putting together these reports.

Each report you will find in this volume provides you with a starting point to understand and explore the currently debated issues in each area of concern. To achieve this, after summarizing the workshop goals, each report offers a critical summary of the participants' position papers as well as a transcript of the actual debates aroused by the talks. You will also find the full list of participants, with contact information, as well as the list of contributed position papers. Several of the reports also add a list of relevant publications and Web sites, including the workshop home page, where you will usually find the contributed position papers themselves as well as other material that goes into each covered topic more closely.

Finally, as editors, we harmonized the report titles to mention only the topics of the workshops and to avoid repeated references to ECOOP 2004. However, each workshop report should be referenced as "Report from the ECOOP 2004 Workshop on ..." where you fill in the blanks with the workshop title.

September 2004

Jacques Malenfant
Bjarte M. Østvold

Organization

ECOOP 2004 was organized by the University of Oslo, the Norwegian Computing Center and Sintef, under the auspices of AITO (Association Internationale pour les Technologie Objets) in cooperation with ACM/SIGPLAN. The proceedings of the conference itself were published as LNCS volume 3086.

Workshop Organization

Workshop co-chairs: Jacques Malenfant (LIP6, Univ. P. et M. Curie and CNRS)
Bjarte M. Østvold (Norwegian Computing Center)

Workshop Selection Committee

Bente Anda	Simula Research Laboratory
Martine Devos	OOPSLA 2003 Workshop Chair
	Avayalabs, Avaya Inc.
Jacques Malenfant	ECOOP 2004 Workshop Co-chair
	LIP6, Univ. P. et M. Curie and CNRS
Bjarte M. Østvold	ECOOP 2004 Workshop Co-chair
	Norwegian Computing Center
Jean-François Perrot	LIP6, Univ. P. et M. Curie and CNRS

Sponsoring Institutions

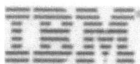  

Table of Contents

Object Orientation and Web Services*

Christian Zirpins[1], Giacomo Piccinelli[2], Winfried Lamersdorf[1],
and Anthony Finkelstein[2]

[1] Department of Computer Science, University of Hamburg, Germany
{Zirpins, Lamersdorf}@informatik.uni-hamburg.de
[2] Department of Computer Science, University College London, United Kingdom
{A.Finkelstein, G.Piccinelli}@cs.ucl.ac.uk

Abstract. The annual European workshop on Object Orientation and
Web Services focusses challenges and potentials of service-oriented computing in relation to object-oriented technologies and methodologies. In
particular it brings together the academic and the industrial perspective
on Web Services. This year's issue was characterised by the competency
and motivation of the participants, both workshop activists who presented their specific results as well as organisers and invited speaker,
who contributed their broad experience. This report outlines the contributions and discussions of the event, as well as the conclusions reached
by the participants.

1 Structure of the Workshop

The second annual European workshop on Object Orientation and Web Services
(EOOWS'04) brought together researchers and practitioners interested in the
relation of service-oriented- and object-oriented computing paradigms (section
2). With this year's event, EOOWS entered its second round since initiation at
ECOOP 2003 in Darmstadt and proved its role as a constant workshop series.
The workshop was lead by Giacomo Piccinelli and Winfried Lamersdorf, who
compiled an attractive mix that included general perspectives of an invited talk,
a brought variety of specific contributions and lively discussions spanning the
whole event. Around fifteen people where participating, including presenting and
non-presenting attendees.

Initially, the invited talk added an interdisciplinary perspective to the workshop and extended the discussions beyond usual Web Service scenarios. The
talk was given by Daragh Byrne from the Edinburgh Parallel Computing Center (EPCC) [1]. Daragh Byrne works at EPCC as an Applications Consultant.
At the time of this writing, he is engaged in the OGSA-DAI project, which involves generalizing data access for the Grid. The talk provided an architectural
blueprint of Grid systems with special focus on the Open Grid Service Architec-

---

* The title of this report should be referenced as "Report from the ECOOP 2004
Workshop on Object Orientation and Web Services".

J. Malenfant and B.M. Østvold (Eds.): ECOOP 2004, LNCS 3344, pp. 1–9, 2004.

ture [2, 3] of the Global Grid Forum [4]. In particular, it detailed the relationship and interplay of Grid- and Web Service technologies.

Presentations of individual contributions made up the main part of the workshop. From the response to the call for papers, nine papers where selected for presentation. The contributions ranged from genuine and upcoming research to industrial experience (section 3). Presentations where given in relaxed 20 minute intervals and where always followed by intense discussion that resulted in further insights for listeners as well as contributors and lead to quite some network building. The workshop was concluded by a plenary discussion (section 4).

2   Themes and Objectives

Web Services are evolving beyond their SOAP, WSDL, and UDDI roots toward being able to solve significant real-world integration problems. Developers of Web Services systems are currently working on new generations of systems that incorporate security, transactions, orchestration and choreography, grid computing capabilities, business documents and processes, and simplified integration with existing middleware systems. Current economic issues continue to force consolidation and reduction in enterprise computing resources, which is resulting in developers discovering that Web Services can provide the foundation engineering and realisation of complex computing systems.

The question of how Web Services could and should change system and solution development is very much open. Are Web Services just about standards, or do they imply a new conceptual framework for engineering and development? Similarly open is the question of how requirements coming from system and solution development could and should make Web Services evolve. In particular, methodologies as well as technologies based on the object-oriented conceptual framework are an established reality. How do Web Services and object-orientation relate? How can Web Services leverage the experience built into current object-oriented practices?

The overall theme of the workshop is the relation between Web Services and object orientation. Such relation can be explored from different perspectives, ranging from system modelling and engineering to system development, management, maintenance, and evolution. Aspects of particular interest are the modularisation of a system into components and the (possibly cross-domain) composition and orchestration of different modules. Components and composition are closely connected with the issue of reuse, and an important thread of discussion within the workshop will address the way in which Web Services impact reuse.

The objective of the workshop is twofold: assessing the current work on Web Services, and discussing lines of development and possible cooperation. Current work includes research activities as well as practical experiences. The assessment covers an analysis of driving factors and a retrospective on lessons learned. The identification and prioritisation of new lines of research and activity is a key outcome of the workshop. In particular, the intention is to foster future cooperation among the participants.

3   Contributions

The workshop contributions can be classified into four categories. Three contributions revolve around software development for and with Web ServicesAnother two contributions where related to interaction processes for the composition of W eb Services. The topic of W eb Service m anagem entwith emphasis on context awareness and autonomy was the main line of two contributions. Finally, two contributions where concerned about architectural patterns and general modelling of W eb Service based system s In the rest of this section, the categories and contributions will be outlined.

3.1   Software Development of and with Web Services

Web Services border on internal software systems at two points. First, the functionality of a Web Service has to be realised by an internal software system. Second, the functionality of a Web Service is to be used by an internal software system. The relation to object-orientation is obvious in the case that these software systems are designed and/or implemented in an object-oriented way. There where workshop contributions for each of these points.

The first contribution came from G uadalupe O rtizfrom the Quercus Software Engineering Group, University of Extremadura, Spain. During presentation of her work on "D ecoupling N on-FunctionalP roperties in W eb Services: An A spect-O riented Approach", she stressed the point that Web Service technologies offer a new and successful way for interoperability among web applications. However, current approaches do not propose an acceptable method to decouple non-functional properties from Web Service implementations, having a large amount of code scattered and tangled all over the application, thus raising problems at design. implementation, maintenance and evolution. She argued that Aspect-oriented techniques allow these properties to be easily modularised and reused. Furthermore, she showed how information about properties can be added in the WSDL file, in order to keep clients informed about the characteristics of the service they are going to use.

A contribution concerning the second aspect came from Takashi K oshida from the Department of Information Engineering, Matsue National College of Technology, Japan. He presented an "Autom ated D ynam ic Invocation System for W eb Service w ith a U ser-defined D ata Type". In particular, he claimed that this system can automatically discover the WSDL file describing a Web Service from a UDDI registry. After analysing the WSDL file, the system extracts and automatically sets up the parameters needed for dynamic invocation. Furthermore, the system dynamically generates and compiles the Java code for a user-defined data type. Finally, he presented experimental results and demonstrated the validity of this system by invoking published Web Services as practical examples.

Finally, Fabien Baligandand Valrie M onfortfrom IBM , MDTVision, France contributed their work on "A pragmatic Use of Contracts and Aspects to gain in Adaptability and Reusability"as an industrial paper that offers a practical perspective on the integration of software application systems based on Web Services. They argue that buying and selling of company departments involves huge changes in their information systems (IS). Often, the technical solution to connect distant IS is based on Web Services. This requires to model organisational structures and business processes, which are used and shared to deploy service-oriented infrastructure and Web Services. However, practice shows that distant IS are supported by different and heterogeneous technical infrastructures. The authors claim experience with SOA and Web Services for industrial projects in heterogeneous contexts. They encountered different problems like the lack of methodology to develop Web Services w.r.t. new emerging standards. Faced with industrial realities, they defined such a methodology for Enterprise Application Integration (EAI) and SOA. Moreover, they propose solutions to lacks of new WS-I standards as Policies and Meta data. They based their technical solution on contracts and aspects to gain in flexibility and reusability.

3.2   Interaction Processes for Web Service Composition

Interactions are significant for Web Service concepts. The interaction between different roles of the Web Service Model is eminent from the basic invocation of a single operation up to the choreography of a complex composite e-Service. In the later case, interactions form the building blocks for collaboration procedures between organisations [5]. Such interaction processes that represent an e-Service are complemented by meta interaction processes that implement a methodology leading to the enactment of e-Services. These complementary perspectives where each represented by one workshop contribution.

Christian Zirpins from the Distributed Systems and Information Systems Group (VSIS) at Hamburg University, Germany based his contribution about "Service Cooperation Patterns and their Customised Coordination"in the first perspective. He argued that service-oriented computing is meant to support loose relationships between organisations. Such relationships constitute cooperation procedures that translates to interaction processes via Web Services. Service composition deals with the specification and automated enforcement of such interaction processes and its predominant approach is orchestration, where a workflow management system (WFMS) is pro-actively coordinating the interaction activities. In most cases, the orchestration process is regarded as an implicit result of cooperation logic (actually, they are often the same) but the reverse impact of operational coordination on cooperation logic are often neglected. Based on that, he claimed that the choice of coordination alternatives impacts the quality of service and has to be customised to actual service cases and their individual participants. He proposed a potential solution approach that revolves around service cooperation patternsTherein, paradigms of patterns/idioms that are well known from object-oriented design/development are applied to cooperation procedures and orchestration processes. This approach allows studying a) reusable cooperation patterns typical for service relation-ships and b) for each pattern a range of possible coordination idioms. Finally, he sketched a technique that is intended to refine a composition process based on an analysis of its co-operation patternsand the application of suitable coordination idiom sselected by rules in terms of the service context.

The second perspective is taken by M uham m ad F . K alem from the Technical University Hamburg, Germany who was not present at the workshop. In his contribution about "Interactions for C om position as a M eans for Enacting Robust C om posite Services", he focuses on the importance of the composite service enactment process for robust composite services. He discusses why this focus is necessary, and describes a methodology currently being developed which allows autonomous service providers to interact with each other for composite service enactment.

3.3 Management of and with Web Services

One of the current trends in Web Service research and – in particularly – in practice is the internal and cross-organisational operations management of platforms for atomic and composite Web Services [6]. In particular, Web Services allow for Service Level Management (SLM) of metrics that are close to the application domain (e.g. control of order throughput). Complementary, Web Service technology can act as an instrument for the management of any heterogeneous systems and build a basis for the development of new management paradigms. Two of the workshop contributions where revolving around this topics.

Concerning SLM, C lem ens K erer from the Distributed Systems Group, Information Systems Institute, Vienna University of Technology, Austria presented his work on "Presence-Aware Infrastructure using W eb services and RF ID technobgies". He explained that Web services have the potential to serve as a key enabling technology for environments facilitating collaborative scenarios. His group analysed a same room/same time collaborative scenario, a program committee (PC) meeting. They focus on design and implementation of a service-oriented approach for PC meetings. Their proposed solution includes various Web services for the actual support of the work, Web applications combining those services, and presence-aware technology, in this case RFID (Radio Frequency Identification) tags. The essence of this contribution was to show how a presence-aware infrastructure comprising Web services and RFID technology can be built and how they provide support for the envisaged scenario.

In contrast, Am ir Zeid from the Department of Computer Science at the American University in Cairo, Egypt presented his efforts "Towards A utonom ic W eb Services", that presents management with Web Services. He explained autonomic computing that was introduced with the promise of achieving self management; however, most of the current work does not address the problem of designing autonomic computing systems so that computing systems can be evolved towards self-management paradigm. Regarding this problem, his research ties autonomic computing with Web services to achieve a new approach, which is autonomic Web services, where each entity is a Web service behaving autonomically. Adopting Web services supports the dynamic and seamless integration among computational units. He claimed that this research aims at proving that: with autonomic Web services, computing systems will be able to manage themselves as well as their relationships with each other. To achieve this objective, the research proposes a system that implements the concept of autonomic Web services; a proof-of-concept prototype of this system is currently under development and testing.

3.4   Modelling and Patterns of Web Service-Based Systems

The benefit of modelling in the development cycle of software systems is commonly agreed and Web Service-based systems are no exception to this rule. Many powerful modelling techniques emerged from the field of object-oriented development. Their application to Web Services is promising but has to be verified and customised in order to meet disparities of the paradigms. One of the most prominent approaches is the Unified Modelling Language (UML) [7] that provides fundamental modelling capabilities. A family of more specific approach revolves around capturing mature knowledge in common design- or implementation patterns [8, 9] that can be reused by system engineers as proven solutions for building new systems. The mapping of these approaches to Web Services was the main line of the two concluding workshop contributions.

Concerning the utilisation of UML for Web Service modelling, Raœk Amir from the Department of Computer Science at the American University in Cairo, Egypt presented his contribution about a "UML Proœle for Service Oriented Architectures based on W3C Web Service Architectures." He pointed out again that Service Oriented Computing (SOC) is the new emerging paradigm for Distributed computing and e-business processing that is changing the way software applications are designed, architected, delivered and consumed. Services are autonomous platform-independent computational elements that can be described, published, discovered, orchestrated and programmed using standard protocols for the purpose of building agile networks of collaborating business applications distributed within and across organizational boundaries. He came to the conclusion that engineering and modelling service-oriented architectures need extensions to existing modelling techniques and methodologies. Subsequently, he propose a UML profile for service-oriented architectures.

As an example for service-oriented design patterns, Simon Martin from the Space Science and Technology Department, Rutherford Appleton Laboratory, UK presented "The Service Cache Pattern and Grid Services in the European Grid of Solar Observations (EGSO)." He introduced the EGSO project [10] that has developed a reusable messaging infrastructure for communication between Grid applications, whereby message-relay services transparently leverage directory, storage and logging services in order to provide enhanced functionality to consumer applications. He continued to describe the proposed Service Cache pattern, which has been applied to the engineering of these services. Finally he claimed that the main potential benefits derived from the application of this pattern include improved manageability and predictability of service delivery, and faster response times for consumers.

4 Main Lines of Discussion

The workshop closed with a plenary discussion. It mainly revolved around three topics. First, the invited talk gave reason to question the relationship between Web Services and Grids. Second, the number of contributions that combined aspect oriented techniques with Web Services promoted to fathom the potential of this constellation. Then, after addressing just a few facets of all new trends and standards, the discussion turned to the vast proliferation in the Web Service arena and raised general questions of rationale and expedience of this evolution. Finally, the thread returned to the foundation of it all and evaluated the basic Web Service standards after nearly half a decade since the emergence of WSDL and SOAP.

Web Services and Grids. Motivated by the talk of Daragh Byrne and his brought experience, an initial thread of discussion was about the relation of Web Services and the Grid. Especially the Open Grid Service Architecture (OGSA) [2] and Infrastructure (OGSI) where regarded. In fact, the situation is manifold: On the one hand, it is Web Service technology that facilitates many of the OGSA capabilities. Actually, OGSA builds on an extension of WSDL (GWSDL) that enables inheritance of port types and defines additional such port types for vital features like stable references, state maintenance and lifecycle management. That is, Grid Services are by far more sophisticated then traditional Web Services. On the other hand, Grid Services are intended for much finer grained entities then Web Services. That is, Grid Services are tailored to represent low-level resources while Web Service are normally positioned very close to application-level (business) objects. As a result, the technical relationship must not be confused with the usage of these entities (e.g. in a business-to-business interaction scenario): Web Services (if anything) are the choice for representing organizational endpoints for the cross-organizational interactions while Grid Services offer means to implement them beneath. This answers one of the main questions that emerged: could and should Web Services and Grid Services be integrated? The answer is no, because they reside on a different level of abstraction.

Web Services and AOP. A lively discussion revolved around the relation of Web Services and separation of concerns with aspect oriented programming [11]. The later is around in object-oriented development for quite a while and its application to Web Services should not come as a surprise. However, there are several alternatives for this combination. A first one is to utilize an aspect oriented language to implement Web Services and factor out service properties as aspects. This was the approach presented by Guadalupe Ortiz (see section 3.1) who could report on positive results with using AspectJ [12] for this purpose. More positive experiences in this direction where told by co-attendees from the

AOP workshop. One question here was about the dynamics of such approaches. Certainly, the possibility to use aspects for the static development of Web Services is already a benefit but it would be even better to allow the adaptation of service properties in running systems (e.g. to be used by service management systems). A different idea that was discussed revolved around separation of concerns in service composition. One possibility to do this is to code service composition logic using aspect oriented languages and prevent "hard" coding by factoring out composition aspects. Also aspect oriented concepts have been applied to workflow evolution [13]. As workflow is the underlying principle of many service composition approaches, it might be worthwhile to investigate in the separation of concerns within collaborative service processes.

Evolution of Web Service Standards. In the end of the session, the discussion shifted towards the evolution and future development of Web Services themselves. The ongoing process of organisations including diverse standard bodies (e.g. OASIS, W3C, WSI...) and companies (IBM, Microsoft...) flooding the Web Service scene with an ever-growing number of standard-like specifications was discussed very critically. This is by no means a coordinated process and the fact that numerous of such approaches overlap or contradict each other (sometimes completely) is a clear indicator for that. Not to mention that some of them are obviously not consistent or even complete, the vast majority of new Web Service specifications keeps quite aloof from implementation issues and just state properties of Web Services.

As regards the foundational and by now established core Web Service standards (i.e. WSDL, SOAP), there where little worries and subsequently no pressing need to evolve them was felt by the participants. On the contrary the mind within the plenum was more in the direction of applying and better understanding a stable core. We will return to this point when eventually more complex application scenarios and applications are reached and the Web Service core comes across its conceptual limits dating back to its middleware roots.

5   Conclusion

In the end, the workshop was perceived as a very positive experience by everybody. Thanks to competency and motivation of the participants, there was a concentrated and productive atmosphere in terms of both, interesting presentations of single contributions and fruitful discussions.

As a result, it can be concluded that Web Service research enters a more advanced but still very early stage that is yet far from the goals of business-to-business interaction aimed by the general service-oriented computing paradigm. In fact, the centre of gravity is still close to middleware and system integration. Meanwhile, the basic principles of this setting seem to be well understood and start to become settled knowledge that is represented, for example, as design patterns. On this basis, attention shifts to more sophisticated issues. Concepts that only very recently entered the object-oriented arena are already being aligned with and transferred to Web Services.

An example is the obvious trend towards separation of concerns in Web Services that can be witnessed for service implementation (utilisation of aspect oriented technology) and service models (e.g. aspects of service composition logic). While in the former case Web Services benefit from the experience of the object-oriented community, the later case shows that the relationship is not one-sided: the innovative power of the (still) young Web Service discipline pays back in the currency of new concepts for issues that are out of scope for others. This is one step further towards the final goal: dynamic and flexible mega-programming for open application-level interactions.

References

1. EPCC: Computing for business and science. http://www.epcc.ed.ac.uk/ accessed at:1.8.2004 (2004)
2. Foster, I., Kesselman, C., Nick, J., Tuecke, S.: The physiology of the grid: An open grid services architecture for distributed systems integration. Technical report, Open Grid Service Infrastructure WG, Global Grid Forum (2002)
3. The Globus Project: Towards open grid services architecture. Published on the Globus website: http://www.globus.org/ogsa/ accessed at:1.7.2004 (2004)
4. GGF: Global grid forum. http://www.ggf.org/ accessed at:15.8.2004 (2004)
5. Zirpins, C., Piccinelli, G.: Interaction-driven definition of e-business processes. In: Proc. 26th International Computer Software and Applications Conference (COMPSAC 2002), Prolonging Software Life: Development and Redevelopment, 26-29 August 2002, Oxford, England. IEEE Computer Society (2002) 738–740
6. Casati, F., Shan, E., Dayal, U., Shan, M.C.: Business-oriented management of web services. Commun. ACM **46** (2003) 55–60
7. OMG: Unified modeling language, v1.5. Technical Report formal/03-03-01, Object Management Group (Mar 2003)
8. Gamma, E., Helm, R., Johnson, R., Vlissides, J.: Design Patterns: Elements of Reusable Object-Oriented Software. Professional Computing Series. Addison-Wesley, USA (1994)
9. Buschmann, F., Meunier, R., Rohnert, H., Sommerlad, P.: Pattern-Oriented Software Architecture - A System of Patterns. Wiley and Sons Ltd. (1996)
10. EGSO: European grid of solar observations. http://www.mssl.ucl.ac.uk/grid/egso/ accessed at:15.8.2004 (2004)
11. Czarnecki, K., Eisenecker, U.W.: Generative Programming: Methods, Tools, and Applications. Addison-Wesley, Boston (2000)
12. Kiczales, G., Hilsdale, E., Hugunin, J., Kersten, M., Palm, J., Griswold, W.G.: An overview of aspectj. In Knudsen, J.L., ed.: Proc. ECOOP 2001 - Object-Oriented Programming, 15th European Conference, Budapest, Hungary. LNCS 2072. Springer (2001)
13. Bachmendo, B., Unland, R.: Aspect-based workflow evolution. In Rashid, A., ed.: Workshop on Aspect-Oriented Programming and Separation of Concerns (Lancaster). (2001)

Practical Problems of Programming in the Large (PPPL)

Ralf Reussner[1] and Wolfgang Weck[2]

[1] Software Engineering Group, University of Oldenburg, Germany
reussner@informatik.uni-oldenburg.de
[2] Independent Software-Architect, Zurich, Switzerland
wolfgang.weck@iaeth.ch

Abstract. Practical Problems of Programming in the Large are those issues that IT industry experiences today when working on large software systems or when integrating software within entire organisations. Relevant and current topics include Software Architecture, Component Software, Middleware platforms, Model-Driven-Architecture, but also Enterprise Application Integration, and others.

The workshop had practitioners and researchers concerned with technology transfer presenting their views on problems currently seen as most pressing in the above areas. In addition, the discussions were focussed by an "Example of a problem of programming in the large" concerning the step-wise re-engineering a complex legacy information system. Participants discussed how they would approach this exemplary problem, identified key challenges and compared their solution strategies.

In the afternoon, general problems of transferring academic research results into practice were discussed. The invited talk of Dave Thomas discussed current problematic trends in software engineering research, such as the concentration on general purpose programming languages for developing domain-specific enterprise software. Finally, we discussed specific needs for a software engineering education from industrial perspective.

1 Motivation

Programming in the Large means to handle software with huge amounts of objects, classes, and relations between them. A commonly known problem of this is that people loose track of a system's coarse grained structure. The result is often addressed as object sea.

Current state-of-the-art programming languages use object-orientation mostly for fine-grained structuring. How does this scale up with large systems? What is the practical experience? How does the software industry today experience Programming in the Large and what problems are encountered and should be addressed by the academic world?

J. Malenfant and B.M. Østvold (Eds.): ECOOP 2004, LNCS 3344, pp. 10–22, 2004.

Besides these questions, the workshop was motivated by the observation that academic researchers and industrial developers rarely interact on conferences. So are ECOOP workshops (like workshops of other conferences in our field) mainly populated by academics. We think that a closer interaction between scientific researchers and industrial software developers can create a mutual win-win situation: Researchers get an understanding of pressing "real" problems (hopefully sparking new research motivation) while industrial developers get an understanding of novel research results and how to apply them to specific problems.

Therefore, the ECOOP-Workshop on Practical Problems of Programming in the Large was thought to present a forum for

1. Practitioners to present their currently most pressing problems in the area of programming in the large object oriented systems and
2. Researchers looking for current open questions in object orientation and beyond in IT industry.

This report is organised according to the course of the workshop sessions. Hence, we first sketch the presentations of the accepted papers with their associated discussions of the first morning session. Then we summarise the example of a problem of programming in the large and the following discussion. In the description of the afternoon sessions, we report on problems of transferring academic research results into practice followed by a summary of Dave Thomas thought-provoking invited keynote worse-is-worse The last session presents our discussions about what should be taught to software engineers in academic courses.

2　Presentations

The morning sessions saw four presentations of submitted and reviewed papers:

1. Abdelwahab Hamou-Lhadj, Timothy C. Lethbridge: Reasoning about the Concept of Utilities (presented by Abdelwahab Hamou-Lhadj)
2. Ulf Schreier, Alexander Prack: Dynamically distributable Java Application Components (presented by Ulf Schreier)
3. Jonathan Sillito, Kris De Volder: Tool Support for Working With Large Systems (presented by Jonathan Sillito)
4. Peter Tabeling, Bernhard Gröne: Handling Complexity of Large Software Systems by Mapping Objects and Classes to Conceptual Architectural Elements (presented by Bernhard Gröne)

These papers presented recent research results and work in progress in areas that the authors have experienced as important with programming in the large. Each presentation was followed by a discussion with the audience.

2.1   Reasoning About the Concept of Utilities

The authors realised as one problem of programming in the large, to identify in an existing large system, what is important and what is not, to facilitate reengineering. A common method of reengineering is to run the software and collect execution traces. As to be expected, with large systems these traces get large as well and need to be filtered to allow readers to focus on the relevant issues. The hypothesis of the authors is that we can distinguish between substantial parts of a system and utilities that merely support the substantial system units. UML 1.5 has a definition for utilities. In practice, however, it appears that this definition not always exactly describes what people consider being utilities. The authors hence interviewed software engineers to see, how they characterize the concept of utilities. Three main aspects became apparent: Scope, Packaging, and Role.

1. Scope: Despite the feeling that utilities are usually the components that are used by many other components of the entire system, in reality, there might have narrower scopes such as a specific subsystem. Therefore, any metric that aims at detecting utilities should take into consideration the scope attribute.
2. Packaging: Despite the feeling that utilities are packaged in units that only contain other utilities, local utilities are included in normal packages. This is, because utilities are often designed by and for a specific group of people.
3. Role: Almost by definition, utilities are seen as things the programmer should not worry about when looking at the big picture.

However, the conclusion was, that the subjective conception what a utility is differs from objective conception and that there are always several exceptions to whatever rule one might try.

In the following discussion the question was raised, what to do, once utilities are identified. It is not clear, whether and when they really should be excluded from analysis. This, however, is further research yet to be done.

A further proposal to remedy the lack of general and objective criteria for utility identification was that tools should only suggest classifications to be reviewed by users. This actually links to the third presentation of the session.

2.2   Dynamically Distributable Java Application Components

The second presentation was based on experience with component programming in Java. It addressed the claim that components would exist at a class level only. Here, the term component is used in accordance with the Composite Component Model of UML 2, requiring components to have identified provided and required interfaces according to a connector model. The authors identified seven problems with component programming in Java. These can be roughly categorised as

1. component design, that is how to arrive at a sensible "componentisation"
2. component reuse, when existing components do not completely meet the requirements or internal dependencies occur
3. rediscovering components in the code
4. the schism between components and the units of distribution, which may require to repackage components when adapting local distribution of software parts

Java, in particular, does not support composite components in the language. Packages and jar files are only conventions, and there is no tool support enforcing correct usage. Consequently, there is no protection against programmers spoiling the component architecture when changing code locally. Frameworks, such as EJB, seem not to be the solution either, because they introduce extra overhead both at runtime as well as in development. The proposed solution is an XML-based extension of Java, that allows to express componentisation to be made explicit, allowing for automated checks whether the actual code still meets the specified component structure.

In the discussion it was pointed out that there are possibly further and non-technical issues as well as solutions to consider. The author's experience was, however, that these can be quite unpopular with developers. A second question addressed crosscutting issues, but these are subject to further research.

2.3   Tool Support for Working with Large Systems

The third presentation started from the observation that complexity is inherent with larger software systems. Because of this, long ago modules were proposed as a means of structuring by Parnas and others. The problem is, that modules can only represent a single decomposition at a time, while large complex systems may need to be decomposed in several ways, depending on the perspectives necessary to achieve individual tasks. Modules also require some degree of localization. Hence non-localisable tasks are hard to structure. It gets hard to identify and to maintain mental model what belongs together. The research question put forward by the authors is whether the editing environment can help here, so that one would not have to structure the system explicitly but get structures presented by the editor. The obvious approach today seems to be to use several displays simultaneously to present more information. Experience seems to show, however, that this just presents too much information but no additional structure. The proposed solution is that the programming environment (editor) should somehow know what other parts of a system would be important, when a certain part is being edited. These parts could than dynamically be presented close to the editing focus. Mainly, this research aims at changing the established object or class browser-based editing paradigm, towards a more scratchpad-oriented way of organizing information on screen.

The discussion mostly focused on the obvious open research question, how the editor should select what to display close to the editing focus. One answer was that this needs experimenting. A remark was made, that there is generally too little research done about what those (few?) people, who can keep overview of large systems, actually do and which support they would need. Another suggestion was that the editor should not actually structure a system, that is, produce a mental model, but make a separately specified high-level structure explicit. It could then also ensure conformance between programs and that high-level structure. A final question addressed round-trip engineering tools, which are conceived as being complementary to an editor of the kind described by the authors.

2.4   Handling Complexity of Large Software Systems by Mapping Objects and Classes to Conceptual Architectural Elements

The fourth presentation started from the observation that there are three different structures involved with programming in the large. One is the general system structure or conceptual architecture consisting of large-grained components or subsystems, such as databases and web servers. Second is the software structure, relating to all the software artefacts, such as, programs, database schema, deployment descriptors, and so on, which need to be organized and related. The third and final structure becomes apparent in the running system only and consists of entities such as instantiated objects and references between them. The problem addressed by the authors is the mapping between the various structures, in particular, how to impose a system structure on a collection of objects. A related question is how to map object terminology to system structure terminology. As a first categorization, the authors propose to distinguish between agents and storages. Next, they separate four different views of the system structure: Object Agent View, Abstract Data Type View, Functional View, and Low-Level View. For each of these views a mapping guide can be given, explaining how objects are subsumed under certain system structure entities.

The discussion raised the question for tool support, which does not exist yet. Currently, the proposal is at the level of patterns. Another question was what to do, if there are so many objects instantiated, that the object-agent view (considered as a snapshot of the running system) becomes incomprehensible. In this case, one has to combine objects into higher-level units, which is seen as a task for the human user, who has to develop a mental model for structuring.

3   EoPPPL

While planning the workshop, the organisers thought about presenting an exemplary problem of programming in the large (EoPPPL) to focus discussions and to give authors the possibility to present the benefits of their particular approach, presented in the previous session. The EoPPPL was taken from a cooperation between the OFFIS research institute [1] and the KDO [2], a company developing software for eGovernment, in particular for municipal administration. Given the amount and idiosyncratic complexity of German laws and the over-regulation in any administrative public process of this country, one can easily imagine the complexity of that software. However, as KDO is a market leader in north-western Germany, KDO successfully solved these particular challenges. As it is often the case with market-leader in specific application domains, the company knows the specific domain requirements well. However, as the software had to be enhanced in functionality and had to be adapted to changing government regulations for public administration, it became larger and larger. In addition, technology changes with its own pace. Altogether, the costs for software maintenance increased more and more, and the KDO started a cooperation with the OFFIS research institute to re-engineer the software architecture and to use a modern middleware platform as a base. The old version of the software used a 4GL to code business logic, database access and GUI logic. The user interface ran on remote machines via a terminal emulation (i.e., the GUI code was actually not separated from the parts of the code). However, a standard database system was already used. The aim was to bring that software to a modern three-tier architecture with the "classical" database, business logic and GUI tier where all layers finally should run in a J2EE environment. A more detailed description of the project and the applied solution strategy can be found in [3].

However, in the PPPL workshop we were primarily interested in the problem and in the participants' approaches to that problem rather than in the actual "solution" used in the cooperation. (This solution, the Dublo-pattern [3] for architectural transformation toward s a three tier architecture was presented later upon request from the participants.)

The participants proposed to tackle the EoPPPL in the following steps:

1. Need to figure out what is there. This means to discover code structures or the model in the programmers mind. Problems arise if no structure exists (either right from the beginning or by architectural drift). One approach for architectural discovery could be the monitoring and filtering techniques presented in the first paper of the morning session by Abdelwahab Hamou-Lhadj and Timothy C. Lethbridge.

2. Need to design and describe new structure. Doing so, one should try to avoid the mistakes of the old system design. Although this is an obvious and simple to state advice, it is often not such easy to (commercially) realise. This is because, for a good durable system architecture, one has to design it for the "right" non-functional properties. For doing so, one needs to predict the future. The other contribution of the morning session particularly provide support for this and the following step.

3. Incremental migration: Get from old to new structure. For doing so incrementally and to support quality assurance during the process, it can be of great help to re-use the old text cases (or corresponding translations of them into the new system structure). The stepwise migration can be supported by various wrapping techniques, ranging from wrapping single classes or modules to whole subsystems. Wrapping can be done on the code level (by adapters and interceptors) or data-oriented by filters, including screen-scrapers (i.e., by not touching the code itself).

4   Problems of Transferring Research into Practice

In the first afternoon session, Ralf Reussner presented a summary of key problems when transferring academic research results into industrial software engineering practice. His talk was based on a discussion on this topic that took place during the FESCA workshop at ETAPS 2004 in Barcelona [4, 5]. Basically eight obstacles for transferring research results into software engineering practice were identified:

1. **Many Formal Methods Do Not Scale:** Developed in an academic world, formal methods are applied to rather limited toy examples. Opposed to that, major challenges in industry are originated by handling large and complex systems. Unfortunately, the costs of applying formal methods to large systems most often grow super-linearly.

2. **Insufficient Constructs to Model the Real World:** Increasingly, computer systems use concepts beyond the standard functional model (inputs are mapped by computations to outputs). Examples are distribution, concurrency, mobility, dynamic reconfiguration and ubiquity. Some of these concepts are long running topics for research (such as concurrency) while modelling and analysing others are still challenging. However, as between the practical motivation and the actual research result some assumptions and simplifications have to be made to make the problem tractable, the research result not necessarily solves the original real-world example, but inevitably focuses on specific aspects.

3. **No Time for Validation:** The development of a formal method is a task by itself. Given the usual time frame of academic dissertations, for the validation of the method often no time is left. In addition, there is a hen-egg problem: Without validation, industrial managers are nit inclined to invest into the application of a novel method. However, without any industrial deployment of the research result, it will remain un-validated (which sometimes is erroneously takes as "invalidated".)

4. **Unclear Practical Benefit:** Academic research is often motivated by intriguing mathematical questions. In principle this is justified, because one hardly knows what comes out of research, hence one cannot exclude in principle the value of such motivated research. However, the outcome of such research often has no practical benefits and lies much more in a deeper understanding of the problem. If such research is later for the sake of better selling motivated by practical questions, one has the impression of "solution found, in search for a problem". Obviously, such methods do not really solve real world problems with their many different facets.

5. **Missing Tool Support:** Scientific progress is considered as adding scientific knowledge to a given area of research. The implementation of tools does not create scientific knowledge, at its best it creates experience how to apply software development techniques. Due to that, for many scientists no motivation exists to invest time in the demanding task of tool creation. However, without tool support, the application of most formal methods does not scale up (see reason 1).

6. **Lack of Industrial Experience for Academics:** Many academics spend their life-time in universities but have not worked in industry or in industry cooperation projects. Consequently, researchers provide a deep understanding of mathematical techniques for solving problems, but may have a rather limited knowledge of "real" problems. In particular, real problems are multi-faceted, including non computer science issues. Interestingly, single aspects are often rather trivial, annoying researchers having solutions to this single aspect. The complexity of industrial systems often simply stems from their sheer size while the single algorithms and data-structures are simple.

7. **Up-Front Costs in Industrial Processes:** Formal methods, like nearly all software engineering techniques, increase the up-front costs of software development. Additional effort has to be spend during the specification or design of the product, while hoping to save costs during implementation, testing and maintenance. Generally, this is problematic: (a) Even if the over-all savings effort of a technique is demonstrated several times, (e.g., in case of software reviews and inspections [6]), managers are often reluctant to deploy these techniques. This is because, managers often still consider the implementation step as the most important one and do not see the project's progress if effort is spent on steps prior to the implementation. (b) Due to a lacking validation in industrial contexts, the saving effects of many formal methods is unclear or at least not quantified. This results in a hen-egg problem: As long a formal method is not deployed, it will not be deployed.

8. **Goals of Research Differ from Industrial Needs:** Probably the most fundamental reason beyond all previously mentioned ones is that the motivation and credit one gets for work fundamentally differs between academic researchers and industrial software developers. Industry projects have to succeed under tight time and cost constraints. Sometimes, time-to-market is of higher concern than the quality of the first version shipped. Success is measured in producing the product with the lowest amount of these constrained resources. The application of a not-yet validated formal method (having the only guaranteed property of increasing up-front costs) is not very appealing. On the academic side, the contribution of research is measured not only in soundness but also in originality and novelty. This is done for good reasons, but often has the drawback, that the work on transitioning existing formal methods into practice (such as tool construction, adapted process models or case studies) are still considered as less scientific compared to the development of new formalisms. As new formalisms have to add something to the old ones (which are also not yet understood and deployed in industrial practice), the gap between research and practice will be widened.

We intentionally omitted the training aspect. Of course, the specific knowledge required to deploy a formal method is most often not present at industrial developers and the awareness of new formal techniques and their benefits are often low. This was usually considered as a problem to be solved by increasing the number of software developers having an academic degree in software engineering or computer science. While this is partially true, the above list of problems still is valid when having teams with academically trained staff. Although the internet-boom is over, current industrialised countries have a lack of academically trained software developers (still or again). As the demand of software professionals still exceeds the capacities of universities, this situation will not change in the near future. Consequently, the transition of formal methods in industrial practice cannot solely depend on trained people (and, as argued above, even that would not solve the above mentioned list of problems). During the discussion the importance of the exchange between research and practice was once more emphasised. However, this exchange has to siple to state pre-conditions:

1. Researchers need to understand the problems of industrial software development and try to solve these problems by their methods. However, one has to be careful: New scientific theories will not occur by simple piecewise research driven by unrelated open industrial questions.
2. Practitioners need to communicate their problems and should also actively invest into research and relations to researchers. However, this usually means to invest in a long-term goal which will most often not pay back for the current project.

Therefore, a cyclic interaction process is proposed. Researchers try to apply novel research results to industrial problems. This should be done in close cooperation. The benefit for the practitioner is (hopefully) support by state of the art techniques and novel approaches, while the researcher be benefits from the validation of a new method which will generate new knowledge on the pros and cons of the research result applied. This will result into the motivation to develop modified or new methods and techniques in research which then itself should be applied in the next cooperational project.

This approach can be seen as a mutually driving mixture from empirical validation and motivation and theoretical or technical work on models, tools, methods or techniques.

5   Worse-Is-Worse

In his very appreciated and thought-provoking keynote W orse is W orse - Challenges Building Large Scale Software with Class Libraries and Frameworks Dave Thomas of Baderra Research Labs put forward the thesis that the current trend to use more and more sophisticated general-purpose languages and frameworks is leading into a dead-end road. Generic programming paradigms, technology, and tools are becoming more and more a source of problems with programming in the large.

The ultimate focus in software engineering is on building applications. On top of the complexity inherent in these applications, the environments to be used add further complexity. Even the supposedly simple and widespread concepts of object-orientation are hard for many people and it does not make sense to express everything with objects at any rate. For some (parts of) applications functional descriptions, transformation rules, algorithms or other approaches can be much more appropriate.

By putting layers on layers not only the demands for programmers to master specific abstractions grow but also the performance requirements. More and more computing power is needed, just to drive that overhead.

To overcome this general trend to use the same generic and standardized mechanisms all over, regardless of the application, more diversity in computing should be fostered. Here organizations such as ACM and IEEE are in charge.

With technology becoming more and more complex, mastering it becomes more and more important and consequently the importance of knowledge shifts from professionalism (competence) to short-term knowledge (certification). This trend needs to be reversed.

However, when looking over several decades of computing, there is progress where domain is understood very well. Anyhow, currently there is a doubtful tendency to use generic system programming, tools, languages, knowledge to build domain-specific applications.

6   Teaching

During the course of the workshop it became apparent that the different backgrounds of the participants could provide an interesting discussion on the specific requirements from industry for an academic software engineering education. Although we were ready to moderate a controversial discussion, surprisingly the views of academics and practitioner's were quite similar (which means, both were different from that politician's sometime argue for). The following list is a result of those discussions, detailed by some after-thoughts of the organisers.

- University courses should teach the fundamentals. Timely and technical details should be left to industrial training programs (possibly on-the-job training). There are at least two reasons for that:
  1. Knowledge on technology is not only timely, but most often is also highly specific to the particular tools used in a project. Furthermore, these tools can be domain-specific. As universities cannot cover this broad range of tools and knowledge, students should be trained to acquire technology knowledge fast. For a fast acquisition of knowledge, a thorough understanding of fundamental principles shared across different tools is required.
  2. Practical technical knowledge cannot be taught by reading books and solving text book exercises. Much more, the necessity of specific tools and processes only becomes clear in large projects. For universities, it is hard to simulate these environments. However, approaches to simulate medium-sized industrial software development projects in universities are certainly beneficial, as they lower the "shock of practice" of graduates starting their careers.
- Train students to be different (better)! Make students clear that they increasingly have to compete with graduates from developing countries that are in many ways cheaper to hire. If they are not superior in their qualifications, it is easy to be inferior in this global competition.

- Teach non-technical skills, such as communication. Successful teamwork is the absolute, indispensable pre-requisite of any software engineering project. It is easy to see that communication skills are needed to communicate with customers (requirements engineering, etc) and to colleagues.
- Educate to think! Creative solutions to technical problems often use an original solution based on a very individual view of the problem. Students should be able to use different views on the same problem to find an appropriate solution.
- Teach to deliver! Students should understand that their work in industry is not judged by the originality of the solution or they way they develop products. The most important indicators of success is to finish a project.
- Try to acquire domain knowledge! In most projects, sheer technology knowledge is not sufficient for a successful completion of the project. A wrong understanding of domain-specific requirements is one of the most common reasons for software engineering project failures. Therefore, successful developers must be able to communicate with customers and "speak their language", i.e., understand the meaning of the terms used in a specific domain.

Most of these ideas are shared between academics and practitioners. However, as many academics have a solid understanding of computer science fundamentals but not of application domain specific concepts, one obviously has to enhance computer science or software engineering curricula by courses taught by experts of application domains.

7   Conclusions

Looking back, the organisers found the workshop most interesting in discussing the various facets of the complex relationship between research and software development practice. Having tackled a wide variety of related topics ranging from problems of transferring research results into practice to academic education for software developers made that workshop a success. Besides the lively discussions of all participants, a vital component of that success certainly was the thought provoking key-note of Dave Thomas. His identification of the current trend towards general purpose languages in the domain of business software as erroneous was as surprising as his view on the role of academic software engineering teaching was surprisingly academic.

All documents of the workshop, such as the papers, presentations, descriptions of the EoPPPL, Ralf's talk on the problems of transferring research into practice and Dave's keynote are available from the workshop's web page at

http://se.informatik.uni-oldenburg.de/pppl

List of Participants

Name	E-mail	Affiliation, Country
Abdelwahab Hamou-Lhadj	ahamou@site.uottawa.ca	University of Ottawa, Canada
Tomáš Opluštil	oplustil@nenya.ms.mff.cuni.cz	Charles University, Prague, Czech Republic
Andrzej Krzywda	andrzej@64pola.pl	University of Wroclaw, Poland
Guido Poschta	guido@poschta.de	TU Darmstadt, Germany
David Cok	david.cok@kodak.com	Eastman Kodak, USA
Jean-Guy Schneider	jschneider@swin.edu.au	Swinburne Univ. of Technology, Australia
Bernhard Gröne	bernhard.groene@hpi.uni -potsdam.de	Hasso-Plattner-Institute, Potsdam, Germany
Kris de Volder	kdvolder@cs.ubc.ca	Univ. of British Columbia, Vancouver, Canada
Doug Janzen	dsjanzen@cs.ubc.ca	Univ. of British Columbia, Vancouver, Canada
Alexander Prack	ap@sernet.de	SerNet GmbH, Germany
Ulf Schreier	schreier@fh-furtwangen.de	Univ. of Applied Sciences Furtwangen, Germany
Jonathan Sillito	sillito@cs.ubc.ca	Univ. of British Columbia, Vancouver, Canada
Dave Thomas	dave@bedarra.com	Bedarra Research Labs, Canada
Ralf Reussner	reussner@informatik.uni -oldenburg.de	University of Oldenburg, Germany
Wolfgang Weck	wolfgang.weck@iaeth.ch	Independent Software Architect, Zurich, Switherland

References

1. Oldenburg research institute for computer science tools and systems, http://www.offis.de/index_e.php.
2. Kommunale Datenverarbeitung Oldenburg, http://www.kdo.de/.
3. W. Hasselbring, R. H. Reussner, H. Jaekel, J. Schlegelmilch, T. Teschke, and S. Krieghoff, "The dublo architecture pattern for smooth migration of business information systems," in *Proceedings of the 26rd International Conference on Software Engeneering (ICSE-04)*. Los Alamitos, California: IEEE Computer Society, May 23–28 2004.

4. J. Küster-Filipe, I. H. Poernomo, R. H. Reussner, and S. Shukla, Eds., *Proceedings of the Workshop Formal Foundations of Embedded and Component-based Software Architectures (FESCA 2004)*. Barcelona: Published at ETAPS 2004, March 2004.
5. R. H. Reussner, J. Küster-Filipe, I. H. Poernomo, and S. Shukla, "Report on the Workshop on Formal Foundations of Embedded Software and Component-based Software Architectures (FESCA)," Newsletter of the European Association of Software Science and Technology (EASST), 2004.
6. R. L. Glass, *Facts and Fallacies of Software Engineering*. Addison-Wesley, Reading, MA, USA, 2002.

8th Workshop on Quantitative Approaches in Object-Oriented Software Engineering (QAOOSE 2004)[*]

Coral Calero[1], Fernando Brito e Abreu[2], Geert Poels[3],
and Houari A. Sahraoui[4]

[1] ALARCOS Research Group, Departamento de Informática, Universidad de
Castilla-La Mancha, Ciudad Real, Spain
`Coral.Calero@.uclm.es`
[2] QUASAR Research Group, Departamento de Informática, Faculdade de Ciências e
Tecnologia, Universidade Nova de Lisboa, Monte da Caparica, Portugal
`fba@di.fct.unl.pt`
[3] Faculty of Economics and Business Administration - Ghent University and Centre
for Industrial Management - Katholieke Universiteit Leuven
`geert.poels@rug.ac.be`
[4] Département d'Informatique et Recherche Opérationnelle, Université de Montréal,
Montréal, Quebec, Canada
`sahraouh@IRO.UMontreal.CA`

1 Summary

The workshop was a direct continuation of seven successful workshops, held at previous editions of ECOOP in Darmstadt (2003), Malaga (2002), Budapest (2001), Cannes (2000), Lisbon (1999), Brussels (1998) and Aarhus (1995). This time, as in previous editions, the workshop attracted participants from both academia and industry that are involved / interested in the application of quantitative methods in object oriented software engineering research and practice.

As a result of the previous edition and in order to open the workshop participation to a broader audience, the 2004 edition extended the scope of the workshop to quantitative approaches to other than object-oriented modelling, specification and programming methodologies and technologies. In particular component-based systems (CBS), web-based systems (WBS) and agent-based systems (ABS) will also fit into this new edition.

Like in previous years, submissions were invited, but not limited, to the areas of metrics collection, quality assessment, metrics validation, and process management.

This year we received 15 position papers. 9 authors were invited to present theirs positions as discussion topics and 3 others to present posters. Informal proceedings of QAOOSE'2004 were distributed to the participants.

---

[*] The title of this report should be referenced as "Report from the ECOOP 2004 8th Workshop on Quantitative Approaches in Object-Oriented Software Engineering (QAOOSE 2004)".

J. Malenfant and B.M. Østvold (Eds.): ECOOP 2004, LNCS 3344, pp. 23–35, 2004.
© Springer-Verlag Berlin Heidelberg 2004

The workshop was divided in four sessions, which follow:

- Session A. Metric definition and validation
- Session B. Methodology and application of measurement
- Session C. Functional size and quality
- Session D. Short papers

At the end a "Discussion and closing session" took place.

The workshop had 17 participants (included de four organizers). Among them, we had people from several European countries and Canada and also from industry and from University.

As each year the workshop was very active and new topics and future directions for the workshop were addressed at the end. Among them, were selected for be included as a topics on next editions of the workshop the following: metrics visualization, components and services, aspect oriented software development, paradigm independent product metrics, metrics and reengineering, process aspects vs. product aspects, early phase metrics, relationships between cost and quality aspects, influence of context on quality.

2   Organizers

This year, the workshop was organized by:

Coral Calero
ALARCOS Research Group
Escuela Superior de Informática,
Universidad de Castilla-La Mancha. Ciudad Real, Spain

Fernando Brito e Abreu
QUASAR Research Group
Faculdade de Ciências e Tecnologia, Universidade Nova de Lisboa
Monte da Caparica, Portugal

Geert Poels
Faculty of Economics and Business Administration - Ghent University, and
Centre for Industrial Management – Katholieke Universiteit Leuven
Gent, Belgium

Houari A. Sahraoui
Département d'Informatique et Recherche Opérationnelle
Université de Montréal
Montréal, Canada

3   Workshop Attendants

The information about the workshop attendants is shown in this section. Name and affiliation is shown for each attendant:

- **Miguel Goulão.** Faculty of Sciences and Technology, Lisbon New University, Portugal

- **Manuel F. Bertoa** Dpto. Lenguajes y Ciencias de la Computación. Universidad de Málaga
- **Valerie Paulus.** CETIC. Charleroi, Belgium
- **Olivier Beaurepaire.** SNCF - Délégation aux Systèmes d'Information Voyageurs. Nantes, France
- **Benjamin Lecardeux.** SNCF - Délégation aux Systèmes d'Information Voyageurs. Nantes, France
- **Christine Havart.** SNCF - Délégation aux Systèmes d'Information Voyageurs. Nantes, France
- **Parastoo Mohagheghi.** Department of Computer and Information Science, Trondheim, Norway
- **Silvia Abrahão.** Department of Computer Science and Computation. Valencia University of Technology. Valencia, Spain
- **Houari Sahraoui.** Département d'Informatique et Recherche Opérationnelle. Université de Montréal. Montréal, Canada
- **Mario Piattini.** ALARCOS Research Group. Escuela Superior de Informática, Universidad de Castilla-La Mancha. Ciudad Real, Spain
- **Denis Kozlov.** Department of Computer Science and Information Systems, University of Jyväskylä. Jyväskylä, Finland
- **Jean-François Gelinas.** Département de Mathématiques et d'Informatique. Université du Québec à Trois- Rivières Canada
- **Sherif Gurguis.** Department of Computer Science. The American University in Cairo
- **Briand Henderson-Sellers** University of Technology, Sydney
- **Coral Calero** ALARCOS Research Group. Escuela Superior de Informática, Universidad de Castilla-La Mancha. Ciudad Real, Spain
- **Fernando Brito e Abreu** Faculty of Sciences and Technology, Lisbon New University, Portugal
- **Geert Poels** Faculty of Economics and Business Administration - Ghent University, and Centre for Industrial Management – Katholieke Universiteit Leuven. Gent, Belgium

4   The Call for Papers

The call for papers of the workshop was distributed by e-mail basically through distribution lists (among them the one created during the 7 years of previous workshops with all the workshop attendants) but also with direct e-mails to the workshop organizers contacts. The Call for Papers was structured as follows:

4.1   Introduction

A brief introduction of the workshop including an explanation about the number of editions, the main goal of the workshop, etc.

4.2   List of Topics

Topics for the workshop submissions. This year, submissions were invited, but not limited, to the areas of metrics collection, quality assessment, metrics validation, and process management.

Area C (Metrics Collection)

- Automatic support for sharing research hypotheses, data and results
- Standards for the collection, comparison and validation of metrics
- Embedding metrics in CASE and application development tools
- Evaluation of metrics collection tools
- Automating collection from formal metrics definition
- Metrics collection in the development process (measurement planning)
- Public repositories for measurement data
- Metrics visualization (*)
- Metrics for component-based systems (*)
- Metrics for web-based systems (*)

Area A (Quality Assessment)

- Measuring non-functional requirements of OO systems
- Quantitative OO and CB design heuristics
- Metric-based design refactoring
- OOD and CBD quality characteristics assessment
- Quantitative impact analysis in OO and CB architectures
- Quantitative assessment of OO analysis/design patterns and frameworks
- Quantitative assessment of behavioral modeling in OO models
- Quantitative assessment of OR and OO database/datawarehouse schemata
- Measurement and quality assessment of components (*)
- Measurement and quality assessment of agent-based systems(*)
- Agent-based Web service architecture as a means of providing QoS(*)
- Quality of Service models(*)
- Instrumentation of Web services for QoS (*)

Area V (Metrics Validation)

- Meta-level metrics
- Formal and empirical validation of metrics
- Metrics and Measurement Theory
- Validation techniques and their limits
- Standard data sets for metrics validation
- Limitations of quality estimation techniques

Area P (Process Management)

- Reliability and rework effort estimates based on design measures
- Reuse evaluation
- Resource estimation models for OO and CB software development

- Quantitative tracking of OO, web services, and CBS development activities
- Empirical studies on the use of measures for process management
- Measurement support in a CBD life cycle

We explicitly solicited position papers related to topics marked with an asterisk (*) as well as papers that document and/or motivate the use of quantitative methods in industrial software processes. These topics were identified as important open research issues in QAOOSE'2003 workshop.

4.3   Important Dates Information

Information about the important dates of the workshop were included on the call for papers

4.4   Web Page

The web address of the workshop was included on the call for papers. On this page the people could find all the information related to the workshop. The address of the workshop is: http://alarcos.inf-cr.uclm.es/qaoose2004.

5   The Workshop Sessions

The day started with the session on M etric deɐnition and validationIn this session we had three presentations (one of the presenters failed and another from the short papers session asked for a change).

Independent Validation of a Component Metrics Suite. Miguel Goulão, Fernando Brito e Abreu.

The session started with the paper of Miguel Goulão titled "Independent Validation of a Component Metrics Suite". The paper describes an independent validation study for a suite of reusability metrics for component based design. The authors present a formalization that combines the UML 2.0 metamodel with OCL. By doing that they provide a formal, portable and executable definition of the metrics set that can be used by other researchers and practitioners to perform independent validations of the metrics suite. Also they present a prototype working environment to perform such independent validation experiments. A workshop attendant asked about the formalization of implementation metrics and Miguel asked that this approach cannot be used for this kind of metrics because only works with structural metrics. A question about the definition of one of the metrics (the RCO) used for the technique utilization example was done. Problems related to the difficulty of filling values in the metamodel and the validation of the metrics was discussed and the ideas for solving them were exposed by the presenter. A participant asked if the technique was limitative because the authors use reverse engineering and Miguel asked that no because it can be used in forward engineering as well, in fact with less effort since component diagrams will be available for obtaining the required information. The only thing to be in mind is that, sometimes, another meta-model would be needed, for instance, when applying the work to relational database metrics (planned as future work). Also a question about the accuracy of the experimental results presented was done and the speaker explained that their objective in this paper was not to assess the accuracy of the results presented by Washizaki et al., but rather showing that a better formalization of their metrics allows the replication of their experiment in a far more reusable (because OCL interpreters are becoming widespread), efficient (because OCL clauses are executable and as such can help automate the collection process) and objective way (as long as the corresponding metamodel is made available). The next question was if the results mean that the analyzed components are of bad quality and Miguel said that they didn't get experts opinion on the components quality to perform such kind of conclusion. However their aim here was not to discuss the appropriateness of the thresholds proposed by Washizaki el al., but rather showing how independent cross can be easily performed without the typical problems of metrics definition interpretation, metrics collection (lack of tools), among others.

Usability Metrics for Software Components. Manuel F. Bertoa and Antonio Vallecillo

The session followed with the paper presented by Manuel F. Bertoa about usability metrics for software components. The work presented on this paper is justified on the need to select a component among a set of possible candidates that offer similar functionality and the fact that this selection can be done using metrics. In the paper they define, in a consistent way, usability metrics for software components based on the ISO 9126 Quality Model. They also define the basic concepts on software measurement used in the paper, what they understand for usability in a CBSD framework, and the component information available to be measured. One of the attendants asked about how the authors had considered the fact that, when a component has been used more than one time, it becomes easier and so, perhaps a more complex component become easier than other that using the proposed approach is considered as the easier one. Manuel answered telling that this was a good point to consider for future work because now they are centring their work only considering that the components to select are not known by the user. The difference between understandability and learnability was explained by the author after a question of one of the workshop attendees. Also someone asked about the metamodel the authors have used and Manuel explained that as a result of the research, the metamodel is always under revision. The importance of the 'point of view' concept was pointed to the speaker who answered that they mainly take the user point of view, and make it explicit. About the relationship between the metrics and the quality sub-characteristics Manuel said that they investigate this in future work when they have external metrics for the quality sub-characteristics. This investigation is done by means of empirical studies. The fact that the usability metrics cannot have an absolute value was remarked by an attendant and Manuel said that their point of view is to support the selection of components, meaning the choice between alternative components and so, absolute values are not needed.

Finally a question about how to evaluate non-functional aspects like QoS was raised and the speaker explained that this was not included yet, but they plan to extend the proposal in this respect.

Classification of Metrics Related to the Software Development Process as a Prerequisite for Its Improvement. Denis Kozlov

The session finished with the short paper of Denis Kozlov about Classification of metrics related to the software development process as a prerequisite for its improvement in which the author points out that estimation of object-oriented software quality remains as very urgent because there is a lack of generally accepted classifications of metrics related to final software and to the software development process, despite of numerous articles devoted to it. Then, the focus of the article is the classification of metrics of the software development process. The correlations between quality characteristics and metrics of the software development process have been revealed. An approach for using the presented classifications for improvement of the software development process was also proposed. At the end of the presentation some attendees remarked to Denis that the fact of mixing the ISO9126 (which is a product norm) with the process could be a bit dangerous and he would take this into account. Briand Henderson-Sellers remarked to Denis that his work links somehow to SPI&A framework and he suggested him look into the SPICE standard where process enactment is assessed, based upon the metamodel. Another attendant recommended the author to think about the existing relationship between his work and CMM and SPICE. A question about how where "correlations" presented in the paper determined was done and Denis answered that the "correlations" were just a personal view of the strength of. He plans to detail the criteria in a follow-up version of this paper.

After a break, the second session, on Methodology and application of measurement, was held. There were three presentations:

On the Application of Some Metrology Concepts to Internal Software Measurement. Miguel Lopez, Simon Alexandre, Valerie Paulus, Gregory Seront

This paper was presented by Valerie Paulus. The authors investigate the applicability of classical metrology concepts to software measurement. In particular they explore the concepts of systematic and random error, repeatability and reproducibility, uncertainty, calibration, and etalon when measuring internal attributes of software with metric tools. Using a laboratory experiment the uncertainty of McCabe's measure of the cyclomatic complexity of a Java class was examined. Although several factors can impact the measurement method, the experiment did not show the occurrence of systematic or random errors. Hence the authors conclude that uncertainty might not be a relevant concept for internal software measurement. On the other hand, it was shown that calibration is relevant when different measurement instruments for the same measure are available. This was shown using three tools that measure the cyclomatic complexity of a Java class. Measurement results obtained with these tools can be different as they implement some counting rules differently. However, with calibration, the correctness of the measurement results can be ensured. One workshop participant questioned the relevancy of the research question as measurement results are deterministic when a same tool is used (unless there is some software bug). Valerie replied that this was not sure, and therefore they wished to examine this. In future work the authors intend to introduce themselves some errors to further investigate the usefulness of the metrology concepts. It was further remarked that concepts like calibration are surely relevant when there is ambiguity in the measurement methods, such as with functional size measurement. Valerie responded that new functional size measures such as COSMIC-FFP even incorporate calibration and other metrology concepts (e.g. conversion) as part of their method. Another question related to the use of McCabe's cyclomatic complexity as the object of study in the experiments, given that it is not an object-oriented measure. Valerie admitted, but McCabe's number was only an example and other measures will be investigated. At the end of the presentation, Valerie argued for the introduction of a common terminology for reference fields such as measurement theory and metrology. Currently there is a lot of confusion in software measurement with respect to validation, and the separation of a measure from its methods and instruments could resolve some of these semantic problems. As a final comment it was suggested that the application of metrology is probably very promising for dynamic metrics, where there is uncertainty by definition.

Industrialisation of Software-Quality-Led Project Management Process at the S.N.C.F. (French Railways). Olivier Bearupaire, Benjamin Lecardeux, Christine Havart.

This 'industrial' presentation was made by Olivier Beaurepaire. The industry report of these authors was especially welcomed by the workshop organizers, as in the past there was a lack of participants from industry in the QAOOSE workshops. The contribution by Beaurepaire and colleagues demonstrated that the topic of the QAOOSE workshops is not only of academic interest. In the presentation, Olivier demonstrated the metrics program at the French Railways company. The program was established to assist project managers in assuring the quality of the produced software systems. The core of the program is a decision support tool (called the Software Quality Portal) that helps both managers and developers to interpret the measurement results (e.g. occurrence of anti-patterns, quality over time trend analysis). As a result of the introduction of the metrics program, an improvement in the level of quality has been observed. Further, the metrics initiative establishes a contractual framework for sub-contractors, allowing the French Railways to assure the quality of externally developed software. One of the metrics used is the severity of the software problems that are observed. Workshop participants wondered how this severity could be quantified. Olivier responded that it was based on the end-user's point of view. A participant further remarked that the severity of software problems is not necessarily directly related to their costs. Another question related to the improvements that were observed after the introduction of the metrics program. It was replied that there were improvements, although it was too soon to quantify them. Some results are promised for the near future, in a next paper. One of the workshop organizers further remarked that is could be worthwhile to move to the model level, and not focus metrics efforts exclusively on the code level. This would, amongst other benefits, make the metrics program more independent of the languages used (as for each language other metrics thresholds may apply). Such an approach, though valuable, might be difficult to implement at French Railways, because models are rarely used, or not kept up to date. Unfortunately, this is the rule rather than the exception in software engineering practice.

Exploring Industrial Data Repositories: Where Software Development Approaches Meet. Parastoo Mohagheghi, Reidar Conradi

The presentation was done by Parastoo Mohagheghi. The paper deals with methods and problems of exploring large industrial data repositories in empirical software engineering research, taking into account that software data are not always obtained as part of a measurement program. The presentation gave an overview of recent research results, presented by the authors at other conferences. These are a study of defect reports, a study of change requests, and a study of effort spent in some releases of a large-scale telecommunications system. It was concluded that the integration of the results of such studies with other studies and with theory is a challenge, especially since measurement programs and metrics are tied to particular development approaches. As part of a solution for this problem, the authors present a set of metrics for a combined incremental, reuse-, and component-based development appoach. One workshop participant asked about the granularity of the collected effort data. Parastoo answered that effort data is needed per component and not only per use case, and that this is currently a problem with the repository that was analyzed. It was commented by another participant that components might have considerably different sizes, so the use of 'component' as a normalizing factor for effort is questionable. According to Parastoo this is true, however, in a well-defined context such as the one presented, components have similar sizes. Another participant noticed that the distinction between 'reused' and 'not reused' components is too coarse-grained. There might be a wide range of values between these two extremes with respect to the extent of software reuse. There was also the question of the validity of the data in the repository. Parastoo admitted that all data was used, even without being sure that a validation procedure was used before storing the data. There was however a configuration management system in use, which provides some assurance against storing invalid data. Another question related to the analysis techniques that were used. These were hypothesis testing and correlational analysis, but not multivariate analysis yet.

After lunch we had a session on Functional size and quality where three papers were presented.

Validation Issues in Functional Size Measurement of Object-Oriented Conceptual Schemas: The Case of OOmFP. Silvia Abrahäo, Geert Poels, and Oscar Pastor.

The paper, presented by Silvia Abrahao, introduced a framework for evaluating Functional Size Measurement (FSM) methods, based on a process model for functional size measurement. The authors also show how to apply this framework to evaluate OO-Method Function Points (OOmFP) focusing on the role of theoretical validation within the evaluation framework.

Silvia was asked about the metamodel that during the talk she mentioned that they used for defining the concepts in FP but it cannot be found in the paper. She also was asked about the relationship between Object Points and their approach and she said that they haven't yet come across it but they will have a look. Also an attendant asked about what meta-model was used for the FSM method? and Silvia asked that they used UML to formalize the IFPUG-FPA meta-model that was first mapped into the OO-Method meta-model.

A Proposal of a Multidimensional Model for Web-Based Applications Quality. Ghazwa Malak, Linda Badri, Mourad Badri and H. Sahraoui.

In this paper, authors propose a three-dimensional model for web-based applications quality. Houari, who presented the paper, was asked about the correctness of considering the application domain as a dimension for the web quality model taking into account that it is a nominal scale and he answered that two dimensions is not enough. Also related to the domain dimension he was asked if there should not be a different quality model for each domain instead of having the domain dimension by itself and he said that they looked for orthogonal dimensions and they thought that a dimension, which refers to the profile of the web application, which has its impact on quality characteristics, was necessary. He was also asked about how the information content or volume assessment was considered in their model and he said that they believe assessment is only a problem if the site is not well structured.

Measuring the Effects of Patterns on Object Oriented Micro Architectural Design. Javier Garzás and Mario Piattini.

In OO Micro-Architectural Design Knowledge, design patterns are a key and important technique. "Using design patterns increments design quality" is a famous sentence, but this is an ambiguous and imprecise sentence: what does "design quality" mean? Patterns affects on difference way to the quality of the micro architectural design. In this paper authors propose metrics for answering this important question. An attendant asked Mario, the presenter of the work, that the optimal number of patterns seems to be a magic number and Mario answered that they were conscious of that, especially since there are so many kinds of OO patterns. He also he was asked about the definition of a metric included on the paper.

During the short paper session, we started by a demo on software metrics visualization using perception and simulation presented by Houari Sahraoui. After the demo, two participants presented briefly their positions.

Aspect Cohesion Measurement Based on Dependence Analysis. Jean-François Gélinas, Linda Badri and Mourad Badri

Jean-François argued that Aspect-Oriented Programming is a promising new paradigm. Although several metrics have been proposed in order to assess object-oriented software quality attributes, new metrics must be developed to hold account Aspect's characteristics. As cohesion is considered as one of the most important software quality attributes, he proposes a new approach for aspect cohesion assessment based on dependence analysis. To illustrate his proposal, he introduced several cohesion criteria and built a new cohesion metric using them. After this short presentation a discussion took a place. The first topic that was addressed concerns the alternatives of adapting existing OO cohesion metrics or developing aspect cohesion metrics from scratch. The position of Jean-François is that AOP introduced many new concepts which made any adaptation hard and risky. The second topic addressed the problem of choosing the cohesion rather than other attributes like coupling. Jean-François explained that cohesion is a fundamental principle of aspects. An aspect is supposed to implement a cohesive behavior. The final discussion topic was about the coverage of the proposed metric. Jean-François recognized that more metrics are probably needed to cover all the different factors that can influence the cohesion.

Towards A Minimal Performance Metrics Suite for Agent-Based Systems. Amir Zeid and Maha Abdel Kader.

Sherif Gurguis was the last participant who presented the position of his team. Like the previous position, he claimed that agent-oriented paradigm is gaining popularity. With this respect, each scientific development that claims to provide a "new way" for approaching existing problems needs proper (i.e. formal and quantifiable) evaluation methods and consensus-based criteria for measuring the validity of its claims. As agents present some unique features that should be verified and evaluated, it is important to define useful metrics to measure them. The particularity of this work is that the authors start by defining a large set of metrics and then reduce this set by evaluating the dependency between the metrics using correlation techniques.

The workshop finished with a Discussion and closing session During this session, the first part was devoted to the identification of important issues that emerged from the different sessions of the day.

- Participants from industry and academia agreed the fact that it is difficult to define objective measures for evaluating the ROI of adopting product measurement and quality programs.

- ISO9126 was used during the past years as a starting point for a large part of software measurement research work. Today it is obvious that this model is not application to software applications built using emerging technologies such as component and web-based applications. The adaptation of this model and/or the definition of technology-specific models are crucial issues.
- The adaptation of structural programming-based metrics to OO paradigm have reveled many problems. The same problem is occurring today with the adaptation of OO metrics to emerging technologies (aspects, components, agents, etc. . .). What are the lessons and how can we make this transition more successful that the previous one?
- Although many contributions have been made in the study of the relationships between quality attributes and metrics, the area still suffers from rigorous and exhaustive results.
- The success of evaluating the majority of software quality factors is deeply related to the ability of understanding the phenomena behind them such as software evolution. Even if there is a consensus on this statement, very few work addressed the theory and model that can represent these phenomena.

During the second part of this session, additional issues were identified as future challenges for the community and consequently as important topics for the next year workshop edition. These topics are:

- Quantitative visualization of large sets of software artifacts
- Measurement and quality evaluation of component and service-based application
- Measurement and quality evaluation for aspect-oriented software development
- Rigorous empirical studies for software quality evaluation
- Paradigm independent product metrics
- Process vs product attributes
- Metric-based reengineering
- Early development phase metrics
- Relationship between cost/effort and quality factors
- Influence of context (product and/or organization) on quality

6   Other Information Related to the Workshop

The links to the web pages of the previous editions of the workshop are:

- QAOOSE'2003:
  http://ctp.di.fct.unl.pt/QUASAR/QAOOSE2003
- QAOOSE'2002:
  http://alarcos.inf-cr.uclm.es/qaoose2002
- QAOOSE'2001:
  http://www.iro.umontreal.ca/~sahraouh/qaoose01

- QAOOSE'2000:
  http://ecoop2000.unice.fr/Program/Technical/Workshops/w10.html
- QAOOSE'99:
  http://ecoop99.di.fc.ul.pt/techprogramme/w20.html
- OO Product Metrics for Software Quality Assessment:
  http://www.crim.ca/~hsahraou/oopm.html
- Quantitative Methods for OO Systems Development:
  http://ctp.di.fct.unl.pt/QUASAR/ECOOP95

Eighth Workshop on Pedagogies and Tools for the Teaching and Learning of Object Oriented Concepts*

Jürgen Börstler[1], Isabel Michiels[2], and Annita Fjuk[3]

[1] Umeå University, Sweden
[2] Vrije Universiteit Brussel, Belgium
[3] University of Oslo, Norway

Abstract. This report summarises the results of the eighth workshop in a series of workshops on pedagogies and tools for the teaching and learning of object-oriented concepts. The submissions to this year's workshop mainly covered curriculum issues, tool support for teaching, and case studies. Several contributions dealt with teaching object-orientation to non-Majors (junior high-school students, non-Science students). This aspect permeated most of the discussions at the workshop and is also reflected in the conclusions. The workshop gathered 19 participants from nine different countries.

1   Introduction

Object-orientation has nowadays become the dominant software development paradigm. In most educational programs object-orientation is the first (and sometimes the only) paradigm students encounter. Successfully applying object-oriented methods, languages and tools requires a thorough understanding of the underlying object-oriented concepts. Despite this importance there is still no accepted approach to effectively teach or learn basic object-oriented concepts.

Studies show that there is a great mismatch between language used and paradigm taught. In Australia for example about 82% of the introductory programming instructors use an object-oriented language. Only about 37% however teach their courses using an object-oriented approach [1]. Most educational publications however suggest to introduce objects early on.

Using traditional programming languages, concepts could be introduced step by step. Abstract and advanced concepts, like for example modules and abstract data types could be handled as an afterthought. In the object-oriented paradigm, the basic concepts are tightly interrelated and cannot easily be taught and learned in isolation, making these tasks much more challenging.

---

* The title of this report should be referenced as "Report from the ECOOP 2004 Eighth Workshop on Pedagogies and Tools for the Teaching and Learning of Object Oriented Concepts".

J. Malenfant and B.M. Østvold (Eds.): ECOOP 2004, LNCS 3344, pp. 36–48, 2004.
© Springer-Verlag Berlin Heidelberg 2004

Switching to object-oriented development is not just a matter of programming languages. Focusing on the notational details of a certain language prevents students from grasping the "big picture." Most students therefore have difficulties taking advantage of object-oriented concepts. Many traditional examples are furthermore not very suitable for the teaching and learning of object-oriented concepts. Many popular examples (like for example 'Hello World') actually contradict the rules, guidelines and styles we want to instill in our students [2].

Educators must therefore be very careful when selecting or developing examples and metaphors. Rules and misconceptions that students develop based on doubtful examples will stand in the way of teachers and learners as well.

This was the eighth in a series of workshops on issues in object-oriented teaching and learning. Reports from most previous workshops in the series are available [3, 4, 5, 6, 7, 8]. Further information and links to the accepted contributions of most workshops can be found at the workshop series home page [9].

The objective of the workshop series is to share experiences and discuss ideas, approaches and hypotheses on how to improve the teaching and learning of object-oriented concepts. The organisers particularly invited submissions on the following topics:

- successfully used examples and metaphors;
- approaches and tools for teaching (basic) object-oriented concepts;
- approaches and tools for teaching analysis and design;
- ordering of topics, in particular when to teach analysis and design;
- experiences with innovative CS1 curricula and didactic techniques;
- learning theories and pedagogical approaches / methods;
- representation of learning resources;
- distance education / net-based learning;
- collaborative learning;
- guiding the learners;
- learners' view(s) on object technology education;
- development of the learner's competence.

2   Workshop Organisation

Participation at the workshop was by invitation only. The number of participants was limited to encourage the building of few small interest groups working on specific topics. Potential attendees were required to submit position papers.

Out of the 11 position papers that were submitted, 9 papers were accepted, of which 7 were formally presented at the workshop. Two papers were rejected. All accepted contributions were made available on the workshop's web site some weeks before the workshop, in order to give attendees the opportunity to prepare for the discussions. All formal presentation activities were scheduled for the morning sessions. The afternoon sessions were dedicated to discussions in small working groups.

After the formal presentations all attendees had the opportunity to present their main "message(s)" in a round-robin presentation (materials had to be

Table 1. Workshop program

TIME	TOPIC
9:00	**Welcome and Introduction**
9:15	**Session 1: Curriculum Issues** Why Structural Recursion Should Be Taught Before Arrays in CS 1, *K. Bruce (15 min)* Teaching Object-Oriented Programming–Towards Teaching a Systematic Programming Process, *M.E. Caspersen (15 min)* Object-Orientation by Immersion–Teaching Outside the CS Department, *M. Lindholm (10 min)* Discussion (10 min)
10:05	**Session 2: Tools** OCLE, a Tool Supporting Teaching and Learning UML and OCL, the Understanding and Using of Metamodeling, Abstraction and Design by Contract, *D. Chiorean (10 min)* Online Assessment of Programming Exercises, *G. Fischer (10 min)* Discussion (5 min)
10:30	**Coffee Break**
11:00	**Session 3: Case Studies** Junior High School Students' Perception of Object-Oriented Concepts, *M. Teif (15 min)* Lego as platform for learning OO thinking in primary and secondary school, *C. Holmboe (15 min)* Discussion (10 min)
11:40	**Round-robin Presentations of Attendee Positions (1 overhead each)**
12:10	**Split up into Working Groups**
11:30	**Lunch Break**
13:30	**Parallel Working Group Sessions**
15:00	**Coffee Break**
15:30	**Parallel Working Group Sessions (cont.)**
16:15	**Working Group Reports, Discussion, Wrap-up**
17:00	**Closing**

submitted in advance). After that three working groups were formed to discuss in more detail the topics they found most interesting or relevant. The full workshop program can be found in table 2.

The workshop gathered 19 participants from nine different countries, all of them from academia. A complete list of participants together with their affiliations and e-mail addresses can be found in table 4.2.

3   Summary of Presentations

This section summarises the main points of the presented papers and the most important issues raised during the morning discussions. More information on the presented papers can be obtained from the workshop's home page [10].

Table 2. Overview of the presentations

	Bruce	Caspersen	Lindholm	Chiorean	Fischer	Teif	Holmboe
Target Group							
– CS juniors	X	X			X		(X)
– CS seniors				X			
– Non-CS			X		(X)	X	X
– Pre-Univ.						X	X
Target Area							
– OOP	X	X			X	(X)	(X)
– OO concepts	X	(X)	X	(X)		X	X
– Design			X				
– Modelling		X		X			(X)
– Formal Spec.				X			
– Testing				(X)	(X)		
Paper Type							
– Exp. report	X	X	X	X	X		
– Case study						X	X
Main message	Teach structural recursion before arrays	Teach systematic techniques and processes explicitly	Use sufficiently complex examples from a familiar domain	Tool support is essential for teaching meta-modelling	Automatic assessment is both feasible and effective	Misconceptions don't differ with age	OO is more about a way of thinking as a way of programming

3.1   Curriculum Issues

Kim Bruce (Williams College, MA, USA) described how rearranging topics helped his CS1 students to better understand object-oriented principles, in particular encapsulation. The first half of the course originally took an objects-first, event-driven approach using the objectdraw library, developed at Williams College. The students caught on very well to object-orientation using this approach. However, when introducing non-object-oriented structures, like arrays, strings and files in the second part of the course the students do no longer apply the object oriented principles they have learned. Students for example resisted to encapsulate arrays in purposeful objects and returned to directly manipulating arrays and their elements.

Moving the topic of structural recursion from the end of the course to the beginning of the second part of the course (i.e. before introducing arrays), proved to be a major improvement. Kim argued that recursive structures are much easier to understand than recursive procedures. In their course they use recursive pictures, where the base cases are realised as Java interfaces. The recursion is then an implementation of a Picture interface that has an instance variable of the interface type for the recursive part. Such recursive structures are also very useful to reinforce important object oriented concepts like dynamic method dispatch and interfaces. They also provide a smoother transition to arrays. This revised topic order also helps students to better understand the motives behind explicit encapsulation of arrays (compared to direct manipulation).

The audience found this approach very promising. However, it was not quite clear whether this approach could be used with more mediocre student groups. The concept of structural recursion is not that easy to grasp and even Kim's well designed examples would require a thorough understanding of object-oriented concepts. Kim argued that they hide many language specific details in their library. This makes it easier for the students to concentrate on the important things.

Michael E. Caspersen (University of Aarhus, Denmark) claimed that teaching should focus on systematic techniques to develop programs by means of conceptual modelling and that it is mandatory to train students in the process of applying systematic development techniques. He and his colleagues use a model-driven objects-first approach with a strong focus on systematic techniques and programming processes. In this approach the actual programming is not just a matter of a certain programming language. Students are gradually exposed to more complexity by means of conceptual models and not by means of more complex constructs in a certain programming language.

Systematic (implementation) techniques are taught on different levels. On method level the students deal with algorithm patterns and loop invariants. On class level the students deal with class specifications (contracts). On class structure level the students deal with specification models (class diagrams). This separation of concern makes it easier for students to choose the appropriate technique for the problem at hand. Michael also noted the importance of actually demonstrating how experts use these techniques in practise. The lecturers do a lot of "live" programming and modelling in class, where they say aloud what they do and why the do it in a particular way. They also show videos of actual developers working on real projects.

According to Michael the approach has been very successful. The drop-out rates have decreased from about 50% five years ago to about 10%.

Morten Lindholm (University of Aarhus, Denmark) described his approach to teaching object-oriented concepts to students of the Faculty of Arts. The goal of the two-semester course Programming & Systems Development is to give students a basic understanding of computers and software development. A problem in course development had been to find a suitable textbook for students from the humanities or social sciences. Current textbooks usually aim at students with a Science or Engineering background and are therefore full of problems, examples and exercises that draw on this background. Most solutions (i.e. example programs) lack therefore objects rooted in the "real" world, as for example System.out.

Morten suggested to use language philosophy and logic as the foundation for object-orientation and a way to reason about ways of describing (a model of) the world in a machine. To motivate the students examples, assignments, and projects should always be taken from a domain familiar to the students. There should also be a mapping to the real world in order to grasp what an object is.

The students in this course sequence are exposed to a wide range of techniques to give them a broad view of object-orientation and design (CRC-cards, UML, Pair Programming, Design Patterns, Unified Process). These techniques are then trained by means of team projects. This approach seems to work well except for the actual coding part.

In his talk Morten highlighted the importance of "sufficiently complex" examples[1]. The real power of object-oriented modelling cannot be used in trivial examples. Several attendees choose to disagree here. Micheal Caspersen agreed that examples should not be trivial and, but not more complex than necessary to make their point. He would rather vote for "sufficiently simple" examples. As another important point it was mentioned that every program the students write, should reflect the programs the students use (i.e. no batch-like processing for example).

3.2   Tools

Dan Chiorean (Babes-Bolyai University, Romania) presented OCLE (Object Constraint Language Environment), a tool for the teaching and learning of OCL, UML, metamodelling, and abstraction. Dan presented several examples how the tool can be used to view, evaluate and transform example specifications. OCLE supports modelling on the user model level as well as the metamodel level. By grouping both kinds of models in one project, the user models can then be (statically) validated against the corresponding rules defined in the metamodel.

This kind of parallel modelling on two different levels of abstraction helps the students to appreciate metamodelling and also to better understand the semantics of OCL and UML. The tool can visualise different views of the same information at the simultaneously. This enables students to understand how decisions made at metamodel level affect instances on the user model level.

The tool can even generate (Java) code from OCL specifications. By doing so one can trace the effects of changes in the metamodel down to the generated code. It was however not clear whether the code generation would scale up to more complex examples.

Gregor Fischer (University of Wrzburg, Germany) reported about the usage of Praktomat (see [8]) to automatically assess programming exercises. All attendees agreed that multiple-choice tests are not very reliable for assessing programming skills. However, manually assessing large numbers of exercises in a consistent manner would be very difficult, if not infeasible.

Praktomat is capable of several types of tests; formal (syntax, compiling, coding style and required documentation), program structure, specification requirements, and functional tests. Functional testing is done by means of testing operations written in JUnit. Functional testing against the results of master so-

---

[1] The idea of using *sufficiently complex* examples was originally propagated by Kristen Nygaard using his famous Restaurant example.

lution (working as an oracle) did not work as reliable. This would however put less restrictions on the structure of the solutions that must be delivered by the students.

The tool results are very reliable. Less than 2% of the programs passing all automatic tests were rejected by a human inspector. It was however not clear whether fundamentally good, but imperfect solutions would be rejected by the tool. The examination work load decreased by a factor of four. Developing suitable exercises on the other hand is much more expensive. Gregor did not have actual data on this part, but claimed that there still is a reasonable pay off.

Programming is a skill that requires a lot of training. Automatic assessment can provide the immediate feedback that is necessary to handle large student groups and/ or large numbers of exercises. In the current setting students can perform as many tests as they like before finally submitting their programs. The audience was not sure whether this will teach students bad habits. Nevertheless, since the tool has been introduced Gregor and his colleagues have observed considerable quality improvements in students' solutions. The tool did on the other hand, not affect the course's overall passing rate.

Gregor noted further that currently all test are public. This helped many students appreciate proper testing. For the future it is planned to integrate testing and test development into the course (but how will the tests be tested).

3.3   Pre-university Case Studies

Mariana Teif (Israel Institute of Technology, Israel) presented results from a junior high school course (7th-8th grade) on object-oriented concepts. In the context of a research project, she studied difficulties and misconceptions the students faced while learning basic object oriented concepts. The students developed small programs using a Java-based Turtle-graphics environment. Students did not have to present practical programming skills at the end of the course. Examination was by means of concept-level questions.

The study identified four types of misconceptions. Students did for example confuse an object's attributes with its parts (components) or actions (knowing how to do certain things). They had also difficulties accepting sets as objects and considered set-subset (hierarchy) relationships and whole-part relationships as equal to the class-instance relationship. A follow-up study with undergraduate students as subjects revealed the same results.

Mariana discussed a range of possible explanations for the found misconceptions, which might be based on classification theory. Further research and analysis is planned to explain the underlying reasons for the problems.

Christian Holmboe (University of Oslo, Norway) presented preliminary results from a case study done in the context of the COOL[2] project on teaching primary and secondary school children general principles of object-orientation and computer functionality.

---

[2] Comprehensive **O**bject-**O**riented **L**earning

The study was carried out as an intensive four day course, with two different age groups (6th and 9th grade respectively) at different schools. The object-oriented concepts covered were classification, specialisation and aggregation. The students engaged in various types of classroom activities, like drawing, building with Lego, or written textual definitions. The "products" of these activities were discussed with respect to features, attributes and different kinds of relationships to emphasise the usefulness of different kinds of "specification" mechanisms.

In a group project the students then explored and programmed a Lego vehicle using a small Robot API based on LeJoS, a Java-based development language for Lego. The API and an object diagram for the vehicle were carefully explained and set up on the walls of the classroom. The results of the students' group work were discussed in relation to object-oriented principles, but without using strict object-oriented terminology. After that the students did some exercises using the Restaurant example.

The students solved quite interesting tasks after only four days. Interviews after the course (using another example) showed that the students gained quite some understanding of the covered object-oriented concepts. Teaching (object-oriented) design and technology in this way might enhance the students confidence about information technology. This might help to get more people interested in Information Technology and Computer Science. Further studies of the gathered data are however necessary to draw any safe conclusions.

4   Working Group Discussions

For the afternoon sessions participants formed three working groups to discuss specific topics in more detail. The following subsections summarise the discussions on the topics discussed in more detail.

4.1   Balancing Focus Between Process and Product

The discussion was initiated by trying to establish a common understanding of the notions of "process" and "product." A product is a concrete result of a (planned) development activity, like for example the final executable program code, a diagram or a model. A process is the sum of the developers' actions to produce these products. To develop a product we also have to take care of the pragmatics of software development, like for example the usage of tools and the application of certain guiding principles and rules.

In his analogy with cabinet making, David Gries described nicely how the teaching about products, processes and pragmatics should (not) be didactically and pedagogically organised [11]:

> Suppose you attend a course in cabinet making. The instructor briefly shows you a saw, a plane, a hammer, and a few other tools, letting you use each one for a few minutes. He next shows you a beautifully-finished cabinet. Finally he tells you to design your own cabinet and bring him the finished product in a few weeks.

You would think he was crazy! You would want instructions on designing the cabinet, his ideas on what kind of wood to use, some individual attention when you don't know what to do next, his opinion on whether you have sanded enough, and so on. (p82)

One way of achieving a balance between product and process in teaching, is to expose students to how experienced programmers work. Like how a master shows his or her profession to apprentices. Approaches like projector-programming and live-programming in the classroom were considered important by all group members. However, when a teacher demonstrates the process of programming (with help of a projector or the like), she must also think aloud and make typical errors. Programming is not a straight forward process. Students must be reassured that there are no single correct solutions that will unfold automatically when "doing it right."

4.2   Student Diversity and Core Computer Science

Teaching Computer Science to different groups of students rises the question about a thorough definition about the core of our field. What do we need to teach to students who take only few Computer Science courses? The definition of a "real" core (see 1) of Computer Science must necessarily be much narrower for students outside our field compared to the definition as for example proposed by the CC2001 [12].

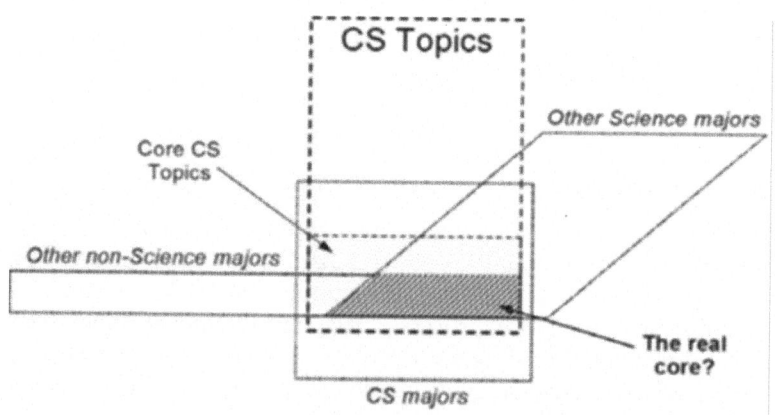

Fig. 1 Points of view of the core of Computer Science

The group concluded that object-oriented programming is not a core topic for students outside our field. However, object-orientation as a way to structure and model problems should be included in some way.

It was also pointed out that different groups of students would need different kinds of "windows" to view the core (see 2). Matlab for example could be a

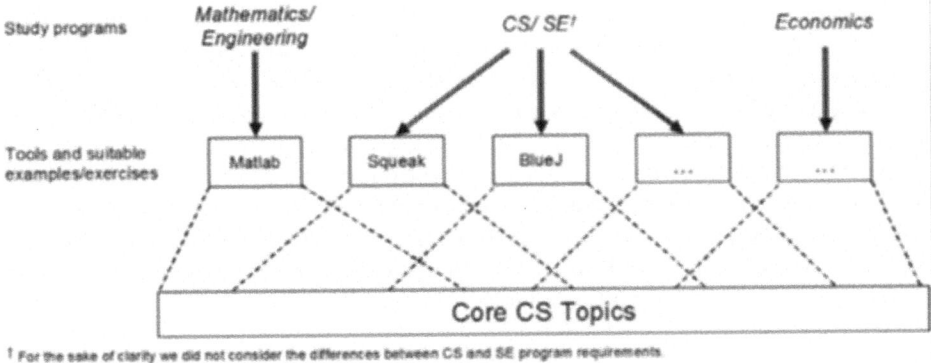

Fig. 2 Windows to approach the core of Computer Science

suitable window for Math or Engineering students to approach Computer Science. For all windows and groups it would be necessary to provide suitable examples.

Table 3. List of workshop participants

Name	Affiliation	E-mail Address
Jrgen Brstler	*Ume University, Sweden*	jubo@cs.umu.se
Isabel Michiels	*Vrije Universiteit Brussels, Belgium*	imichiel@vub.ac.be
Annita Fjuk	*University of Oslo, Norway*	annita.fjuk@telenor.com
Jens Kaasboll	*University of Oslo, Norway*	jensj@ifi.uio.no
Jens Bennedsen	*IT University West, Denmark*	jbb@it-vest.dk
Maria Bortes	*Babes-Bolyai University, Romania*	maria@lci.cs.ubbcluj.ro
Kim Bruce	*Williams College, MA, USA*	kim@cs.williams.edu
Michael E. Caspersen	*University of Aarhus, Denmark*	mec@daimi.au.dk
Dan Chiorean	*Babes-Bolyai University, Romania*	chiorean@lci.cs.ubbcluj.ro
Dyan Corutiu	*Babes-Bolyai University, Romania*	dyan@lci.cs.ubbcluj.ro
Gregor Fischer	*University of Wrzburg, Germany*	fischer@informatik.uni-wuerzburg.de
Roar Granerud	*University of Oslo, Norway*	rgraneru@ifi.uio.no
Arne-Kristian Groven	*Norwegian Computing Centre, Norway*	groven@nr.no
Hvard Hegna	*Norwegian Computing Centre, Norway*	hegna@nr.no
Christian Holmboe	*University of Oslo, Norway*	christho@ifi.uio.no
Morten Lindholm	*University of Aarhus, Denmark*	lindholm@daimi.au.dk
Wilfried Rupflin	*University of Dortmund, Germany*	wilfried.rupflin@uni-dortmund.de
Mariana Teif	*Israel Institute of Technology, Israel*	tmariana@tx.technion.ac.il
Kristina Vuckovic	*Zagreb University, Croatia*	kvuckovi@ffzg.hr

Most importantly examples need to be appealing to students and interesting in itself, but not necessarily depending on context (not everything needs to be real world relevant). Besides that examples must fulfill certain criteria to be meaningful with respect to object-orientation. They should for example comprise at least two classes, where at least one class has multiple instances. There should furthermore happen some real object interaction, where different objects need to (get to) know each other. Examples should also make use of non-static methods and exchange objects as parameters (instead of built-in types only). In addition to that custom designed libraries to hide language specific details would help students to focus on the real problems.

4.3   Student Attitudes

Student attitudes was another topic discussed in this group. The audience agreed that students are not as good as before in solving problems on their own. They quickly give up on exercises and they often rely on help from others when they are stuck with a certain problem. Possible solutions could be (as proposed by Michael Caspersen) to show students the process of working towards a reliable solution. However, it was argued that this is not sufficient. Teachers often ask themselves questions as part of this (implicit) process in specific orders. When this process is not made explicit to students, they do not know how to proceed once they are on their own. The group concluded that we definitely need to teach more programming methodology. This must however be done in a systematic way to enable the students to choose the "right" tool for the right problem. To help students build up confidence some kind of peer-based help to help yourself approach, like Supplemental Instruction, can also be very useful.

5   Conclusions

The objective of the workshop was to share experiences and to discuss ideas, approaches and hypotheses on how to improve the teaching and learning of object-oriented concepts.

Ongoing work was presented by a very diverse group of people with very different backgrounds, which resulted in a broad range of topics, see table 3. The workshop attendees represented a broad range of experiences, which are often not easily accessible and transferable. We can definitely conclude that there are many approaches that can work in certain environments. We can also certainly conclude that there is no is no one-size-fits-all approach to teaching object-oriented concepts and principles. The challenge is to find the right approach (or view on things) for each type of student.

To summarise our discussions we want to suggest the following.

- We must expose students to the real programming process, instead of an idealised linear one. Software development is an inherently incremental process. Students must be made aware of that there is no single correct solution to virtually any programming problem. There is not even a single correct process that will "automatically" reveal a correct solution. This is even more important when students are faced with analysis and design problems.

- Students need "tools" to help them escape when they get stuck on their own, instead of waiting for someone to help them out. The teaching of systematic techniques and explicit processes can help a lot. But, especially weaker students, also need help to improve their self-confidence, for example by means of supplemental instruction.
- Carefully developed examples and exercises are very important. They must be designed with the target group of students in mind. They must also be valid and meaningful with respect to the object-oriented paradigm.
- Object-oriented programming is not a given core subject for non-Majors in Computer Science. However, basic object-oriented concepts or principles, like encapsulation and abstraction, should certainly be taught to any student to enable them to cope with complexity.

References

1. de Raadt, M., Watson, R., Toleman, M.: Introductory Programming: What's Happening Today and Will There Be Any Students to Teach Tomorrow? In: Lister, R., Young, A.: Proceedings ACE2004, Conferences in Research and Practice in Information Technology, Vol. 30, Australian Computer Society (2004) 277-282.
2. Westfall, R.: "Hello, World" Considered Harmful. Communications of the ACM **44** (10) (2001) 129-130.
3. Börstler, J. (ed.): OOPSLA'97 Workshop Report: Doing Your First OO Project. Technical Report UMINF-97.26. Department of Computing Science, Umeå University, Sweden (1997).
4. Börstler, J. (chpt. ed.): Learning and Teaching Objects Successfully. In: Demeyer, S., Bosch, J. (eds.): Object-Oriented Technology, ECOOP'98 Workshop Reader. Lecture Notes in Computer Science, Vol. 1543. Springer-Verlag (1998) 333-362.
5. Börstler, J., Fernández, A. (eds.): OOPSLA'99 Workshop Report: Quest for Effective Classroom Examples. Technical Report UMINF-00.03. Department of Computing Science, Umeå University, Sweden (2000).
6. Michiels, I., Börstler, J.: Tools and Environments for Understanding Object-Oriented Concepts. In:Malenfant, J., Moisan, S., Moreira, A. (eds.): Object Oriented Technology, ECOOP 2000 Workshop Reader, Lecture Notes in Computer Science, Vol. 1964. Springer (2000) 65-77.
7. Michiels, I., Börstler, J., Bruce, K.: Sixth Workshop on Pedagogies and Tools for Learning Object-Oriented Concepts. In: Hernández, J., Moreira, A. (eds.): Object Oriented Technology, ECOOP 2002 Workshop Reader, Lecture Notes in Computer Science, Vol. 2548, Springer (2002) 30-43.
8. Michiels, I., Börstler, J., Bruce, K., Fernndez, A.: Tools and Environments for Learning Object-Oriented Concepts. In: ECOOP 2003 Workshop Reader, Lecture Notes in Computer Science, Vol. 3013, Springer (2004) 119-129.
9. Workshop series homepage: Pedagogies and Tools for the Teaching and Learning of Object Technology. http://www.cs.umu.se/research/education/ooEduWS.html

10. ECOOP04 workshop homepage. http://www.cs.umu.se/~jubo/Meetings/ECOOP04
11. Gries, D.: What Should We Teach in an Introductory Programmming Course. Proceedings of the fourth SIGCSE Technical Symposium on Computer Science Education. ACM SIGCSE Bulletin **6** (1) (1974) 81-89.
12. CC2001 Task Force: Computing Curricula 2001-Computer Science. Final Report (2001).

2nd Workshop on Object-Oriented Language Engineering for the Post-Java Era: Back to Dynamicity*

Sebastián González[1], Wolfgang De Meuter[2], Pascal Costanza[3],
Stéphane Ducasse[4], Richard Gabriel[5], and Theo D'Hondt[2]

[1] Département d'Ingénierie Informatique, Université catholique de Louvain – Belgium
[2] Programming Technology Lab, Vrije Universiteit Brussel – Belgium
[3] Institute of Computer Science III, Universität Bonn – Germany
[4] Software Composition Group, Universität Bern – Switzerland
[5] Sun Microsystems – USA

Abstract. This report covers the activities of the 2nd workshop on "Object-Oriented Language Engineering for the Post-Java Era". We describe the motivation that led to the organisation of a second edition of the workshop. Relevant organisational aspects are mentioned. The main part of the report consists of a summary of Dave Thomas's invited talk, and a recount of the presentations by the authors of position papers. Comments given along the way by the participants are included. Finally, some pointers to related work and events are given.

1   Introduction

As stated in the workshop's first edition, the advent of Java has always been perceived as a major breakthrough in the realm of object-oriented languages. And to some extent it was: it turned academic features like interfaces, garbage-collection and meta-programming into technologies generally accepted by industry. Nevertheless Java also acted as a brake especially to academic language design research. Whereas pre-Java ECOOP's and OOPSLA's traditionally featured several tracks with a plethora of research results in language design, more recent versions of these conferences show far less of these. Those results that do make it to the proceedings very often are formulated as extensions of Java. Hence, they necessarily follow the Java doctrine: statically typed, single-inheritance, class-based languages with interfaces and exception handling.

Recent academic developments seem to indicate that a new generation of application domains is emerging for whose development the languages adhering to this doctrine will probably no longer be sufficient. These application domains

---

* The title of this report should be referenced as "Report from the ECOOP 2004 2nd Workshop on Object-Oriented Language Engineering for the Post-Java Era: Back to Dynamicity".

J. Malenfant and B.M. Østvold (Eds.): ECOOP 2004, LNCS 3344, pp. 49–61, 2004.

have recently been grouped together under the name of Ambient Intelligence
(AmI). The visionary idea of AmI is that in the future, everybody will be sur-
rounded by a dynamically defined processor cloud of which the applications are
expected to cooperate smoothly. AmI was put forward as one of the major strategic research themes by the IST Advisory Group of the European Commission
for the financing structure of the 6th Framework of the European Union [1, 2].
Meanwhile, the first European symposium on AmI has recently been organised
and institutions like the MIT and Phillips have published their visions on the
matter. Currently, AmI seems to group previously "unrelated" fields such as
context dependency, domotics, ubiquitous/pervasive computing, mobility, intelligent buildings and wearable hardware. Early experiments in these fields already
seem to indicate that their full development will need a new generation of programming languages that have dedicated provisions to deal with highly dynamic
hardware and software constellations. As such, AmI will open up a new "market"
for a new generation of programming languages which are designed to write software that is expected to operate in extremely dynamic hardware and software
configurations.

The big success of the workshop's first edition at ECOOP 2003 [3] confirmed
the feeling that many researchers in the object-oriented community are still interested in object-oriented language design, and moreover, many are interested
in languages that move away from Java's main design lines. The goal of this
second edition of the workshop was to address object-oriented languages that
diverge from Java's doctrine but support a much more dynamic way of constructing software. In the near future, this dynamicity will be required in order
to construct software that is highly context-dependent due to the mobility of
both the software itself and its users, as is the case in AmI. There is a new
future for languages based on Lisp, CLOS, Scheme, Self, Smalltalk and loads of
less well-known academic languages. This new generation of programming languages will exhibit a mix of new and old ideas. Many position papers submitted
to the workshop support this view.

2   Organisation

This section summarises some organisative aspects of the workshop and gives
information about attendance.

The submitted position papers, the invited talk slides, and complementary
information about the workshop can be found at the workshop website:
http://prog.vub.ac.be/~wdmeuter/PostJava04/

2.1   Call for Contributions

The call for contributions invited researchers to submit a position paper or an es-
say (6 pages maximum) about new language features or about existing ones that
cover solutions to problems that are currently getting relevant in mainstream
languages. Provocative and visionary contributions were especially encouraged.

Dynamicity as required by the AmI vision was selected as the common theme of the workshop, i.e. a new context in which we can talk about the object-oriented language features of the future. Hence the "Back to Dynamicity" part in the workshop's title. Topics of interest were formulated as follows:

- agent languages,
- distributed languages,
- actors, active objects,
- delegation,
- mixins,
- prototypes,
- multi-paradigm programming,
- meta-programming and reflection,
- mobile languages,
- (distributed/mobile) virtual machines,
- other exotic dynamic features which could be categorised as OO.

2.2   Organisers

Wolfgang De Meuter
wdmeuter@vub.ac.be

Pascal Costanza
costanza@web.de

Stéphane Ducasse
ducasse@iam.unibe.ch

Richard Gabriel
rpg@dreamsongs.com

Theo D'Hondt
tjdhondt@vub.ac.be

The affiliations of the organisers are mentioned in the title of this report.

The organisers asked the first author to write this report (even though he is not an organiser himself), since he played the role of reporter of the workshop. The cooperation was natural given that the workshop proposal was actually a merge of two earlier proposals, one of which was co-submitted by the first author.

2.3   Format

The workshop started with an invited talk by Dave Thomas (see section 3.1). The presentation of each position paper followed, in 30-minute slots including questions. The more "technical" papers were first in the lineup. The more "philosophical" papers were presented after lunch. A plenary discussion session was held afterwards, and the workshop finished with a short wrap-up / evaluation part.

2.4   Attendance

A total of 9 position papers were received. PDF files can be found at the workshop website (see section 4). Of those 9 submissions, 7 authors attended the workshop. Other 13 attendees were present for a total of 20 people:

1. Christopher Anderson, Imperial College London – UK
2. Marie Beurton-Aimar, University of Bordeaux – France

3. Ilia Bider, Ibisoft – Sweden
4. Alex Buckley, Imperial College London – UK
5. Raphaël Collet, UCL – Belgium
6. Marc Conrad, University of Luton – UK
7. Pascal Costanza, University of Bonn – Germany
8. Wolfgang De Meuter, VUB – Belgium
9. Theo D'Hondt, VUB – Belgium
10. Jean-François Gélinas, UQTR – Canada
11. Sebastián González, UCL – Belgium
12. Christian Heinlein, University of Ulm – Germany
13. Jonne Itkonen, University of Jyväskylä – Finland
14. Erik Meijer, Microsoft – USA
15. Sven-Olof Nyström, Uppsala University – Sweden
16. Maximilian Störzer, University of Passau – Germany
17. Eric Tanter, University of Chile – Chile
18. Dave Thomas, Bedarra Research Labs – Canada
19. Richard Torkar, BTH – Sweden
20. Jianguo Zhou, University of Leicester – UK

3   Presentations

This section accounts for the workshop presentations. Two main lines were observed in the contributions this year: concurrency and dynamic system adaption. Some position papers were in one extreme (e.g. concurrency in Erlang) or in the other (e.g. object shadowing), but most of them are influenced by both forces. An approximate classification of the presentations (including Dave Thomas's invited talk) could be:

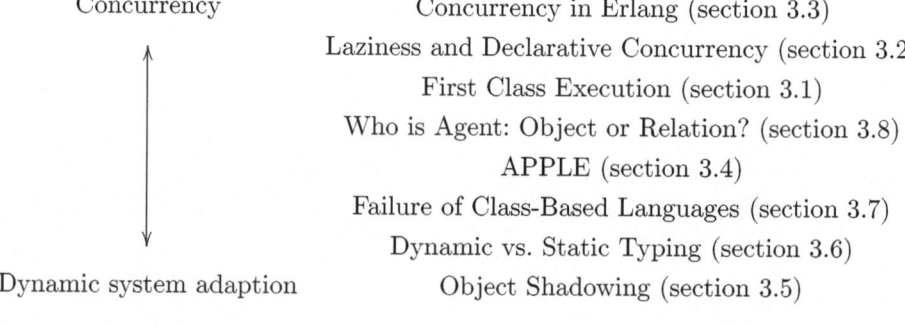

In the reminder of this section, we hope to give a complementary view of the position papers by describing the presentations rather than the papers themselves. The highlights of the discussions by the participants are marked with a [**Discussion**]. label so that they can be easily spotted, although we don't aim at covering each and every nit. The presentation order here is the same as in the workshop.

3.1 Invited Talk: *First Class Execution – Messages and Actors*
Dave Thomas and Brian Barry, Bedarra Research Labs

In his invited talk, Dave Thomas advocated the reification of messages in object-based programming languages. Current commercial OO languages lack support for first class execution (unlike Beta, ABCL etc.). One symptom is that messages have no meta-messages, while classes do have meta-classes. A second one is that message dispatch (evaluation) is usually "hidden", i.e. performed using internal machinery hidden in the compiler or virtual machine. Ideally, messages should have first class status. Many applications are considerably simpler if the viewed from the perspective of the message rather than the object/process. This message-centric view, baptised M essage-O riented P rogramm ingby Dave Thomas [4], is aligned with the ideas presented by Ilia Bider (see section 3.8).

Method dispatch can be abstractly defined in message-oriented programming as: *eval(message, args, sender, receiver)*, where the sending and receiving objects are explicit parameters to the message evaluation in addition to the arguments. A quick comparison shows the differences with two other fundamental approaches:

- Scheme: given the function (method) find the environment.
- Smalltalk: given the environment, find the function (method).
- Message-oriented programming: given the message determine the function (method), knowing the message definition and the value of the sender (environment) and the receiver (environment).

Message-oriented programming is one part of a broader view on how to structure Service Oriented Architectures (SOAs) [5]. The coordination of services (nowadays web services) has proved to be difficult using petri nets or state machines. Dave Thomas turned attention to Carl Hewitt's actor model [6] to tackle this problem. Actors are autonomous and concurrent objects that communicate asynchronously and are intended to be a model of an intelligent person. When an actor receives a message, it executes according to its script and communicates with a well-defined and finite set of other known actors. Actors allow one to model computations as an organisation of communicating active objects and to apply anthropomorphic roles such as Workers, Coordinators, Managers, Couriers, Notifiers, or more application-specific ones like PulseCourier, RadarTrack, TrackManager. Hence, workflow in the system mimics real-world workflow. This Anthropom orph ic P rogramm ingapproach allows business processes to be expressed using common organisational design principles.

Anthropomorphic programming was used for process structuring in the Harmony operating system: tasks are assigned personified roles such as the already mentioned Servers, Administrators, Workers, Couriers, Notifiers, etc. Each of these roles has well known pre-defined semantics. Servers must be responsive, so they delegate most of the work. Processes spend most of their life in a "receive any" loop, while Workers do most computations. The Administrator helps organise this. All these tasks are very lightweight (in Harmony, tasks = processes = threads). Harmony is a message-based operating system, with a simple set of primitives: Blocking Send, Blocking Receive, Reply, Create, Terminate and special forms for Non-Blocking Receive and Interrupts.

Harmony was used as a foundation for the Actra project. Actra sought to show how far Smalltalk could be used in the development of complex embedded applications. The Actra project combined Smalltalk, actors and multiprocessors. An actor encapsulates cooperating passive (non-actor) objects. Actors synchronize and communicate by sending messages. Actors execute in pseudo parallel on a single processor and in parallel on multiple processors. Actors have the granularity of lightweight processes (threads/tasks). There are uniform semantics for remote/local processes and these processes have a well defined life cycle. In Actra, programmers create their own application-specific actors by specialising the generic ones. The complete taxonomy of known actors, some generic, many more application specific, creates a vocabulary that populates the programming model and defines its semantics.

[**Discussion**]. One participant asked why Smalltalk is not considered to have first-class messages, given that the `doesNotUnderstand:` message can be over-ridden to get an instance of the `Message` class. This was considered a hack by Thomas, rather than a true first-class mechanism. Apart from this, the sender of the message is not available, unless a complex inspection of the runtime stack is performed.

3.2   Laziness and Declarative Concurrency
Raphaël Collet, Université catholique de Louvain (Belgium),
raph@info.ucl.ac.be

Raphäel Collet presented an extension of the concurrent declarative framework of the Oz language with by-need synchronisation Oz has a store consisting of constraints over logic variables. There are two operations, ask and tell Telling a constraint simply adds it to the store. Asking a constraint makes the thread wait until the store can logically infer it or its negation.

Programming a demand-driven computation in a dataflow concurrent language is easy. The computation is put in a thread and is suspended until another thread manifests its need for the result. The way of manifesting the need is by telling `need(x)` to the store, where x is the variable. This constraint does not restrict the possible value of x. In this way dataflow synchronisation of multiple threads is achieved.

3.3   Concurrency in Java and Erlang
Sven-Olof Nyström, Uppsala University (Sweden), svenolof@csd.uu.se

Java's threads are rather nicely integrated with the class system. Unfortunately, the implementations use the threads of the underlying operating system, which means that threads are expensive. Many operating systems only allow a very restricted (a few hundred) number of threads. What is even worse is that the behavior of threads depends on the operating system, so that a Java program written for one OS might not work when run on an other OS. The use of OS threads is discouraged by the Erlang designers.

In contrast, all Erlang processes under a specific node share the same OS-process. An Erlang process is a data structure, containing a stack, a heap and a program counter. The stack and the heap are small at creation, and allowed to grow when necessary, so the minimum size of a process is a few hundred bytes. Erlang can easily support thousands of threads.

[**Discussion**]. An operating system based on Erlang could be developed, given its reliability and concurrent design.

3.4   APPLE: Advanced Procedural Programming Language Elements

Christian Heinlein, University of Ulm (Germany),
heinlein@informatik.uni-ulm.de

Christian Heinlein started by observing that current programming languages, in particular aspect-oriented languages such as AspectJ, are considerably complex, in contrast with traditional procedural languages, such as Pascal or C, which provided just two basic building blocks: data structures and procedures. The gain in complexity is not reflected proportionally in the gain of expressive power.

He pointed out that there are many features in aspect-oriented languages which could be dropped from the kernel of these languages and implemented in terms of other features. After many conceptual reductions, he argues that "around advice" (i.e. the possibility to freely override an existing procedure, either with completely new code or with code that augments the original code) remains as one of the few essential (i.e. really necessary) mechanisms.

His position was to go back to the starting point of procedural programming languages and extend them in a different direction, not leading to OO or AOP programming, but to "advanced procedural languages" which are significantly simpler than aspect-oriented languages while offering comparable expressiveness and flexibility.

Three points are the key:

1. Replacing statically bound procedures with dynamically overridable procedures (roughly comparable to around advice) covers the whole range of dynamic dispatch strategies usually found in object-oriented languages. Dynamic procedures remain a single, well-defined concept, hardly more complex than traditional procedures.
2. Replacing record types having a fixed set of fields with modularly extensible "open types" and "attributes" (roughly comparable to empty classes extended by inter-type field declarations) covers a wide range of (practically all) OO abstractions. Again, open types constitute a single, well-defined concept which is little more complex than traditional record types.
3. Preserving (resp. (re-)introducing) the module concept of modern procedural languages with clearly defined import/export interfaces and a strict separation of module definitions and implementations, provides support for encapsulation and information hiding.

Instances of open types differ from instances of classes in object-oriented languages such as Java or C++ in two ways. First, their set of attributes is dynamic, again in two ways: because the attributes of a particular type can be defined in different modules, the set of all attributes is unknown when compiling a single module. Furthermore, since modules containing attribute definitions might be loaded dynamically at run time, the set of all attributes belonging to a type is even unknown at link or program start time. If an attribute is accessed that is not present yet, a well-defined null value is returned for read accesses, while a new attribute/value pair is added for write accesses. Second, the dynamic type of an object, which is equal to its static type immediately after creation, can be changed at run time.

Because procedures are not directly associated with types or objects, such manipulations cannot lead to "message not understood" or other run time type errors, i.e., the system remains statically type-safe.

[**Discussion**]. If a dynamic procedure is overridden in different modules, the linear "module order" that is uniquely determined by the modules' import relationships, determines the order of the procedure redefinitions.

[**Discussion**]. Dynamic procedures solve the well-known "expression problem" (it is hard to add both new types and new operations to an existing type hierarchy) in a simple and straightforward manner – so simple that some of the participants found it hard to believe.

3.5   Object Shadowing – A Key Concept for a Modern Programming Language

Marc Conrad, Tim French, and Carsten Maple, University of Luton (UK), {marc.conrad, tim.french, carsten.maple}@luton.ac.uk

Shadow objects mask one or more methods in a target object (the "shadowed" object). A shadow is applied at run-time rather than compile-time, in response to dynamic needs. Every message sent to the shadowed object is processed by the shadow, if the shadow defines it, or otherwise it is passed to the shadowed object as if there were no shadow in between. More characteristics of the shadow mechanism are described in the position paper. The shadow mechanism has for long been available in LPC (a highly pragmatic language used for text based computer games, see http://wwwlysator.liu.se/mud/lpc.html) but has not been evaluated academically so far.

Marc Conrad presented possible application areas for this mechanism:

1. Deprecated Methods: a shadow system could help the developer of a library to separate an object into two parts. The actual, official version of the object where the deprecated methods have been removed and a collection of shadows that implement deprecated methods. The shadows avoid breaking existing (legacy) clients.
2. Prototyping: a shadow could be used to adapt the behaviour of objects in a library, in situations where the objects cannot be directly manipulated because the library has been bought from an external supplier or because of copyright issues.
3. Reclassification: reclassification and a special case of it, dynamic inheritance, is the process of changing the class of an object at run-time. The main goal

in reclassification is to modify the behaviour of an object. This could be achieved by the application of a shadow to the object. For example a player having a temporal "frog shadow" might change its nature by replacing it with a "prince shadow" (but it remains a player).

4. Interclassing: the basic principle in interclassing is the insertion of a new class in an existing inheritance hierarchy. Suppose an existing hierarchy has `Parallelogram` as a parent of `Square`, and that `Rectangle` is introduced as a specialization of `Parallelogram`. Now, `Square` should inherit from `Rectangle`, and to this end, one could shadow `Square` with a `SquareShadow`, which inherits from `Rectangle`. All the clients of `Square` will now see the behaviour of `Rectangle`, even if `Square` itself is not modified.

5. Inheritance and Specialization: A shadow could even be used to emulate inheritance. In particular, a programming language that has shadows as a first class feature and derives inheritance as a special application of shadows can be envisioned. However the presenter expressed fears that this particular idea may be too wild and not relevant for any practical implementation.

At the end of his talk Marc Conrad raised the (provocative) question, why such a useful feature is not available in mainstream languages?

[Discussion]. It was pointed out that the last feature, emulation of inheritance by shadows (the feature that has been considered as too esoteric by the presenter), could be the most useful, as it would allow the implementation of different roles that an object may have during its lifetime.

[Discussion]. The class `java.lang.reflect.Proxy` of Java may serve a similar purpose as a shadow but it was pointed out that this Java class works only for interfaces and cannot shadow classes or objects.

There was some agreement in the audience that shadows may be a useful feature and the question why it is not available in mainstream language is valid.

3.6 Dynamic Versus Static Typing – A Pattern-Based Analysis
Pascal Costanza, Universität Bonn (Germany), costanza@web.de

The main point Pascal Costanza made is that statically typed languages sometimes force solutions which in dynamic typed languages could be expressed more naturally or are even available by default. Furthermore, statically-typed languages introduce new sources of potential bugs, contrary to conventionally perceived wisdom. He presented three examples of these situations, in the form of patterns. Java was chosen as a representative example of a statically typed language. The three examples shown were the following:

Statically Checked Implementation of Interfaces. When implementing an interface in Java, usually the programmer "fills in" the required methods with dummy bodies (e.g. which simply return `null`, `0` or `false`), so that the program compiles. Clean compilation is needed for incremental development of the class. The problem with these dummy implementations is that they are a potential bug which might be hard to find later on. The solution is to throw dynamically checked exceptions indicating that the involved methods are currently not implemented, instead of providing a dummy implementation, as in the following example:

```
public class FileCharSequence implements CharSequence {
    public FileCharSequence() {...}
    public char charAt(int index) {...}
    public int length() {...}
    public CharSequence subSequence(int start, int end) {
        throw new UnsupportedOperationException
            ("FileCharSequence.subSequence not implemented yet.");
    }
}
```

But the main point is, dynamically typed languages do exactly this by default: the sending of a message which is not implemented will raise an exception, à la Smalltalk's "message not understood".

[**Discussion**]. The problem could be seen as an IDE support issue rather than a programming language flaw: for example in Eclipse, one can configure the IDE so that code similar to the above is generated automatically. But by default, Eclipse generates dummy code.

Statically Checked Exceptions. This issue is better explained with an example. Assume that a class performs some heavy computations based on statistical data. It should be possible to deploy this class by itself, in which case the data is read from a local file, or else it will fetch the data from a remote file via an RMI service. In the latter case, this class needs to deal with the statically checked RMI exceptions. The problem is that declaring RMI exceptions is not appropriate to the abstraction provided by the statistical class.

The solution is to use dynamically checked exceptions. They are passed on by any code without the need to even mention the exceptions. A class only needs to explicitly deal with exceptions it is concerned with. The point in favour of dynamically typed languages with exception handling mechanisms, is that they have this functionality by default.

[**Discussion**]. In the case of Java, the RMI exception can be wrapped with a RuntimeException so that the exception declaration can be omitted.

Checking Feature Availability. Checking if a resource provides a specific feature and actually using that feature should be an atomic step in the face of multiple access paths to that resource. Otherwise, that feature might get lost in between the check and the actual use. Example:

```
System.out.println("Name: " + person.getName());
if (person instanceof Employee) {
    System.out.println("Employer: " +
        ((Employee)person).getEmployer().getName();
}
```

If the value of persons is changed by another thread between the type check and the type cast, an exception will be raised. Static typing promotes the notion that the availability of a particular feature should be checked before it is actually used. For example, fields and methods can be regarded as features of classes.

The solution is to make the check and the use an atomic step:

```
System.out.println("Name: " + dilbert.getName());
try {
    System.out.println("Employer: " +
        ((Employee)dilbert).getEmployer().getName();
} catch (ClassCastException e) {
    // do nothing
}
```

The point in this example is, dynamically typed languages throw "message not understood" errors by default. One only has to catch them instead of Class-CastException. Apart from that difference, the resulting behavior is the same.

[**Discussion**]. Some found that this problem is related to concurrent execution and is not inherent to static typing.

3.7 The Unavoidable Failure of Class-Based Languages in the Processor Cloud Era

Sebastián González, Wolfgang De Meuter, Kim Mens, Theo D'Hondt, Université catholique de Louvain (Belgium) and Vrije Universiteit Brussel (Belgium), {sgm, kim.mens}@info.ucl.ac.be, {wdmeuter, tjdhondt}@vub.ac.be

The point made by this presentation was that class-based languages are not adequate for the programming of the so-called "processor clouds", i.e. ad-hoc mobile networks of wirelessly interconnected computers where nodes can enter and leave the network at any moment, for instance if a user enters or leaves a certain building. The use of object-based languages without the concept of class are advocated as a good alternative. The main problem with classes is that they are a universal, stateful resource sharing mechanism, which is a bad combination of ingredients for open distribution (processor clouds). For example, a node containing the same class as another node may appear in the network, but with a different value for a class variable or a different method implementation; this is an unsolvable conflict since none of the two versions is the "right" one. Other problems with classes mentioned were the fact that classes grow monotonically, getting deprecated methods, which waste resources (storage space, network bandwidth) in a context where resources are scarce: mobile computing. Another problem is that idiosyncratic behaviour is even more important in mobile computing, which is harmed by the usage of classes. A last problem was mentioned: upon sending a message to a node, a class and its superclass(es) need to be sent along, and if the language is statically typed, argument-type, result-type and exception-type classes need to be sent also.

3.8   Who Is Agent: Object or Relation?
By Ilia Bider, IbisSoft (Sweden), ilia@ibissoft.se

Starting from the observation that any object-oriented system can be considered as consisting of objects and relations between them, Ilia Bider proposed a rather different perspective for the role these objects and relations play. In his programming model, the centre of attention is on the relations. This contrasts with traditional OO programming where attention is mainly put on objects, and relations are usually simple pointers. In the new perspective, while objects are passive, relations are active. The relations or connectors represent laws which are to be maintained throughout the system. Whenever the state of an object changes (e.g. because of an external user action), the relations connected to that object are verified. If necessary, these relations change the state of other connected objects in order to bring the system back to an acceptable state. Changes are propagated in this way through object networks. The relations are perceived as the "agents" in the system: the active elements which perform computation and evolve its state. This motivates the title of his position paper.

The described object-connector model is proposed as a method of distributed programming. The whole system is expressed in terms of local laws, with communication and execution control being automatically provided by the environment.

[**Discussion**]. The workshop participants found the programming model quite different from what they are used to in standard OO programming. No flaws or problems were pointed out.

4   Related Work

The submitted position papers, Dave Thomas's slides, and complementary information about the workshop can be found at the workshop website:
http://prog.vub.ac.be/~wdmeuter/PostJava04/

The website for the previous edition of the workshop is located at:
http://prog.vub.ac.be/~wdmeuter/PostJava/

And there is already a followup event planned at OOPSLA 2004, the 1st Workshop on the Revival of Dynamic Languages:
http://pico.vub.ac.be/~wdmeuter/RDL04/index.html

This workshop was inspired by Richard Gabriel's Feyerabend events at past OOPSLAs and ECOOPs. The home page of the Feyerabend Project is located at:
http://www.dreamsongs.com/Feyerabend/Feyerabend.html

References

1. Ducatel, K., Bogdanowicz, M., Scapolo, F., Leijten, J., Burgelman, J.C.: Scenarios for ambient intelligence in 2010. Technical report, EC Information Scociety Technologies Advisory Group (ISTAG) (2001) Available [2004-07-12] at http://www.cordis.lu/ist/istag-reports.htm.

2. Shadbolt, N.: Ambient intelligence. IEEE Intelligent Systems **18** (2003) 2–3
3. De Meuter, W., Ducasse, S., D'Hondt, T., Madsen, O.L.: Object-oriented language engineering for the post-java era. In Buschmann, F., Buchmann, A.P., Cilia, M., eds.: Object-Oriented Technology: ECOOP 2003 Workshop Reader. Volume 3013., Springer-Verlag (2004)
4. Thomas, D.: Message oriented programming. Journal of Object Technology **3** (2004) 7–12 Available [2004-07-12] at http://www.jot.fm/issues/issue_2004_05/column1.
5. Thomas, D., Barry, B.: Using active objects for structuring service oriented architectures. Journal of Object Technology **3** (2004) 7–14 Available [2004-07-12] at http://www.jot.fm/issues/issue_2004_07/column1.
6. Hewitt, C.E.: Viewing control structures as patterns of passing messages. Journal of Artificial Intelligence **8** (1977) 323–364

Philosophy, Ontology, and Information Systems*

Petra Becker-Pechau[1], Pierre Grenon[2], Mark Lycett[3], Chris Partridge[3],
Jörg Pechau[4], and Dirk Siebert[2]

[1] Hamburg University, Fachbereich Informatik, Software Engineering Group,
Vogt-Kölln-Straße 30, 22527 Hamburg, Germany,
becker@informatik.uni-hamburg.de
[2] IFOMIS, University of Leipzig, Härtelstraße 16-18, 04107 Leipzig, Germany,
{pierre.grenon|dirk.siebert}@ifomis.uni-leipzig.de
[3] Department of Information Systems and Computing, Brunel University, Uxbridge,
Middlesex, UB8 3PH, United Kingdom,
{mark.lycett|chris.partridge}@brunel.ac.uk
[4] CoreMedia AG, Ludwig-Erhard-Straße 18, 20459 Hamburg, Germany
joerg.pechau@coremedia.com

Abstract. The workshop aimed at providing a forum to discuss the use
of philosophical ontology in object-oriented information systems. Whilst
ontology is now more widely used in computing circles - knowledge representation, system integration, legacy transformation, and the semantic
web for example - initial attempts have been modest in their outcomes.
This is because computing ontology to-date has been used primarily for
(often competing) concept definitions: Pragmatically, ontologies have either been developed in an abstract sense (based on some authorative
perspective), or people have taken materials at hand (data models and
the like) and tried to glue them together. A sound basis on which to
properly align different views on aspects of the world in order to work
towards a consistent whole is missing. With this in mind, the workshop
aimed to secure a measure of agreement on:

- What philosophical ontology is,
- How ontology can assist in software development,
- Key obstacles to the deployment of ontology, and
- Possible collaborative efforts among the participants.

Selection of participants was based on short position papers and/or
previously demonstrated interest in related areas of activity.

Participants

The workshop was attended by:

- Naci Akkøk, Department of Informatics, University of Oslo, nacia@ifi.uio.no,
- Petra Becker-Pechau, Fachbereich Informatik, Software Engineering Group,
  University of Hamburg, becker@informatik.uni-hamburg.de,

---

* The title of this report should be referenced as "Report from the ECOOP 2004
Workshop on Philosophy, Ontology, and Information Systems".

J. Malenfant and B.M. Østvold (Eds.): ECOOP 2004, LNCS 3344, pp. 62–66, 2004.
© Springer-Verlag Berlin Heidelberg 2004

- José María Cavero, Rey Juan Carlos University, jmcavero@escet.urjc.es,
- Yannis Charalabidis, Singular Software SA, yannisx@singular.gr
- Jim Coakes, School of Business, University of Westminster, j_m.coakes@which.net,
- Martin Gladwell, IBM, martin_gladwell@uk.ibm.com,
- Mass Soldal Lund, Department of Informatics, University of Oslo, Mass.S.Lund@sintef.no,
- Mark Lycett, Brunel University, Mark.Lycett@brunel.ac.uk,
- Esperanza Marcos, Rey Juan Carlos University, emarcos@escet.urjc.es,
- Palle Nowack, Maersk Institute, University of Southern Denmark, nowack@mip.sdu.dk,
- Chris Partridge, Brunel University Chris.Partridge@42objects.com,
- Jörg Pechau, CoreMedia AG, joerg.pechau@coremedia.com,
- Jan Pettersen Nytun, Faculty of Engineering, Agder University College, Jan.P.Nytun@hia.no,
- Andreas Prinz, Department of Informatics, University of Oslo, Andreas.Prinz@hia.no,
- Dirk Siebert, Institute for Formal Ontology and Medical Information Science, University of Leipzig, Dirk.Siebert@ifomis.uni-leipzig.de,
- Mircea Trofin, School of Electronic Engineering, Dublin City University, Mircea.Trofin@eeng.dcu.ie

Summary

Chris Partridge set the scene for the workshop. A sequence of individual presentations and ensuing discussions consumed most of the workshop's time. In the wrap-up we noted:

- Agreement
    - Philosophical ontology is applicable to information systems. Therefore more than 2000 years' worth of ontological research in philosophy should actually be leveraged.
    - There are different views on philosophical ontology, though. But given the state of the art - the differences are of minor importance right now.
    - Metaphysical choices
        * Explicitly to be made
        * Consequenses and implications can and should be made clear.
    - What is (an) O/ontology?
    - Deployability needs to be solved.
    - Sophistication is important to manage quality and complexity.
    - Different views / concerns / aspects can in general be handled in a single ontology - there might be exceptions.
- Disagreement
    - Realism / anti-realism resp. discovery / design.

– Open issues
  • Is there only one ontology?
    * Depends on metaphysical choices (to be) made.
    * Design choices (short term gains)
  • How to reap the benefits?
  • People issues:
    * How to bring people up to speed?
– Query-ability of ontologies
– What is the role of representation in the discussion of ontology? How formal does philosophical ontology need to be?

Literature

– Partridge, Chris: Introduction to the Workshop,
  http://www.ifomis.uni-leipzig.de/Events/ECOOP/2004/
  WS_PhilosophyOntologyInformationSystems/papers/Partridge.pdf
– Accepted papers:
  • Cavero, Jos Mara , Esperanza Marcos: A Schematical View of the Ontologies Concept,
    http://www.ifomis.uni-leipzig.de/Events/ECOOP/2004/
    WS_PhilosophyOntologyInformationSystems/papers/CaveroMarcos.pdf
  • Coakes, J. M., D. Rosenberg: Bringing IS Ontologies Closer to the Real World,
    http://www.ifomis.uni-leipzig.de/Events/ECOOP/2004/
    WS_PhilosophyOntologyInformationSystems/papers/
    CoakesRosenberg.pdf
  • Martin N. Gladwell: Position Paper on Philosophy, Ontology and Information Systems,
    http://www.ifomis.uni-leipzig.de/Events/ECOOP/2004/
    WS_PhilosophyOntologyInformationSystems/papers/Gladwell.pdf
  • Nowack, Palle: Conceptual Modeling for Ubiquitous Systems,
    http://www.ifomis.uni-leipzig.de/Events/ECOOP/2004/
    WS_PhilosophyOntologyInformationSystems/papers/Nowack.pdf
  • Nytun, Jan Pettersen, Andreas Prinz: Metalevel Representation and Philosophical Ontology,
    http://www.ifomis.uni-leipzig.de/Events/ECOOP/2004/
    WS_PhilosophyOntologyInformationSystems/papers/NytunPrinz.pdf
  • Schneider, Luc: Foundational Ontologies and the Realist Bias, http://ceur-ws.org/Vol-94/ki03rao_schneider.pdf
– Late submission:
  • Akkøk, Naci: Proliferation of Ontology in Software Engineering and its Consequences
    http://www.ifomis.uni-leipzig.de/Events/ECOOP/2004/
    WS_PhilosophyOntologyInformationSystems/papers/Akkok.pdf

- Suggested reading:
  - The following papers shed light on different aspects of workshop topics:
    * Smith, Barry, Werner Ceusters: Towards Industrial-Strength Philosophy. [Introduces ontology in philosophy and medical information science.]
    http://ontology.buffalo.edu/medo/tisp.pdf
    * Partridge, Chris: Note: A Couple of Meta-Ontological Choices for Ontological Architectures. Padova, The BORO Program, LADSEB CNR, Italy: 2002. LADSEB-CNR - Technical report 06/02. [Key aspects of a philosophical ontology.]
    http://www.boroprogram.dsl.pipex.com/ladsebreports/ladseb_t_r_06-02.pdf
    * Partridge, Chris: The Role of Ontology in Integrating Semantically Heterogeneous Databases. Padova, The BORO Program, LADSEB CNR, Italy: (2002). LADSEB-CNR - Technical report 05/02. [The link between inter-operability and philosophical ontology.]
    http://www.loa-cnr.it/Papers/ladseb_tr05-02.pdf
    * Daga, Aseem, Sergio de Cesare, Mark Lycett, and Chris Partridge: An Ontological Approach to Sophisticating Legacy Business Content. [The importance of sophistication for a philosopical ontology.]
    http://www.ifomis.uni-leipzig.de/Events/ECOOP/2004/
    WS_PhilosophyOntologyInformationSystems/sr/
    DagaDeCesareLycettPartridge_
    AnOntologicalApproachToSophisticatingLegacyBusinessContent.pdf
  - These provide deeper insight/background:
    * Mealy, G. H.: Another Look at Data. Proceeding of AFIPS 1967 Fall Joint Computer Conference Vol. 31: 1967. [Showing that an interest in ontology manifested itself at a very early stage.]
    * Kent, W.: Data and Reality: Basic Assumptions in Data Processing Reconsidered. North-Holland, Amsterdam, New York: 1978. [Showing that an interest in philosophical questions was also present at an early stage.]
    * Grenon, Pierre: Knowledge Management From the Ontological Standpoint.
    http://www.uni-leipzig.de/ pgrenon/Downloads/grenon-wm2003.pdf
    * Daga, Aseem, Sergio de Cesare, Mark Lycett, and Chris Partridge: Software Stability: Recovering General Patterns of Business Content. [Making the connection between software stability and ontology.]
    http://www.ifomis.uni-leipzig.de/Events/ECOOP/2004/
    WS_PhilosophyOntologyInformationSystems/sr/
    DagaDeCesareLycettPartridge_SoftwareStability.pdf
    * Partridge, Chris: Business Objects: Re-Engineering for Re-use. Butterworth Heinemann, Oxford: 1996. [Tying in O-O implementation with philosophy/ontology.]

* Partridge, Chris: What is Pump Facility PF101? Padova, The BORO Program, LADSEB CNR, Italy: 2002. LADSEB-CNR - Technical report 04/02. [An example of the use of philosophical ontology in the offshore process industry.]
http://www.loa-cnr.it/Papers/ladseb_tr04-02.pdf
* Smith, Barry: Ontology. [For a more general and much more thorough account than the one provided in "Towards Industrial-Strength Philosophy".]
http://www.ifomis.uni-leipzig.de/Events/ECOOP/2004/
WS_PhilosophyOntologyInformationSystems/sr/SmithOntology.pdf

Communication Abstractions for Distributed Systems*

Antoine Beugnard[1], Ludger Fiege[2], Robert Filman[3], Eric Jul[4], Salah Sadou[5], and Eiko Yoneki[6]

[1] ENST-Bretagne, Brest, France
antoine.beugnard@enst-bretagne.fr
[2] University of Technology, Darmstadt, Germany
fiege@gkec.tu-darmstadt.de
[3] RIACS/NASA Ames Research Center, USA
rfilman@mail.arc.nasa.gov
[4] University of Copenhagen, Copenhagen, Denmark
eric@diku.dk
[5] Université de Bretagne Sud, Vannes, France
sadou@iu-vannes.fr
[6] University of Cambridge, UK
eiko.yoneki@cl.cam.ac.uk

Abstract. Communication is the foundation of many systems. Understanding communication is a key to building a better understanding of the interaction of software entities such as objects, components, and aspects. This workshop was an opportunity to exchange points of view on many facets of communication and interaction. The workshop was divided in two parts: the first dedicated to the presentation of eight position papers, and the second to the selection and discussion of three critical topics in the communication abstraction domain.

1 Introduction

Applications have become increasingly distributed. Distribution complicates systems building and exacerbates problems such as dealing with failure, and providing security, quality of service, reliability, and manageability.

System development is eased by abstraction and modeling. How should we model distributed systems? Distributed systems can be understood as communicating objects. To tackle the problems of building distributed systems, it is useful to focus on the abstract issues of inter-component communication. Examples of distributed communication mechanisms include messaging systems, remote procedure calls, distributed objects, peer-to-peer and publish-and-subscribe. Within any such paradigm, there are many opportunities for specialized and detailed engineering decisions. While mechanisms such as these are a good foundation for

---

* The title of this report should be referenced as "Report from the ECOOP 2004 Workshop on Communication Abstractions for Distributed Systems".

J. Malenfant and B.M. Østvold (Eds.): ECOOP 2004, LNCS 3344, pp. 67–75, 2004.

dealing with the problems of distribution, there remain many issues about how to mold these ideas to deal with the problems of real systems.

At the previous ECOOP workshops, we identified some problems (security, privacy, partial failure, guaranteeing quality of service, run-time evolution, meta-object protocols, and ordering of events) that are important concerns of any communication abstraction. The goal of this workshop was to contrast and compare communication abstractions for distributed systems. Participants were asked to submit a position paper on some aspect of communication abstractions for distributed systems. To focus the groups discussion, this year we considered the distributed aerospace information problem, described in the call-for-papers. Prospective participants were requested to relate their contribution to some facet of that that problem. The workshop itself consisted of short presentations, discussion of those presentations, and division into smaller topic study groups.

We received 8 positions papers. All were reviewed by at least two members of the program committee and 6 were considered bringing an interesting point of view and deserving a chance to be discussed. We organized the workshop as follows:

- The morning was dedicated to short, 15 minute presentations of selected papers. The paper authors entertained questions from the workshop attendees and provided clarifying responses.
- In the afternoon, we formed two working groups for deeper discussion of particular issues in communication abstractions. The group reported their conclusions to the collected workshop at the end of the day. This year, the chosen topics were "Events" and "Dealing with Errors"

2   Position Papers Abstracts and Discussions

2.1   Communication Abstraction and Verification in Distributed Scenario Integration [1]

Paper written by Aziz Salah, Rabeb Mizouni and Rachida Dssouli and presented by A. Salah from the department of C.S. University of Quebec, Montreal (Email: salah.aziz@uqam.ca)

Successfully modeling and analysing requirements are among the main challenges to face up when it is time to produce a formal specification for distributed systems. Scenario approaches are proposed as an alternative to make this process easier. They are based on the decomposition of the system behaviour into intuitive pieces that are distributed scenarios. In this paper, we propose an approach to detect the unspecified reception errors by the integration of scenarios. The decision about such property is made possible according to an architectural communication model, which states the communication abstraction level we are considering. We synthesize from message sequence char a set of automata, one per object. Then, we give decision procedure for unspecified reception faults.

2.2 Realizing Large Scale Distributed Event Style Interactions [2]

Paper written by A Vijay Srinivas, Raghavendra Koti, A Uday Kumar and D Janakiram and presented by D Janakiram from the Distributed & Object Systems Lab, Dept. of Computer Science & Engg., Indian Institute of Technology, Madras, India (Email: fdjram@cs.iitm.ernet.in).

Interactions in distributed object middleware that are based on Remote Procedure Call (RPC) or Remote Method Invocation (RMI) are fundamentally synchronous in nature. However, asynchronous interactions are better suited for large scale distributed systems. This paper presents the design and implementation of an asynchronous event based communication paradigm. Typed events, fully distributed hierarchical event dispatching as well as causal delivery of events are the key features that are supported. The paradigm has been realized over Virat, a wide area shared object space that we have built. Virat uses replication, caching and distributed services as the main concepts and provides a well published interface, as well as various relaxed consistency models. This communication abstraction is especially beneficial to applications such as modernizing Airspace Systems, where scalable asynchronous event notification is a critical issue.

2.3 Event Brokering Over Distributed Peer-to-Peer Environments [3]

Paper written and presented by Eiko Yoneki from University of Cambridge Computer Laboratory Cambridge, United Kingdom (Email: eiko.yonekig@cl.cam.ac.uk).

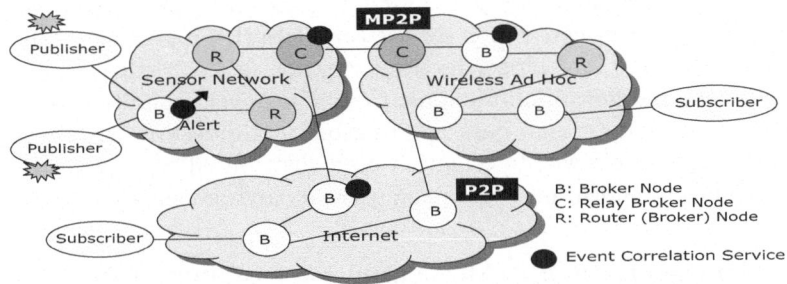

Fig. 1. Event Broker Grids over P2P and MP2P Networks

Peer-to-peer (P2P) networks offer a promising paradigm for developing efficient distributed systems. Event-based middleware (EBM) is becoming a core architectural element in such systems. EBM is based on publish/subscribe communication paradigms that became popular providing asynchronous and multipoint communication. Most distributed EBM contains three main elements: a producer who publishes events, a consumer who subscribes his interests to the system, and an event broker with responsibility to deliver the matching events to the corresponding consumers. The first event-based middleware systems were based on the concept of channel or topic communication. In an attempt to overcome the limitation on subscription declarations, the content-based model has been introduced, which allows subscribers to use flexible querying languages to declare their interests with respect to event contents.

There are diverse network environments from Internet-scale P2P systems to sensor networks. Event broker grids need to communicate over wired P2P networks, wireless ad hoc networks (WAHN) or even Web services. In WAHN, the combination of mobile devices and ad-hoc networks are best managed by the creation of highly dynamic, self-organizing, mobile P2P systems (MP2P). Mobile hosts continuously change their physical location and establish peering relationships with each other based on proximity. Asynchronous communication is essential to support anonymous coordination of communication in such ubiquitous environments. We previously introduced publish/subscribe semantics in WAHN [4]. Note that when publish/subscribe becomes powerful in WAHN environments, all the nodes may not be in pure ad hoc topology, and some nodes must be connected to the Internet backbone or relay nodes from different network environments. For example, a broker node can act as a gateway from sensor networks operating data aggregation and distributes them to the other mobile networks based on its contents (see Fig. 1). Broker nodes that offer event correlation services can coordinate data flow efficiently. Thus, the way publish/subscribe systems can be constructed based on the data contents, which triggers related chained actions. Unusual events will be detected by the embedded sensors triggering distribution of subsequent events to the entire system.

This paper presents a vision of an event brokering system over mixed P2P networks in a multi event broker model. In addition, an event condition action engine will be integrated that is required to perform event correlation services within brokers. Event correlation service combines the information collected by individual resources into higher level information or knowledge. Events reflect the movement and flow of information. Combining event-condition-action-rules, complex event composition, data aggregation, and detection with event-based systems will provide a way to construct large distributed systems providing abstraction of communication over mixed network environments.

2.4   Homogenization: A Mechanism for Distributed Processing Across a Local Area Network [5]

Paper written by Mahmud Shahriar Hossain, M. Muztaba Fuad, Debzani Deb, Kazi Muhammad Najmul Hasan Khan, and Dr. Md. Mahbubul Alam Joarder. (Email: shahriar-cse@sust.edu)

Distributed processing across a networked environment suffers from unpredictable behavior of speedup due to heterogeneous nature of the hardware and software in the remote machines. It is challenging to get a better performance from a distributed system by distributing task in an intelligent manner such that the heterogeneous nature of the system do not have any effect on the speedup ratio. This paper introduces homogenization, a technique that distributes and balances the workload in such a manner that the user gets the highest speedup possible from a distributed environment. Along with providing better performance, homogenization is totally transparent to the user and requires no interaction with the system.

2.5 Modelling a Distributed Network Security Systems Using Multi-agents Systems Engineering [6]

Paper written by Gustavo A. Santana Torrellas from Instituto Mexicano del Petrleo Mantenimiento y Perforacin de Pozos (Email: gasantan@imp.mx)

Recent developments have made it possible to interoperate complex business applications at much lower costs. Application interoperation, along with business process reengineering can result in significant savings by eliminating work created by disconnected business processes due to isolated business applications. However, we believe much greater productivity benefits can be achieved by facilitating timely decision-making, utilizing information from multiple entreprise perspectives. To stay competitive in this current scenario, it is crucial for organizations to react quickly to changing security factors, such as virus attack, active intrusion, new technologies, and cost of disaster recovery. Such information security changes often encourage the creation of new security schemas or security improvements. Accommodating frequent systems information changes requires a network security system be more flexible than currently prevalent systems. Consequently, there has recently been an increasing interest in flexible network security and disaster recovery systems.

2.6 But What If Things Go Wrong? [7]

Paper written and presented by Johan Fabry from Vrije Universiteit Brussel (Email: Johan.Fabry@vub.ac.be)

Nowadays, building distributed systems is said to be easy: just use one of the many distribution frameworks out there, and all the hard stuff will be taken care of for you. However, when we focus on what to do when things go wrong, i.e. consider partial failure, we see that examples in the literature will either ignore these kinds of exceptions, or stop the program, which is clearly inadequate.

A generic and useful failure-handling mechanism for distributed systems exists in the from of transactions, however a significant issue with transactions is that they may be rolled back by the transaction manager to break deadlocks. Again, looking at the literature, we see no thorough treatment of this extra kind of failure, except for the proposal of a number of Advanced Transaction Mechanisms (ATM) that handle this. A large number of ATMS can be found in the literature, and two books have been published about the subject. So, while ATMS exist to solve these problem, we still see no use of them in commercial systems, even although this is research from the 80s and 90s. Indeed, we cannot even find the most well-known model: nested transactions, commercially.

It is our position that the problem with ATMS lies in the difficulty for the application programmer to specify how to use these mechanisms. Given their nature, an ATMS needs more information about the transaction than a classical system. We think that, since letting the developer specify error-handling code is already troublesome, going the extra mile to use a ATMS is nigh-on impossible.

Therefore, we should support the application programmer when specifying these advanced transactions. The programmer should reason about this extra information at a higher level of abstraction, and can specify the required transactional properties at this higher level, e.g. by using a Domain Specific Language.

We have implemented a first prototype tool, outlined at the workshop, as a first step toward this goal. Notable functionality is the ability to provide generic deadlock- or exception-handling strategies for a transaction such as simply retrying the transaction. The question to attendees was what generic deadlock- or exception-handling strategies that are worthwhile to offer the programmer.

Questions and Answers. A first question was how our generic error-handling strategies interact with possible recovery work already done by the transaction monitor. The answer is that we do not really see any interaction, we consider our work more as a 'second line of defense' for when the transaction monitor fails to recover.

The remainder of the discussion was more related to the depth of generalized error-handling strategies: we can go very deep, e.g. do investigations of the program history, and apply AI techniques, which is done by NASA. We do not aim to cover such complex situations, and imagine everything that can possibly go wrong. Instead we are looking for general and simple ways in which things get fixed when something goes wrong, and providing programmer abstractions for these fixes.

3   Discussions

The second part of the workshop was dedicated to discussions and working groups. After a brainstorming session where attendees suggested several subjects of discussion, we selected two of them for further exploration: dealing with errors and event based communication in distributed systems

3.1   Dealing with Errors

We started with the point that usually, specifications focus on what should happen and forget, sometimes voluntarily, the description of what to do when things go wrong! May be because the former is a single description (that obviously can be complex in itself) while the latter is very, very open.

In an attempt of modelling what is needed to deal with errors we identified four tasks:

1. Monitoring. It is essential to be able to observe what happens in the system. Where is this code? Complex architectures are layered, and monitoring code is probably scattered. Error management has to be taken into account from the lowest levels to the application level.

2. Detecting. From the low-level monitoring data, the system must infer bad risky situations. Perhaps a dedicated language is needed to define theses unexpected events. A more elaborate error mechanism may also be able to express the level of risk and urgency of reaction required for particular situations.
3. Repairing actions. A set of "atomic" corrective actions is needed. For instance: restart, do something & restart, do something & continue, abort, do something & abort, abort & do something. Any real system will have to deal with the problem that these actions are themselves subject to errors.
4. Managing. It's easy to imagine situations where not just a single alarm is sounded. Overall, alarms and repairs may occur simultaneously, and rules and mechanisms are needed to arbitrate among them. Rules are required to set up a hierarchy of decisions when things go worst and worst . . .

This view of the world relies on the existence of stable system states (recovery checkpoints) that need to be defined and implemented. However, many errors are not recoverable. This is especially the case for error situations after interactions with the external world — one can not unprint something from the printer or convince the user that he or she didn't really see something on the screen. The procedure to correct or undo wrong or bad real-world side-effects is often out of the scope of the software system. It may require legal or social actions when possible, and sometimes, is completely impossible — all the kings horses and men can reassemble neither Humpty Dumpty nor an Ariane V rocket.

3.2   Event-Based Communication in Distributed Systems

This workshop has always included papers whose communication abstract was based on "events."

Distributed applications usually exist in heterogeneous environments (systems and/or languages). Middleware serves to mediate communications. Its goal is to allow various systems and/or languages to share the same communication protocol. The complexity of the implementation and the use of this common protocol depend on the choice of the communication mode. In this working group, we made a comparison between two modes of communication: event-based and method-based. In object oriented systems, the communication may require the following element:

Interface: the type of the recipient of the message;
Data Type: the signature of the called method or the type of forwarded information;
Identity: recipient's address.

The following table shows the needs for each of the two selected modes:

Comm. mode	Interface	Data type	Identity
Event-based	No	Yes	No
Method-Based	Yes	Yes	Yes

We notice that the communication based on event is less demanding. This implies less dependency between sender and receiver and thus minimizes the role of the common communication protocol in a heterogeneous environment. Indeed, whereas a method-based middleware requires common modes of identification and data representation, an event-based middleware requires only a common mode of data representation. We think that in the future the event-based middleware should be generalized.

How Should We Construct Different Communication Types Using Events? In this section we visit the various types of communication to imagine their implementation in an event-based system:

Asynchronism: In contrary to method-based communication, event-based communication is naturally asynchronous. Objects send events and react to others. No bond is necessary between the sent events and the those received.

Synchronism: On the other hand, the event-based communication requires a mechanism to carry out an equivalent to synchronous calls. An example of such mechanism would be the acknowledgement of receipt, which is sent by the receiver at the end of its task. This defines the termination of the event sender's waiting . The acknowledgement of receipt is an event which contains an identifier provided first by the event sender.

Transaction: In this mode of communication, the receiver must deal with a complete succession of calls and respect its order. This mechanism may be produced by the concept of composite events. A composite event is a structured set of events (a list for example). The structure defines the transaction's order.

Call with Return: As in the case of synchronous calls, to carry out calls with return, it will be necessary to add an identifier to the event in order to associate it with the event representing its result.

Broadcast: Broadcast corresponds to the sending of public events. Any object interested by those events can react.

Multicast/Unicast: This mechanism requires the concept of private event. In the case of method-based calls, it is often the sender object which determines the subset of the concerned objects by its call. To approach this mechanism, we can imagine to add, to the event management system, the concept of filters. On one side the sender gives a filter with its event and on the other side, the receivers can choose filters during the subscribe to a type of events.

How Does This Help? The principal characteristic of the event-based systems is the decoupling between the objects participating in the communication. This characteristic facilitates the implementation of mobile computing and the peer-to-peer network environments. There is a series of workshops on the topic of distributed event-based systems and the last one is co-localized with ICSE'04 (http://serl.cs.colorado.edu/ carzanig/debs04/

4   Workshop Conclusions

A primary goal of this workshop is to enable the sharing of concepts and technologies among various communities. It is clear to us that a critical element for this goal is creating a shared understanding and categorization of communication mechanisms. This is a long-term goal. In this year's workshop, we have made progress on clarifying the nature of event-based communication, and, more innovatively for this workshop series, began to address the issue of dealing with errors in communications. This latter issue is clearly critical to the development of real systems and argues for the development of the right abstractions to support that real system development.

All previous workshop position papers are available via the CADS wiki site http://wiki.enstb.org/cads/

References

[1] Aziz Salah, Rabeb Mizouni, and Rachida Dssouli: Communication abstraction and verification in distributed scenario integration.
http://bscw.enst-bretagne.fr/pub/bscw.cgi/0/2237034, July 2004.
[2] A. Vijay Srinivas, Raghavendra Koti, A. Uday Kumar, and D. Janakiram: Realizing large scale distributed event style interactions.
http://bscw.enst-bretagne.fr/pub/bscw.cgi/0/2237034, July 2004.
[3] Eiko Yoneki: Event brokering over distributed peer-to-peer environments.
http://bscw.enst-bretagne.fr/pub/bscw.cgi/0/2237034, July 2004.
[4] E. Yoneki and J. Bacon: Content-based routing with on-demand multicast. In: Proc. 23rd ICDCS Workshop - WWAN, March 2004.
[5] Mahmud Shahriar Hossain, M. Muztaba Fuad, Debzani Deb, Kazi Muhammad Najmul Hasan Khan, and Dr. Md. Mahbubul Alam Joarder: Homogenization: A mechanism for distributed processing across a local area network.
http://bscw.enst-bretagne.fr/pub/bscw.cgi/0/2237034, July 2004.
[6] Gustavo A. Santana Torrellas: Modelling a distributed network security systems using multi-agents systems engineering.
http://bscw.enst-bretagne.fr/pub/bscw.cgi/0/2237034, July 2004.
[7] Johan Fabry: But what if things go wrong?
http://bscw.enst-bretagne.fr/pub/bscw.cgi/0/2237034, July 2004.

Formal Techniques for Java-Like Programs (FTfJP)*

Alessandro Coglio[1], Marieke Huisman[2],
Joseph R. Kiniry[3], Peter Müller[4], and Erik Poll[3]

[1] Kestrel Institute, USA
[2] INRIA Sophia-Antipolis, France
[3] Radboud University Nijmegen, The Netherlands
[4] ETH Zürich, Switzerland

Abstract. This report gives an overview of the sixth Workshop on Formal Techniques for Java-like Programs at ECOOP 2004. It explains the motivation for the a workshop and summarises the presentations and discussions.

1 Introduction

Formal techniques can help one analyse programming languages or individual programs and precisely describe and verify their properties. Languages such as Java and C# are interesting targets for the application of formal techniques, for a variety of reasons: their reasonably clear and standardised semantics, their type systems play a crucial role in guaranteeing security through type safety, and their novel paradigm for program deployment, which improves interactivity, portability and manageability, but also opens new possibilities for abuse and raises concern about security.

Work on formal techniques and tools for programming and on the formal underpinnings of the programming languages themselves complement each other. This workshop aims to bring together those people working on the formal underpinnings of, and those working on the formal techniques and tools for, programming Java-like languages. The topics covered thus include: language semantics, type systems, dynamic linking and loading, and specification and verification techniques.

The workshop was organized by Sophia Drossopoulou (Imperial College) Gary T. Leavens (Iowa State University), Peter Müller (ETH Zürich), Arnd Poetzsch-Heffter (Universität Kaiserslautern) and Erik Poll (Radboud University Nijmegen).

The selection of papers was done by a larger program committee, consisting of Armin Biere (ETH Zürich), John Boyland (University of Wisconsin), Alessandro Coglio (Kestrel Institute), Matthew Dwyer (Kansas State University), Susan

---

* The title of this report should be referenced as "Report from the ECOOP 2004 Workshop on Formal Techniques for Java-like Programs (FTfJP)".

J. Malenfant and B.M. Østvold (Eds.): ECOOP 2004, LNCS 3344, pp. 76–83, 2004.

Eisenbach (Imperial College), Michael Ernst (MIT), Marieke Huisman (INRIA Sophia-Antipolis), Joe Kiniry (Radboud University Nijmegen), Doug Lea (State University of New York at Oswego), Peter Müller (ETH Zürich), David Naumann (Stevens Institute of Technology), James Noble (Victoria University of Wellington), Erik Poll (Radboud University Nijmegen), and Wolfram Schulte (Microsoft Research).

Twenty-three persons attended this full-day workshop, 18 representing universities and academic research institutes, and 5 from industry. A complete list of participants is given at the end of this report. A number of other participants dropped by for specific presentations, to chat with particular speakers, etc.

2   Overview of the Presented Papers

Twenty position papers were submitted, of which eleven were accepted for presentation at the workshop. In a way it was disappointing to have such a high rejection rate for a workshop, but we deliberately chose for accepting fewer papers to make for a relaxed presentation schedule and allow plenty of time for discussion.

The position papers submitted were collected in an informal proceedings that appears as technical report, nr. NIII-R0426, Radboud University Nijmegen[1], 2004. This technical report, and the individual position papers, are available on the web via the FTfJP home page (http://www.cs.ru.nl/~erikpoll/ftfjp).

The topics addressed by the presented papers were:

- type systems for Java-like languages,
- Java implementation and compilation,
- program specification and verification,
- invariants, and
- ownership types.

There are connections between these topics, of course. The papers about type systems and Java implementation and compilation in a sense all revolve about the flexibility of Java-like languages, providing subtyping and dynamic class loading. There are connection between the last three topics. Invariants play a crucial role in specification and verification for OO languages, and ownership types are about ensuring encapsulation, which is clearly relevant in specification and verification, and is of particular importance in dealing with invariants.

3   Typing

The first session of the workshop was about to type systems, either for more flexible approaches for type checking, separate compilation and linking, or to provide more expressive type system that allow more code reuse.

---

[1] The University of Nijmegen was renamed Radboud University Nijmegen as of 1 September 2004.

Davide Ancona talked about joint research with Ferruccio Damiani, Sophia Drossopoulou, and Elena Zucca into maximising the possibilities for separate compilation. He presented a type system which allows compilation of an individual class in isolation, i.e. without any information available about other classes. The (polymorphic) type system infers the minimal assumptions on other classes needed to guarantee type correct of a class, as a set of constraints on type variables, allowing separately type-checked classes can be safely linked provided these assumptions are met. As discussed, this opens up several possibilities for compilation schemes that support stronger forms of separate compilation and allow a more selective and lightweight approach to recompilation.

Alex Buckley talked about joint work with Sophia Drossopoulou which took a further step in the line of research presented in Davide's talk, namely using type systems like the one discussed by Davide to allow a more flexible approach to dynamic linking. Rather than hard-coding type names in bytecode, as in current dynamic linking schemes for Java or C#, he considered the possibility of leaving type variables in bytecode, which can then lazily be instantiated to concrete types only at run time.

Christopher Anderson presented a different strain of work on type systems than the previous speakers: he was interested in more expressive type systems that provide programmers with more flexible patterns of code reuse. He presented The type system of the language Concord, which was joint work with Paul Jolly, Sophia Drossopoulou, and Klaus Ostermann. This work used a simple form of dependent types to express relationships between collections of classes called groups. This resulted in quite some discussion about the relation with other approaches, notably the use of virtual types in Beta. The main advantage of Concord over other attempts to use dependent types for similar purposes, notably Scala (http://scala.epfl.ch/) appears the simplicity of the language, with allowed of decidability of the type system and soundness to be proved.

4   Java Implementation and Compilation

The work presented by Alessandro Coglio and Neal Glew concerned the use of formal techniques to improve JVM implementation and Java compilation.

Alessandro Coglio talked about checking access to protected members in Java, one of the trickiest aspects of enforcing visibility (or access control) in Java. Indeed, as he had discovered, there are existing JVM implementations which accept incorrect programs and reject correct ones. He gave a very clear explanation of the rules involved, and presented an optimal strategy for checking protected access that demanded the minimal amount of rechecking when new classes are dynamically loaded. There was quite some discussion about why checking access to protected members is so tricky in the first place, which could be traced by to the possibility of subclasses being in different packages.

Neal Glew talked about joint work with Jens Palsberg about method inlining. Method inlining is a standard optimisation performed by compilers, but it can be invalidated by later class loading. He presented a framework for reasoning about this, and presented a technique for inlining method invocations that could be proved sound using this framework. The idea of the technique is that at the moment of dynamically loading a class, a whole program analysis is done to inline methods calls in the loaded code if possible (devirtualisation), and to patch invalidated inlinings in all previously loaded code (revirtualisation).

There was some discussion about the way in which the dynamic class loading, which caused much of the complications in the topics discussed by Coglio and Glew, were also the inspiration for much of the work presented in the first session.

5   Invariants

Class invariants play a crucial role in any approach to specification and verification for object oriented code.

Cees Pierik talked about joint work with Dave Clark and Frank de Boer, about a special kind of invariant that seems to play an important role in some "creational" design patterns for OO programming. In particular, he was interested in design patterns that control the way in which objects of a certain class are created, such as the singleton or factory patterns. These invariants belong to a class rather than an individual object, and could thus be called static rather than instance invariants thereby quantifying over all objects of a given class.

Andreas Roth talked about joint work with Peter Schmitt in the KeY project into the possibility of verifying that Java programs satisfy invariants in a modular way. He began by demonstrating that in the presence of subtyping and aliasing, "local" verifications that each class satisfies its invariants do not suffice to guarantee that invariants are never broken. Andreas proposed a notion of module that would allow sound modular verification of invariants. His solution involved a notion of ownership, a topic which was further discussed in the last session of the workshop.

There was some discussion about the surprising fact that, although class invariants play such a central role in any approach to program specification and verification for OO languages, the precise meaning of the notion is so tricky. It clearly remains a very interesting topic for further research. Cees Pierik raised the possibility of using techniques developed in the concurrency community, more specifically the rely-guarantee approach, to tackle the problem of reasoning about invariants dealing with shared state.

6   Specification and Verification

There were two talks involving the specification languages Spec# (for C#) and JML (for Java) which are related in many ways. Both of these talks were about the use of method calls in specification, e.g. in pre- and post-conditions, as a natural and convenient abbreviation mechanism.

Typically, one insists that such methods are pure, meaning they should not have any side-effects. However, this is a very strong requirements that rules out many obviously harmless method calls from being used in specifications. Mike

Barnett talked about joint work with David A. Naumann, Wolfram Schulte, and Qi Sun, about extending the category of methods than can be used in specifications. He discussed a weaker notion of observationally pure and argued that methods used in specifications need only be observationally pure rather than pure. Mike gave some typical examples to show that many non-pure methods that one would like to use in specifications are indeed observationally pure, so that this is a very useful notion.

In the subsequent discussion Erik Poll noted that one would like to extend the category of methods that could be used in specifications even further, in particular to include the method that came up in the Singleton pattern in Cees Pierik's talk earlier, which does have a (clearly harmless) side effect the very first time it is called.

David Cok talked about his work on extending the program verification tool ESC/Java2 to support reasoning with specification that contained method calls. David considered some of the design decisions involved and raised some more fundamental design decisions about how to reason about the heap in verifying object oriented languages. This led to some discussion with Rustan Leino about how this is done in the new Boogie prover. David also expressed some dissatisfaction with the current notion of "purity" in JML, in line with the previous talks. However, he also noted that the possibility that pure methods can throw exceptions causes complications in reasoning about specifications containing method calls, and suggested that maybe the notion of (observationally) pure should be strengthened to disallow this.

7   Ownership Types

The last session of the workshop was devoted to ownership type systems, which continues to be a hot topic both at FTfJP and the main ECOOP conference.

Alex Potanin presented joint work with James Noble, Dave Clarke, and Robert Biddle. They developed a new type system, OGJ, which combines generic types and ownership [5]. Their type system supports the full type genericity of Generic Java as well as parametric ownership. The talk by Potanin focused on defaulting, a lightweight alternative to type inference. Defaulting allows one to integrate code that does not have ownership annotations. This approach is certainly relevant to all researchers in the area of ownership types, in particular, since type inference for ownership type systems does not yet produce practically useful results, as remarked by Jonathan Aldrich who was one of the several special visitors for this session.

Werner Dietl discussed joint work with Peter Müller on how exceptions can be supported on ownership type systems. He analysed four viable designs (1) cloning exception objects during propagation; (2) using unique references to transfer exceptions between contexts during propagation; (3) treating exceptions as global data; (4) handling exceptions by read-only references that may cross context boundaries. His presentation lead to an interesting discussion among the participants about the design principles of different ownership type systems, contrasting parameterised type systems in the tradition of Clarke, Potter, and Noble's work [1] and Müller's more lightweight Universe type system [4].

This session on ownership type systems was effectively continued the next morning at the main ECOOP conference, where the papers presented in the first session after the invited talk were also about notions of ownership.

8   Discussion

At the end of the workshop there was some more general discussion about topics people wanted to raise then and there. The discussion quickly focused about the pros and cons of typing versus annotations as means of allowing more information to be expressed in programs, and possibilities of moving more annotations into type systems, the latter having the advantage of easier acceptance by programmers and offering more automation. Rustan Leino talked about efforts of moving 'non null'-ness, one of the most fundamental properties that crops up in any attempt to support code analysis or verification, into the type system of Spec#. Joe Kiniry raised the issue of overcoming programmer resistance to new type or annotation system and that a considerable amount of preparatory work, such as annotating APIs, was needed before one could begin to convince programmers of the usefulness. David Cok remarked that for this he would like to see a tool in the style of Daikon [2], which infers likely annotations by observing runtime behaviour of programs, that uses static checking instead of runtime verification; others observed that this is essentially what has been pursued in the Houdini work [3].

9   Conclusions

We were pleased to be able to announce at the workshop that two special journal issues dedicated to previous editions of the workshop had appeared in the month preceding this year's ECOOP. A special issue of the journal Concurrency and Computation: Practice and Experience (CCPE) appeared about FTfJP'2002 (CCPE, Volume 16, Issue 7, 2004), and a special issue of the online Journal of Object Technology (JOT), appeared about FTfJP'03 (JOT (http://www.jot.fm), Volume 3, Number 6, 2004). The fact that these issues appeared almost simultaneously proves one clear advantage of online only journals! There are plans for a special issue of JOT about FTfJP'2004, for which Joe Kiniry and Susan Eisenbach have volunteered to serve as editors.

Even though this is now the sixth workshop in the series, the workshop is still going strong. The focus of the workshop has shifted somewhat over time, as different topics become more or less popular, or essentially resolved. For instance, it was interesting to note that there was not a single presentation about bytecode verification this year. It is nice to observe that the workshop has helped in raising some interesting topics for research, with some papers addressing issues raised at earlier editions of the workshop, and to observe the way it has contributed to fostering collaborations, all of which has resulted in good work presented not just at this workshop but also at the main ECOOP conference.

The workshop has somewhat outgrown the standard workshop format, given the number and quality of submissions it typically received, and the number of people that want to participate. But the interest it generates and the audience it attracts proves that it clearly serves a useful purpose and we look forward to organising another FTfJP workshop at next year's ECOOP.

List of Participants

- Davide Ancona (University of Genua, Italy)
- Christopher Anderson (Imperial College, UK)
- Mike Barnett (Microsoft Research, USA)
- Alex Buckley (Imperial College, UK)
- Alessandro Coglio (Kestrel Institute, USA)
- David Cok (Kodak Eastman, USA)
- Adam Darvas (ETH Zürich, Switzerland)
- Werner Dietl (ETH Zürich, Switzerland)
- John Field (IBM's T. J. Watson Research Center, USA)
- Neal Glew (Intel, USA)
- Johan Glimming (KTH, Sweden)
- Marieke Huisman (INRIA Sophia-Antipolis, France)
- Bart Jacobs (K.U. Leuven, Belgium)
- Joe Kiniry (Radboud University Nijmegen, Netherlands)
- Peter Müller (ETH Zürich, Switzerland)
- Rustan Leino (Microsoft Research, USA)
- Cees Pierik (University of Utrecht, Netherlands)
- Frank Piessens (K.U. Leuven, Belgium)
- Alex Potanin (Victoria University of Wellington, New Zealand)
- Erik Poll (Radboud University Nijmegen, Netherlands)
- Andreas Roth (University of Karlsruhe, Germany)
- Mirko Viroli (University of Bologna, Italy)
- Joe Zhou (University of Leicester, UK)

References

1. D. G. Clarke, J. M. Potter, and J. Noble. Ownership types for flexible alias protection. In *Proceedings of Object-Oriented Programming Systems, Languages, and Applications (OOPSLA)*, volume 33(10) of *ACM SIGPLAN Notices*, October 1998.
2. Michael D. Ernst, Jake Cockrell, William G. Griswold, and David Notkin. Dynamically discovering likely program invariants to support program evolution. *IEEE Transactions on Software Engineering*, 27(2):1–25, 2001.
3. Cormac Flanagan and K. Rustan M. Leino. Houdini, an annotation assistant for ESC/Java. In J. N. Oliveira and P. Zave, editors, *FME 2001*, volume LNCS 2021, pages 500–517. Springer, 2001.

4. P. Müller. *Modular Specification and Verification of Object-Oriented Programs*, volume 2262 of *Lecture Notes in Computer Science*. Springer-Verlag, 2002.
5. A. Potanin, J. Noble, D. Clarke, and R. Biddle. Generic ownership. Technical Report CS-TR-03-16, Victoria University of Wellington, 2003.

Component-Oriented Approaches to Context-Aware Computing[*]

Simon Dobson

Department of Computer Science, Trinity College, Dublin IE
simon.dobson@cs.tcd.ie

1   Motivation and Goals

Context-awareness is emerging as an essential component of many user-focused software domains. It is especially integral to pervasive or ambient computing, but can be used to control the behaviour of any system that adapts to the circumstances in which it is used.

Like most new software projects, many existing context-aware systems have been constructed using object- or component-oriented programming techniques. Experience has shown that objects have difficulty in addressing some of the facets of highly adaptive and highly contextualised systems. These include:

- the need to create object views over information with significant ontological structure;
- consistently supporting multiple views of the same information at different levels of abstraction;
- the complexity of selecting and matching components and interfaces; and
- the mixing of concerns across different levels of the design space.

Many of the techniques being used ad hoc in context-aware applications might be better captured in tools, languages or methods; conversely new developments in infrastructure might be helpful – or not! – to the developers of context-aware systems.

Goals and Organisation

The workshop was organised to address these issues. We requested short contributions in two strands:

1. Research and practitioner contributions on topics highlighting both the contributions object and component technology makes to context-aware distributed computing and the issues and shortcomings of current approaches
2. "What if we could" systems that can be used as a basis for case studies to be expanded during the workshop to drive discussion

---

[*] The title of this report sould be referenced as "Report from the ECOOP 2004 Workshop on Component-oriented approaches to context-aware computing".

J. Malenfant and B.M. Østvold (Eds.): ECOOP 2004, LNCS 3344, pp. 84–93, 2004.
© Springer-Verlag Berlin Heidelberg 2004

We received a wide range of contributions covering middleware issues, interface adaptation, navigating large information spaces and embedded systems, each highlighting some particular aspect of constructing context-aware adaptive systems from components.

The workshop was divided into three parts: short presentations and two discussion groups exploring a different issue in more detail. The rest of this report summarises the contributions (section 2), explore two discussion topics (section 3), and offers some conclusions (section 4). Appendix A contains the names and contact details of the participants.

2   Summary of Contributions

Three major themes were identifiable in the contributions:

- contributions focusing on the extension of object models to provide context-awareness within a largely standard programming infrastructure;
- work on component selection and discovery, and the problems inherent in performing these tasks in an open environment; and
- systems integrating software closely with real-world artefacts which need to provide virtual analogues of physical capabilities.

In introducing the workshop, Simon Dobson posed four questions for context-aware systems:

1. How do we engineer systems that are stable under minor perturbations?
2. How can we compose components into larger functions in a way that users can grasp clearly?
3. How do we balance information collected to inform adaptability against the privacy and security concerns arising from its abuse?
4. What does it mean for an adaptive system to be "correct", when some of its function derives from the changing environment?

Most of these questions occur in "ordinary" systems engineering with components and distributed objects[1], but are thrown into high relief by the introduction of context and adaptability. The use of components can be used to address issues of composition and correctness, but it is not sufficient for a context-aware system to behave correctly in any given context: it must also behave correctly dynamically, retaining continuity and stability for users even in the presence of adaptation.

Extending object models involves allowing objects to sense and adapt to context, without compromising the encapsulation properties of the underlying object model. Aline Senart gave an overview of the "sentient objects" model for pervasive systems. A sentient objects system is composed of a number of entities encapsulating a local view of the system's context and communicating via events. The event system is built around a scalable core that provides location-awareness, robust group management, and a predictive routing infrastructure for managing the sporadic disconnections of devices from the network.

From a programming perspective, sentient objects provide a local context model in which contexts are arranged into a hierarchy. An inferencing system determines which context the system is in, and triggers actions based on this. The view of context is strictly local, making sentient objects behave externally like "normal" objects hiding their context-sensitivity.

The "contextors" system described by Joëlle Coutaz and Gaëtan Rey provides a well-developed approach to "plastic" user interfaces that can be re-modelled and re-presented on a range of devices without compromising the intention or usability of the interface. The system is based around the description of abstract meta-interfaces and associated meta-data, together with a family of possible implementations. As the context of the user and the task being pursued evolve, the implementation can select a different implementation of the interface that is best able to satisfy the environmental and task constraints, and re-map the interface without losing application continuity.

Contextors can both produce and consume context and communicate via events. They are best regarded as context transformers – closer to actors than fully stateful objects.

The problem of component discovery is made even more complex by populations of adaptive components whose matching requirements follower a richer model. Peter Rigole presented a model of resource-aware components in which each component declares the external resources it needs in its interface. The interface then forms a contract which is satisfied and settled when the component is instanciated. The supporting middleware signs the contract to confirm that its requested resources are available, allowing better run-time confidence in and analysis of the component system. Component requirements may be parameterised by the context, allowing run-time adaptation through the re-negotiation of the components satisfying the contract or altering the contract as the task evolves.

Maomao Wu presented a version of the standard Microsoft COM component framework extended with interface meta-data and rules for composition, using the CLIPS engine for inference and matching. A number of factors make component composition harder in context-aware systems including the increased intelligence and adaptability of the individual components, their increased autonomy, and the time- and safety-criticality of some applications.

Otso Virtanen addressed the problem of terminal integrity, ensuring that an adaptive end-point device retains the capabilities and assurances necessary to remain integrated into a full network. Components are downloaded onto the device using a secure protocol from a component broker, which manages the dependencies of the various components sets.

In an extensible and dynamic environment, however, it is impossible to guarantee the correct functioning of every combination of components. Incompatible combinations are recognised at the device, flagged and reported to the component broker to prevent the propagation of clashes across the system. This improves the integrity of users' devices, since faulty compositions are less likely to propagate once a problem has been detected. It also allows "roll-back" of devices to component populations known to be stable.

Dhouha Ayed described an extension of the CORBA component model to express assembly descriptions of components. An assembly descriptor includes information allowing the choice of components to be constrained by location, structure, type and so forth, and may be linked to a discovery service to facilitate more adaptive component location. A rule-based selection system and adapter-filter architecture allows components to be connected in the presence of minor inconsistencies in their interfaces.

Many context-aware systems include a close correspondence between physical objects and informational activities, means that the underlying context model is more closely aligned to individual objects rather than to situations. Trung Dung Ngo reported on embedding sensing and processing into LEGO bricks. Connecting bricks together provided automatic composition, to (for example) use a sensor to directly control a motor. While limited in the complexity of possible compositions, the system is easy enough for children to build with – and indeed the children can work out how the bricks work together themselves, with only a minimal explanation. Other applications include cognitive rehabilitation and other sensory integration therapies.

Micael Sjölund described SensAid, a tablet PC platform for experimenting with mixed physical and virtual entities. A room containing artefacts augmented with RFID tags allows physical objects to have a corresponding virtual presence carrying their meta-data and allowing interaction through the SensAid desktop (or tablet-top) application.

3   Discussions

As seeds for discussion, the workshop addressed two issues arising from the submissions:

1. How is adaptability best represented, presented and understood, both by users and developers?
2. How can designers of middleware and platforms help support the continuity of user experience in the face of adaptation while keeping the complexity of applications development under control?

3.1   Adaptation

Adaptability means changing some aspect of a system's detailed behaviour while keeping the gross behaviour of the system consistent. From a contextual systems perspective, adaptability means matching behaviour to changes in environment, task, user population, preferences or some other factor; from a component systems perspective, it means selecting and/or configuring the component set to provide the optimum behaviour. There are any number of design solutions that can be applied to this process, with the design space being governed by the issues (among others) discussed below.

Context as Process *Versus* Context as Data. Many systems use a context model based around context-as-data the model stores a representation of the state of the world as seen by the application and its sensors, which is then used to inform the behaviour of applications. Adaptability comes from the way in which components respond to changes in the context model, or from how they are selected and interconnected based on it. This approach tends to lay stress on responses to the changing environment.

An alternative view is to adopt a model of context-as-process where the context is the task the user is involved with – a task inferred from the sensor (and other) data. This can be used to provide a stronger sense of continuity, in that the task (and hence the users' goals) are more clearly articulated, and can therefore lay stress on the responding to the changing task priorities[2].

There does not seem to be a clear-cut case for either view as being more powerful or natural. While using the context-as-process model potentially offers a more holistic an continuous view around which to structure adaptation, such models are often more error-prone trough having to infer the task from sensor data. Conversely the context-as-data view can fragment adaptations by not retaining the "flow" of a task-level interaction. Integrating both views in the same model may lead to conflicts between different levels.

Are the Components Context-Aware? Another dimension in systems design is where in the design the adaptability resides. The design space lies between two extremes:

1. A static collection of components is constructed to handle the task, with each component adapting itself to the changing context
2. Each component presents a fixed behaviour, and the collection of components is changed according to the environment by some external agent

The systems described in the presentations fell into both categories, but with an emphasis on the former.

An important notion in this area is that of open- versus closed-adaptive systems, deriving from the work of Rick Taylor and others (e.g. [3]). A closed-adaptive component provides a set of adaptive behaviours itself that can be selected; an open-adaptive component accepts new behaviours from outside. Closed-adaptive systems are less flexible over the long term but possibly more reliable, stable and secure than open-adaptive components.

Open-adaptive components offer a better long-term solution for choreography and re-purposing, but would accentuate the need to pay careful attention to fallback and roll-back behaviours if an adaptation proved unsuitable.

Choosing the "Right" Components. In either of the above cases there is an issue in choosing the correct components for a given situation – a decision that may be repeated over the application's lifetime.

Many of the participants work in this area. The main approaches involve adding meta-data to component interfaces – something that should probably be emphasised and standardised as part of the evolution of component frameworks.

The decision process itself is very subtle, since most systems will not have access to all the information that they could potentially use. Several systems are rule-based, although it was recognised that "crisp" logic may not be the ideal way to deal with the inherent uncertainties.

An uncertain process must face the possibility that a decision is made incorrectly. The impact of wrong decisions can vary, from preventing the system working (with possible loss of data) to generating a system that works sub-optimally. Systems that select component populations dynamically are able to recover from non-fatal compositions by re-selecting as soon as the problem arises. More static composition systems require more explicit recovery strategies.

Semantic Compatibility. Component selection depends on a degree of semantic compatibility between the various components, either inherent or introduced through adapters.

Again, one may take a static on dynamic position on the issue. The extreme static position is to assume that interface meta-data is an infallible guide; the extreme dynamic position is that consistency checks are continuously required to ensure that the components are working together. What is important, however, is to embrace the fact that compatibility is an issue in the on-going evolution of systems and to address it in the basic structure of the design.

Complex Components *Versus* Choreography. Another aspect of component selection involves the relative "weight" or "intelligence" of components. Components may perform a single, simple function, or they may perform a larger set of functions. A good example is two ways of building a messaging system: using components that each support a single messaging protocol (e-mail, SMS, IM), or as a single messaging component offering all protocols. Both are valid decision decisions, and both are orthogonal to the issue of whether the components offer adaptive interfaces to their services.

Using large populations of small components involves quite complex coordination (sometimes referred to as "choreography"), but allows very finegrained adaptation. Larger components allow simpler plumbing but force the system developer to take larger "chunks" of functionality.

This argument is common in all component- or object-based systems. It has a particular impact for contextual systems in which the component composition decisions are uncertain and may be hard to undo.

One part of the design space that is definitely concerning is large components offering adaptive interfaces internally. There is a real risk that the component will be selected for functional reasons (i.e. it offers messaging functions), but will not offer the best adaptive interface functions. Separating these two concerns is therefore an important goal for populating a component framework.

Autonomous *Versus* Human-in-the-Loop. One of the goals of pervasive computing is to be able to offer some services autonomously, matched to context. This includes adapting the user interface. The question is whether, and to what extent, services can or should be provided without user intervention, and how to integrate the human into the loop in a natural fashion.

This question divides into two parts. At an interface level it may be possible (and indeed preferable) to provide for user "guidance" of adaptations where possible. At the system level, imprecise reasoning may require disambiguation by the user. In effect this is a "whole system" issue rather than being tied to components per se.

Observability of Relevant State in the Interface. Closely related to the above is the inclusion of relevant state in the interface. It is evident that human decision-making relies on presenting the information needed for the decision; it also seems to be the case that autonomous or semi-autonomous adaptations should be indicated in the interface, either before ("this change may happen") or after ("this is what just happened").

3.2   Continuity and Complexity

If the "software crisis" challenges our ability to build correct software for desktop and server-based systems, then context-aware systems raise the bar even higher. Engineering such systems means that we need to identify the areas of context-awareness that generate additional complexity, and develop ways to keep it under control.

Complexity has a user dimension as well as a programmer one. A system that adapts too often may appear to "flicker" and prevent users forming a coherent mental model of its behaviour and services. This is why it is important to mirror the users' notions of the continuity of an interaction across modifications in detailed behaviour.

A number of major issues affecting complexity are discussed below.

Retain Task Models at Run-Time. Maintaining continuity of interaction across adaptation relies either on knowing that adaptations inherently preserve continuity or on being able to intervene to preserve the experience. The former is difficult to conceive of in an open system; the latter is considerably simplified by keeping task models available at run-time.

"Introspective" systems architectures are moderately common, occurring on a small scale in reflective programming languages and on a large scale in facilities management systems such as Tivoli. It is far less common to encounter run-time descriptions of the use cases or tasks the system addresses. However, having an abstract, machine-readable description of the task being supported by a system makes it far easier to ensure that adaptations "maintain the place" in the workflow.

Separate Functions from Interface. Interface adaptations form a large part of the adaptations a system makes to changes in context – although by no means all the possible adaptations involve interface changes.

The separation of function from interface is a common one in many systems, being the basis for the Model-View-Controller (MVC) design pattern. Maintaining this separation into adaptive and multi-modal interfaces – although challenging – is essential to allow tested functionality to be re-used under different usage models.

This design constraint lends itself well to open-adaptive and choreography-based component strategies, since one may select base behaviour and then provide multiple changing interfaces without modifying it.

Make "Seams" Observable. A lot of pervasive computing is characterised as "seamless" interaction, characterised as meeting Mark Weiser's vision of presented the right service at the right time in the right way with minimal cognitive load[4].

However, there are many ways in which the world is inherently "seamed", and these seams should be reflected in the behaviour of a context-aware system. The key observation is that discontinuous behavioural change should occur in response to clear changes in the environment. A system may change interface mode better to match the task or environment: but if this change introduces a cognitive disruption then there should be a clear rationale for the change that the user can relate to. There are strong arguments for elevating this notion to being a fundamental design driver for tools and languages (see for example [5]).

Externalise Strategies. Any function that is embodied solely as code is essentially a black box that can only be manipulated according to its meta-data. While essential for core low-level tasks, higher-level co-ordination tasks can often be externalised as process descriptions. A number of emerging standards exist in this domain, often targeted at web services. While perhaps not completely applicable to pervasive computing as they stand, they offer a promising direction.

As well as task descriptions of this kind, adaptation also requires adaptation strategies that are followed to determine component configurations or re-configurations. Again, if these strategies are articulated as descriptions rather than code, they can be analysed and manipulated by other strategies to solve conflicts or introduce additional concerns. A good example might be delaying an adaptation that will radically change the system's interaction mode until the user reaches a natural "break" in the task.

4   Conclusions and Recommendations

If one had to distill three recommendations for systems design from the presentations and discussions, they would be the following:

Keep Components Simple. Simple components allow greater flexibility in composition. The separation of user interface from function – a "contextualised MVC" – provides better adaptability than larger-grained components with hard-wired adaptation.

Externalise Adaptations. A systems' reaction to contextual changes is itself a subject for analysis. The strategies and decision processes used should be represented explicitly and in machine-readable form to allow second-order effects to be generated.

Retain a Global View. Contextual systems have an unavoidable holism, which implies taking a global view on the system and its behaviour as well as a local view per-component. This includes a view of the tasks the system is supporting and the way it is supporting them. The global view should be clearly expressed rather than being implied.

In conclusion, a wide range of techniques from object- and component-oriented software engineering are contributing strongly to the development of context-aware systems. Several extensions are needed, especially in handling dynamic component composition in the face of imperfect information, and in maintaining a continuous user experience with adaptive interfaces. Some of these extensions can be provided conservatively by adding meta-data and processing to component interfaces within largely standard frameworks; others require a hange in the way we think about, design and analyse component systems and their relationship to their operating environment.

References

1. Enmerich, W.: Engineering distributed objects. Wiley (2000)
2. Dobson, S.: Applications considered harmful for ambient systems. In: Proceedings of the International Symposium on Information and Communications Technologies, ACM Press (2003) 171–176
3. Oreizy, P., Gorlick, M., Taylor, R., Heimbigner, D., Johnson, G., Medvidovic, N., Quilliei, A., Rosenblum, D., Wolf, A.: An architecture-based approach to self-adaptive software. IEEE Intelligent Systems **14** (1999) 54–62
4. Weiser, M.: The computer for the 21st century. Scientific American (1991)

5. Dobson, S., Nixon, P.: More principled design of pervasive computing systems. In: Proceedings of Engineering for Human-Computer Interaction and Design, Specification and Verification of Interactive Systems (EHCI-DSVIS'04). LNCS, Springer-Verlag (2004) To appear.

A   Participants

Name	Affiliation
Dhouha Ayed	CNRS INT-Evry, FR dhouha.ayed@int-evry.fr
Joëlle Coutaz	CLIPS-IMAG, FR joelle.coutaz@imag.fr
Simon Dobson	Trinity College, Dublin IE simon.dobson@cs.tcd.ie
Jasminka Matevska-Meyer	University of Oldenburg, DE matevska-meyer@informatik.uni-oldenburg.de
Trung Dung Ngo	University of Southern Denmark, DK dungnt@mip.sdu.dk
Gaëtan Rey	CLIPS-IMAG, FR gaetan.rey@imag.fr
Peter Rigole	KU Leuven, BE peter.rigole@cs.kuleuven.ac.be
Aline Senart	Trinity College Dublin, IE aline.senart@cs.tcd.ie
Micael Sjölund	Linköping University, SE x03micsj@ida.liu.se
Otso Virtanen	Helsinki Institute for Information Technology, FI otso.virtanen@cs.helsinki.fi
Maomao Wu	University of Lancaster, UK maomao@comp.lancs.ac.uk

Copies of all the submitted papers and presentations may be found on the workshop web site, http://www.cs.tcd.ie/COA-CAC-04/.

B   Programme Committee

Simon Dobson	Trinity College Dublin, IE
Paddy Nixon	University of Strathclyde, UK
Siobhán Clarke	Trinity College Dublin, IE
Achilles Kameas	University of Patras, GR
Dominic Duggan	Stevens Institute of Technology, US
Gaetano Borriello	University of Washington, US

The Combined 14th Workshop for PhD Students in Object-Oriented Systems and Doctoral Symposium[*]

Susanne Jucknath[1], Jan Wloka[2], Eric Jul[3],
Sari R. Eldadah[4], and Ademar Aguiar[5]

[1] Technical University of Berlin, Germany
[2] Fraunhofer Institute FIRST, Berlin, Germany
[3] DIKU, University of Copenhagen, Denmark
[4] Method Building Capacity Cooperation, Jordan
[5] University of Porto (FEUP), Portugal
http://swt.cs.tu-berlin.de/ecoop04

Abstract. The PhDOOS workshop differs from other workshops because the range of participants is much smaller (only PhD students) but has a wide scope of topics. Even with the limitation to PhD students in Object Oriented Systems, the presentations covered topics such as Generic Ownership, Generic Algorithms, Model Driven Architecture, Prediction of Size, QoS assessment, Frameworks, Teaching of Frameworks and Object Calculus.

Several topics of shared interest were identified and targeted in separate discussion groups on a general theme on the future of object oriented programming. As the participants had various research interests covering very different parts of the OO spectrum, we can confidently state that these topics reflect actual concerns and needs of the OO community, and emerge from its concrete needs.

This document is to be complemented by a workshop proceedings online document which will contain the full versions of the presented papers.

1 Introduction

The 14th workshop for PhD Students in Object Oriented Systems (PhDOOS'04) was for the first time combined with a Doctoral Symposium. The combined event was held on June 14-15 2004 in Oslo, Norway in association with the 18th European Conference on Object Oriented Programming (ECOOP). The workshop was part of the series of PhDOOS workshops held in conjunction with ECOOP each year, same as the Doctoral Symposium. The decision to unite

---

[*] The title of this report sould be referenced as "Report from the ECOOP 2004 combined 14th Workshop for PhD Students in Object-Oriented Systems and Doctoral Symposium".

J. Malenfant and B.M. Østvold (Eds.): ECOOP 2004, LNCS 3344, pp. 94–100, 2004.

these events was made due to the similar group of participants. Students at the beginning of their research should attend the PhD workshop, where they can discuss their ideas with researchers at a similar stage of work and similar difficulties. Students near the finishing of their dissertation should attend the Doctoral Symposium, where they present their work in front of a group of senior researchers who will evaluate their work from a different point of view. Both – participants of the PhD workshop and the Doctoral Symposium – were free to enter the other event. The invited talk and the workshop discussion were relevant for both groups.

The participation was by invitation only, selected after a review process that included at least two reviews for each submission. Each aspirant for the Doctoral Symposium had to sent a package containing general information (name of student, name of advisor, full address, university or department), a research abstract (title of the dissertation, research area, problem to be solved, research hypothesis, approach to solve the problem) and a letter of recommendation from the students advisor. Two students have been selected to join the Doctoral Symposium (Alex Potanin and Sameh Elnikatney) and were supervised during the session by Professor Eric Jul and Professor Markku Sakkinen. The students had to give a 45 minute talk in front of them and later answer their questions for another 45 minutes.

Students, who were interested in joining the PhD-Workshop, had send a package containing general information about the authors and a paper which was limited up to 10 pages. Eight submissions were selected after the review process, so that eight students actually presented at the workshop (Po-Hao Chang, Jerome Darbon, Gregory de Fombelle, Johan Glimming, Guillermo Jimenez-Diaz, Raquel Hervas, Gabor Stikkel and Istvan Zolyomi). Each of these participants had to give a talk about her paper including a discussion part, altogether strictly limited to 45 minutes.

2   Workshop Structure

A large diversity of topics was presented, the submissions might be divided into three general groups: General Problems in Object Oriented Programming, Model Driven Architecture and Frameworks. There has also been two other works, which don't fit into this scheme. The individual topics were the following:

1. General Problems in Object Oriented Programming
   (a) Generic Ownership
   (b) C++ template Introspection Library
   (c) Generic Algorithmic Blocks dedicated to Image Processing
   (d) Design Pattern
2. Model Driven Architecture
   (a) Prediction of Size in Executable Model Driven Architecture
   (b) QoS assessment
3. Frameworks
   (a) Adaptive Distributed Object Framework for the Web
   (b) Case-Based Approach for Teaching Frameworks

4. Others
   (a) Object Calculus
   (b) Dynamic Content Delivery Network

Besides discussions of these topics Professor Eric Jul gave a talk about how to do PhD studies and how to work toward actually completing the studies with a readable PhD dissertation as a result.

The following sections summarize the contributions and discussions that took place in the various sessions.

2.1   General Problems in Object Oriented Programming

Alex Potanin presented Practical Ownership Control in Programming Languages where he outlines a general problem in object-oriented languages and one solution in Java. An object is aliased whenever there is more than one pointer to that object. Aliasing can cause a range of difficult problems within object-oriented programs, because one referring object can change the state of the aliased object, implicitly affecting all the other referring objects. To deal with such problems, object instance encapsulation has been widely studied in literature. But most of the former approaches do not take the introduction of generic in modern programming languages into account. The approach here is to combine ownership and generic types and developed a compiler extension, called Ownership Generic Java (OGJ)

Istvan Zolyomi presented A general C++ template introspection library mentioning Zoltan Porkolab as his advisor. Generic programming is heavily based on parametric polymorphism, what is provided by templates in C++. To ensure the correctness of template based constructions, constraints on template parameters are especially useful. Unlike other languages (Ada, Eiffel, etc), C++ does not directly support checking requirements on template parameters (concept checking), but many authors mentions ad hoc solutions based on special language features. The here presented solution is a template meta-programming library which supports an easy expression of basic concepts, providing the possibility to avoid re-implementation of simple checks for every single concept. Based on this library there is also a checking method that takes the advantages of both traditional concepts and static interfaces.

Jerome Darbon presented Generic Algorithmic Blocks dedicated to Image Processing, mentioning Thierry Geraud and Patrick Bellot as his advisors. The focus is here on the implementation of algorithms in the specific domain of image processing. Although many image processing libraries are available, they generally lack genericity and flexibility. Many image processing algorithms can be expressed as compositions of elementary algorithmic operations referred to as blocks. Implementing these compositions is achieved using generic programming. As a conclusion this solution is compared to previous ones and demonstrated on a class image processing algorithm.

Raquel Hervas presented Using Design Patterns to Abstract a Software Architecture for Natural Language Generation joint work with Pablo Gervas. There are several problems of Natural Language Generation (NLG), including the fact that there is no consensus about the architecture a NLG must follow. The approach here is a reusable software architecture for a NLG systems by applying design patterns to abstract the main design decisions involved in the construction of a system of this kind. Its applicability had been tested through the development of a particular instantiation of a simple NLG application.

2.2   Model Driven Architecture

Gabor Stikkel presented Prediction of Size in Executable Model Driven Architectures, joint work with Zoltan Theisz. Most of the project planning approaches are based on the prediction of the software size. Size is often measured in lines of code. Lines of code as a size measure must be reviewed in the context of Executable Model Driven Architecture as some part of the code is generated automatically. Moreover models which are based on object-orientation are extended with code written in an action semantic language. The outcome of their investigations shows how the amount of action semantic language code can be predicted by using object-oriented design metrics. As one result the number of operations seems to be a good predictor of the lines of code written in the action semantic language.

Gregory de Fombelle presented A model driven engineering chain for early QoS assessment in dynamic federation of systems. Dynamic federation of systems raise the problem's quality of service properties assessment early in the development process. At the moment it is not conceivable to perform cross cutting properties evaluation on operational systems because of combinatory explosion. One should assess those properties with QoS tagged models of systems and QoS tagged models of platforms on which systems will deploy.

2.3   Frameworks

Po-Hao Chang presented An Adaptive Distributed Object Framework for the Web. Currently, coding Web applications is location and platform dependent: programmers entangle code for client and server together with different technologies. Due to the diversity and dynamicity of the Internet, it is hardly believed such inflexible code could deliver good performance in all the cases. The goal is to develop a framework which provide programming abstraction over the heterogeneous Internet, and the mechanism to realize the abstraction. This is composed of two tasks: a scripting language with concurrent object support and the associate retargetable compiler to provide a uniform abstraction over the Internet, and a framework management system for adaptive application deployment and resource management. The main contribution of this work is to extend the control and management of the Web out of the servers without special protocols and software.

Guillermo Jimenez-Diaz presented A Case-Based Approach for Teaching Frameworks, joint work with Mercedes Gomez-Allbarran. There are several learning techniques for computer skills and learning to use an object-oriented framework is a hard task. There has been little work done to develop effective techniques to reduce the effort and time taken to teach how to use a framework.

The solution here is a Case-Based Teaching approach following an active learning process where the learner is involved in resolving exercises based on framework instantiation examples.

2.4   Others

Johan Glimming presented D ifunctorial Sem antics of O bject C alculus where he gives a new denotational semantics for Abadi and Cardelli s object calculus (without sub-typing). The model is a Cartesian closed category which gives a self-application semantics of objects and model object types as fixed points of mixed variance functors. A prove is also presented that the denotational semantics agrees with Abadi and Cardelli s operational semantics. As a conclusion there are some further research directions for the denotational model explained.

Sameh Elnikety presented D ynaServer:D ynam ic C ontent D elivery N etwork for E -com m erce Traditionally a website generates dynamic web content by running a web server, application server and database server, all located in one place. The approach here is to use a network of proxies to generate and deliver dynamic web content to users. These proxies should be located at strategic points in the Internet to be close to users, achieving both low latency and high availability as perceived by uses. Each proxy maintains a complete replica of the database and should have a web server and application server that execute application code locally. To maintain data consistency among the databases replicas, the system provides generalized snapshot isolation to database transactions.

3   Workshop Discussions

A large variety of approaches were presented, spanning from foundations of object orientation over language improvements and several domain specific problems to the teaching of object oriented frameworks. In contrast to preceding Ph-DOOS workshops this workshop wasn't dominated by a certain new "wonder" technique, like extreme programming, refactoring or aspect-oriented programming. Single sharp bordered problems and their solutions using well known OO techniques and their improvements were in the focus of this years' PhD work. For example, problems of domains like image processing, natural language generation and web application development were presented to motivate interesting drawbacks of object oriented means.

In several discussions many different OO techniques were individually depicted and their problems and applications discussed in small groups. Some features of C++, framework based solutions and generative programming built the core of presented PhD work. The improvement of OO programming language or the creation of a specific framework seems to help usual developers to keep focussed to their actual problem solution.

C oncluding D iscussion Participants:Jerome Darbon, Jan Wloka, Susanne Jucknath, Po-Hao Chang, Raquel Hervas, Guillermo Jimenez-Diaz, Sameh Elnikety

In a concluding discussion we tried to identify next hot topics in object orientated research. To start with a tangible base, requirements for descriptions of certain computation in different domains were identified. For example, the composition of functional units seems to be an important capability in image processing whereas a transparent distribution of objects is essentially needed for the development of web applications. Developers struggle in every domain with different abstractions. At first most participants agreed in the need for more flexibility in programming languages. However, a small excursion to the obstacles in teaching frameworks gave enough suitable examples for difficulties in handling flexibility. Recognizing the fact that the lost of comprehension and control is the effect caused by to much flexibility, the wish of bit more "on demand" adaptation was generated. A kind of adaptation mechanism that could be easily configured to the specific needs of a certain domain.

After many and also partially turbulent discussions a lot of different views, ideas and techniques have been exchanged. As a common agreement could be seen that developers need to describe their application at various abstraction levels. On the one hand there are non-computer scientists, like mathematicians or engineers, writing programs focussed on algorithms that solve abstract computation problems. There is usually no specific need to describe the underlying implementation details. On the other hand in high-constraint environments, where a certain performance in terms of response time or physical data cache is important, one can be interested in very low level implementation details. Hence, developers are still eager for a mean that combines simplified abstraction and "on-demand" flexibility in descriptions of computation.

Acknowledgments

We would like to thank AITO for financial support, which was important for many students. AITO provided support to partially cover student travel expenses. As we had participants from Sweden, France, Spain, Germany, Hungary, USA, and New Zealand—and most of them were not financially provided for as they are students—we were most grateful for support.

Participants List

1. Ademar Aguiar, University of Porto, Portugal
   ademar.aguiar@fe.up.pt
2. Patrick Bellot, ENST - INFRES, France
   bellot@enst.fr
3. Po-Hao Chang, University of Illinois at Urbana-Champaign, USA
   pchang2@uiuc.edu
4. Jerome Darbon, EPITA - LRDE, France
   darbon@lrde.epita.fr, darbon@enst.fr
5. Sari R. Eldadah, Method Building Capacity Cooperation, Jordan
   Sdadah@MethodCorp.com

6. Sameh Elnikety, School of Computer and Communication Sciences, Swiss Federal Institute of Technology (EPFL), Lausanne, Switzerland
sameh.elnikety@epfl.ch

7. Gregory de Fombelle, Thales Research and Technology, France
gregory.defombelle@thalesgroup.com

8. Thierry Geraud, EPITA - LRDE, France
geraud@lrde.epita.fr

9. Pablo Gervas, Universidad Complutense de Madrid, Spain
pgervas@sip.ucm.es

10. Johan Glimming, Stockholm University, Sweden
glimming@kth.se

11. Mercedes Gomez-Albarran, Universidad Complutense de Madrid, Spain
albarran@sip.ucii.es

12. Raquel Hervas, Universidad Complutense de Madrid, Spain
pgervas@sip.ucm.es

13. Guillermo Jimenez-Diaz, Universidad Complutense de Madrid, Spain
gjimenez@sip.ucii.es

14. Susanne Jucknath, Technical University of Berlin, Germany
susannej@cs.tu-berlin.de

15. Eric Jul, DIKU, University of Copenhagen, Denmark
eric@diku.dk

16. Zoltan Porkolab, Eoetvoes Lorand University, Hungary

17. Alex Potanin, Victoria University of Wellington, New Zealand
alex@mcs.vuw.ac.nz

18. Gabor Stikkel, Lorand Eoetvoes University, Hungary
stiko@compalg.inf.elte.hu

19. Zoltan Theisz, Ericsson Telecommunications Hungary
gmd@alta.hu

20. Jan Wloka, Fraunhofer Institute FIRST, Germany
Jan.Wloka@first.fraunhofer.de

21. Istvan Zolyomi, Eoetvoes Lorand University, Hungary
scamel@alta.hu

MASPEGHI 2004
Mechanisms for Specialization, Generalization and Inheritance*

Ph. Lahire[1], G. Arévalo[2], H. Astudillo[3], A.P. Black[4], E. Ernst[5],
M. Huchard[6], T. Oplustil, M. Sakkinen[7], and P. Valtchev[8]

[1] Laboratoire d'Informatique Signaux et Systèmes de Sophia Antipolis (I3S),
Université de Nice Sophia antipolis, France
Philippe.Lahire@unice.fr

[2] Software Composition Group, Institut für Informatik und angewandte Mathematik,
Bern, Switzerland
arevalo@iam.unibe.ch

[3] Departamento de Informática, Universidad Técnica Federico Santa María
Valparaíso, Chile
hernan@acm.org

[4] Dept. of Computer Science & Engineering, OGI School of Science & Engineering,
Oregon Health & Science University (OGI/OHSU), Beaverton, USA
black@cse.ogi.edu

[5] Department of Computer Science, University of Aarhus, Denmark
eernst@daimi.au.dk

[6] Laboratoire d'Informatique, de Robotique et Micro-électronique de Montpellier
(LIRMM), CNRS and Université de Montpellier 2, France
huchard@lirmm.fr

[7] Department of Computer Science and Information Systems, University of
Jyväskylä, Finland
sakkinen@cs.jyu.fi

[8] Dépt. d'Informatique et recherche opérationnelle (DIRO), Université de Montréal,
Québec, Canada
petko.valtchev@umontreal.ca

Abstract. MASPEGHI 2004 is the third edition of the MASPEGHI workshop. This year the organizers of both the ECOOP 2002 Inheritance Workshop and MASPEGHI 2003 came together to enlarge the scope of the workshop and to address new challenges. We succeeded in gathering a diverse group of researchers and practitioners interested in mechanisms for managing specialization and generalization of programming language components. The workshop contained a series of presentations with discussions as well as group work, and the interplay between the more than 22 highly skilled and inspiring people from many different communities gave rise to fruitful discussions and the potential for continued collaboration.

---

* The title of this report sould be referenced as "Report from the ECOOP 2004 Workshop on Mechanisms for Specialization, Generalization and Inheritance (MASPEGHI 2004)".

J. Malenfant and B.M. Østvold (Eds.): ECOOP 2004, LNCS 3344, pp. 101–117, 2004.

1   Introduction and Summary of the CFP

The MASPEGHI workshop took place on Tuesday, June 15th, at ECOOP 2004 in Oslo. It was the third edition of MASPEGHI (after OOIS 2002 and ASE 2003), but it was at the same time a follow-on to the Inheritance W orkshop at ECOOP 2002 in Málaga (see Section 6) — a case of multiple inheritance. The meaning of the acronym MASPEGHI was modified from M Anaging SPE cializa-tion/G eneralization H Ierarchies to M echAnism s for SPE cialization, G eneraliza-tion and inH erItance, thus broadening the scope of the workshop.

MASPEGHI 2004 continued the discussion about mechanisms for manag-ing specialization and generalization of programming language components. The workshop was organized around concepts such as inheritance and reverse inher-itance, subclassing, and subtyping, and specialized into variants such as single or multiple inheritance, mixins, and traits.

The workshop was concerned with (i) the various uses of inheritance, and (ii) the difficulties of im plem entation and control of inheritance in practical applica-tions. Several communities were represented, including those dealing with design methods, databases, knowledge representation, data mining, object-oriented pro-gramming languages, and modeling: each community addresses these concerns in different ways. Thus, one important goal of this workshop was to bring together a diverse group of participants to compare and contrast the use, implementation and control of inheritance as practiced in their communities.

This report summarizes the workshop. Section 2 lists the organizers, the participants and the written contributions. Section 3 provides an overview of the contributions and debates. Section 4 summarizes the outcome of the three work groups. We end this overview of the workshop with a conclusion and a list of pointers (Sections 5 and 6).

2   People and Contributions

2.1   Organizers

The organizers of this workshop were (in alphabetical order):

- **Gabriela Arévalo:** Software Composition Group, Institut für Informatik und angewandte Mathematik, Bern, Switzerland. (arevalo@iam.unibe.ch)
- **Hernán Astudillo:** Departamento de Informática, Universidad Técnica Federico Santa María Valparaíso, Chile. (hernan@acm.org)
- **Andrew P. Black:** Dept. of Computer Science & Engineering, OGI School of Science & Engineering, Oregon Health & Science University (OGI/OHSU), Beaverton, USA. (black@cse.ogi.edu)
- **Erik Ernst:** Department of Computer Science, University of Aarhus, Den-mark. (eernst@daimi.au.dk)
- **Marianne Huchard:** Laboratoire d'Informatique, de Robotique et Micro-électronique de Montpellier (LIRMM), CNRS and Université de Montpellier 2, France. (huchard@lirmm.fr)

- **Philippe Lahire:** Laboratoire d'Informatique Signaux et Systèmes de Sophia Antipolis (I3S), Université de Nice Sophia antipolis, France. (Philippe.Lahire@unice.fr)
- **Markku Sakkinen:** Department of Computer Science and Information Systems, University of Jyväskylä, Finland. (sakkinen@cs.jyu.fi)
- **Petko Valtchev:** Dépt. d'Informatique et recherche opérationnelle (DIRO), Université de Montréal, Québec, Canada. (petko.valtchev@umontreal.ca)

2.2   Participants and Position Papers

A total of 22 persons participated in the workshop, although some of them only for part of the day. The attendees came from 13 different countries, the largest attendance (4) coming from France. Among them 15 were paper authors (see the table below) and/or members of the organizing committee. Five of the organizers were able to come: A. Black, E. Ernst, M. Huchard, Ph. Lahire and M. Sakkinen. All the papers in the following table are in the proceedings of the workshop [1], which is accessible from the website.

Contribution	Presenter / *Other Authors*
(1) Object Identity Typing: Bringing Distinction between Object Behavioural Extension and Specialization	D. Janakiram, Indian Institute of Technology Madras, India (djram@lotus.iitm.ernet.in) / *C. Babu*
(2) A Reverse Inheritance Relationship for Improving Reusability and Evolution: the Point of View of Feature Factorization	Philippe Lahire (see above) / *C.-B. Chirila and P. Crescenzo*
(3) Mathematical Use Cases lead naturally to non-standard Inheritance Relationships: How to make them accessible in a mainstream language	Marc Conrad, University of Luton, UK (marc.conrad@luton.ac.uk) / *T. French, C. Maple, and S. Pott*
(4) Proposals for Multiple to Single Inheritance Transformation	Michel Dao, France Télécom R&D, France (michel.dao@francetelecom.com) / *M. Huchard, T. Libourel, A. Pons and J. Villerd*
(5) The Expression Problem, Scandinavian Style	Erik Ernst (see above)
(6) The Logic of Inheritance	DeLesley Hutchins, University of Edinburgh, UK (D.S.Hutchins@sms.ed.ac.uk)

(7) An anomaly of subtype relations at component refinement and a generative solution in C++   Zoltán Porkoláb, Eötvös Loránd University, Hungary (gsd@elte.hu) / I. Zólyomi

(8) Java with Traits — Improving Opportunities for Reuse   Philip J. Quitslund, Oregon Health and Science University, USA (philipq@cse.ogi.edu) / A. P. Black

(9) Merging conceptual hierarchies using concept lattices   Marianne Huchard (see above) / M. H. Rouane, P. Valtchev, P. and H. Sahraoui

(10) Behaviour consistent Inheritance with UML Statecharts   Markus Stumptner, University of South Australia, Australia (mst@cs.unisa.edu.au) / M. Schrefl

(11) Domain Modeling in Self Yields Warped Hierarchies   Ellen Van Paesschen, Vrije Universiteit Brussel, Belgium (evpaessc@vub.ac.be / W. De Meuter and T. D'Hondt

(12) Inheritance Decoupled: It's More Than Just Specialization   L. Robert Varney, University of California at Los Angeles, USA (varney@cs.ucla.edu) / D. S. Parker

Among the other participants were the following (alphabetically):

- Antoine Beugnard, Ecole Nationale Supérieure de Télécommunication, France (Antoine.Beugnard@enst-bretagne.fr)
- Kim Bruce, Williams College, Massachusetts, USA (kim@cs.williams.edu)
- Sebastián González, Université catholique de Louvain, Belgium (sgm@acm.org)
- Håvard Hegna, Norwegian Computing Center, Norway (hegna@nr.no)
- Tomáš Opluštil, Charles University in Prague, Czech Republic (oplustil@nenya.ms.mff.cuni.cz)
- Wilfried Rupflin, University of Dortmund, Germany (Wilfried.Rupflin@uni-dortmund.de).

3   Workshop and Contribution Overview

3.1   Workshop Organization

The organizers prepared for the workshop by a quite lengthy process of characterizing and classifying the papers, based on their main topics. In this process it turned out to be useful to apply techniques from concept analysis, which is a core research area for some of the organizers. Here is an early version of the classification[1]; note that some papers match several topics.

- Contradiction between a desired subtyping or specialization relation and available language mechanisms. What should designers and developers do when a desired subtyping relation cannot be expressed in the particular technology (e.g., programming language) employed to create the software? Papers P6, P7, P3, P1, P11, P8, P12, P5, P9, P2 deal with this topic. They propose, roughly, to rearrange the desired hierarchy to fit the language, or to design a new language.
- Is class composition worthwhile? One example of a class composition mechanism is multiple inheritance, and it is well-known that multiple inheritance is hard to do well. People who think class composition is worthwhile emphasize that it is powerful, and the more sceptical people emphasize that the resulting software is complex and hard to maintain. Papers P11, P8, P12, P5, P4 are related to this topic.
- Different kinds of subclassing relationships. How many kinds of inheritance relationships are needed? How many kinds does your technology have? Papers P10, P12, P4, P2 deal with this topic.
- Form and Transform, Dealing with evolution. How can methodologies, languages and tools help us to deal with classification, construction and evolution? Papers P3, P4, P9, P2 deal with this topic.

This process of establishing an overview of the issues and positions represented by the papers continued, and at the workshop we ended up with three sessions:

1. Form and Transform: Dealing with Evolution (papers P3, P2, P4, P10).
2. Class composition (papers P11, P8, P5).
3. Contradiction between a desired subtyping or specialization relation and available language mechanisms (papers P6, P7, P1, P12).

The workshop started with a brief welcome and the introduction of the participants. The three sessions were organized as presentations of the position papers followed by discussion, applying a flexible attitude to timekeeping that prioritized the contents of the discussions rather than adhering rigidly to a schedule. Each presentation lasted about 10 minutes; following that, an opponent—who prepared by carefully studying the paper and other related material—initiated the discussion by asking questions, making comments or proposing an alternate point of view. Gradually, the other participants would also ask questions or make comments. Some ingenuity was needed to schedule this activity around lunch and coffee breaks, but the flexible approach to timing worked quite well.

We now turn to the conduct of the three sessions listed above.

---

[1] In this report, papers presented at the workshop are referred to as *Pn* where *n* is the number of the paper in the table in Section 2.2

3.2   Session 1: Form and Transform: Dealing with Software Evolution

This session dealt with the evolution of designs and of software; papers P4 and P10 addressed the design level with UML whereas P2 and P3 addressed the programming level. Paper P4 focused on the use of meta-information, categorizing applications of multiple inheritance according their semantics, and then using this categorization to select a suitable transformation to single inheritance.

Paper P10 deals with object life-cycles represented with UML statechart diagrams. Inheritance is used to specialize life-cycles, that is, to extend and refine them. The semantics of this kind of inheritance relationship relies on two properties: observation consistency and invocation consistency [2]. Paper P3 investigates how method renaming, dynamic inheritance and interclassing can be used to strengthen the relationships between mathematical reasoning (algebric structuring) and object-oriented techniques [3]. This led to a discussion about benefits and advantages of introducing these ideas within OO languages. The last paper of the session, P2, deals with the introduction of a reverse inheritance relationship to better address the reuse and evolution of hierarchies of classes. This implies the existence of a language that provides both specialization and generalization relationships [4]. The paper introduces a factorization mechanism that enables a programmer to move features up the hierarchy. A discussion ensued about the semantics that should be attached to generalization relationships.

3.3   Session 2: Class Composition

The second session included presentations of three papers that addressed this topic, but based in the culture of three different languages — Self [5, 6], Java and gbeta [7].

In P11 the authors demonstrate that the hierarchies required for proper domain modeling are the reverse of the hierarchies required by the Self programming language for the proper execution of the corresponding code. Self uses a particular kind of prototype object, called a trait object, as a way of sharing behavior. A variation of this idea is explored in paper P8, which led to some discussion on this topic. The paper deals with a mechanism for reusing code in Java, based on previous work on traits in Smalltalk [8]. One of the common ideas is that the class is not the best unit of reuse; the authors demonstrate this through a detailed study of code duplication in the Java Swing library.

The third paper, P5, is influenced by the expressiveness of the gbeta language and explains how higher-order hierarchies [9] can be used to solve the expression problem [10]. One of the main advantages of gbeta is that it makes it possible to adapt and evolve whole hierarchies of classes rather than individual classes. A discussion dealing with other possible solutions to the expression problem, especially reverse inheritance, followed the presentation of the paper.

3.4   Session 3: Subtyping and Specialization

The third session dealt with incompatibilities between the subtyping and specialization relations and the available mechanisms, and involved four papers. In P6 the author argues that inheritance is fundamentally concerned with the categorization of objects, and that OO languages should thus be founded upon a formalism that supports categorical reasoning. He proposes a formal language called SYM, which is aimed at representing class/object types in a way that avoids classical inheritance problems such as conflict resolution and the dichotomy between subtyping and implementation inheritance. During the discussion we noted that classes in SYM are like traits or mixins [11, 12] and that SYM enables the handling of both virtual methods and Beta-style virtual classes.

Paper P7 describes a limitation of inheritance that the authors call the chevron shape anomaly. It is based on the fact that (i) classes in a hierarchy may be extended by inheritance in order to add new functionality and (ii) an application may use several hierarchies and use them at different levels. The authors explain that it implies an increase of complexity and propose a solution based on generative programming [13]. Paper P1 is concerned with the expressiveness of inheritance in conventional OO languages, which do not make a clear distinction between object behavioral extension (which needs to preserve object identity) and behavioral specialization (where a new object is created). The authors propose to capture this distinction by representing object identity as a type. The paper P12 pointed out another deficiency of object-oriented languages: that they do not provide sufficient support for interface abstraction and implementation inheritance, thus spreading implementation bias and impairing evolution. To address these issues, the authors propose interface-oriented programming (IOP) [14], which decouples the client of an abstraction from the code that binds it to a specific implementation and provides an interface-oriented form of inheritance that keeps implementation bias in check and is useful for both specialization and adaptation.

3.5   Group Discussions

An important part of the workshop was the group discussions held in the afternoon. Three work groups were formed; the topics of the workgroups reflect the interests of participants. They were largely derived from the session topics: two of them came directly from session topics, whereas the third was formed during the earlier discussions. The topics were as follows:

- Composition of classes
- Subtyping and subclassing
- Inheritance relations applied to components

After one hour of discussion, one representative from each group (Erik Ernst, Andrew Black and Marianne Huchard, respectively) explained to the other participants the perspectives of their groups and the result of the discussion. The next section summarizes these discussions; the summary from each work group is written by its participants, and organized by the group representatives above.

4   Summary of Group Discussions

In the following subsections we describe the working groups held during the afternoon.

4.1   Composition of Classes

The members of this group were Marc Conrad, Erik Ernst, Philippe Lahire, Philip Quitslund, and Markku Sakkinen. It quickly became clear that nobody in the group was vehemently against class composition, even though they acknowledged what Alan Snyder said many years ago: "multiple inheritance is good but there is no good way to do it" (reported by Steve Cook [15]).

Consequently, we implicitly responded to the question of whether class composition is worthwhile with a 'Yes!', qualified by the realization that there will probably always be wrinkles in the design of each concrete class composition mechanism, and then continued to explore the similarities and differences between our approaches to it.

One line of exploration was to find features of each approach that other approaches could not readily match. For traits, represented by Philip, the feature we selected was the symmetry of trait composition: two traits may both import and export from each other, thus satisfying the requirements of both of them. In contrast, with mixins the dependency is strictly unidirectional. Symmetric dependencies enable the creation of composite entities, e.g., classes created by composing traits, in a more flexible manner than is possible with strict unidirectional dependencies.

The selected feature of gbeta, represented by Erik, was that of composing nested entities, e.g., families of classes or even families of families of classes, and having the composition propagate recursively into the structure. This enables disciplined and well-defined composition of many classes in parallel with a very concise syntax. In contrast, a single class composition mechanism is generally more error-prone and typically lacks the ability to ensure compatibility among many classes.

Reverse inheritance, which is a main topic in the paper by Philippe and also the subject of earlier work by Markku under the name exheritance, is unique in that it allows for non-intrusive modification of existing classes (i.e., changing their meaning without editing them). The precise scope of this kind of modification depends very much on the details of the mechanism, but generally it enables addition of new supertypes to existing classes even in a type system based on name equivalence, and some kinds of inverse inheritance or exheritance allows for semantically significant changes, too, such as overriding an inherited method or even adding state to the specified subclasses. Non-intrusive modification improves on the flexibility in system development, especially where large amounts of existing source code must be modified, but cannot be edited.

It is difficult to evaluate the quality of programming language mechanisms because this would ideally require that we look at all programs that could ever be written using the mechanism and evaluate whether those programs would be of higher quality without the use of the mechanism, or using an alternative version of it. Obviously, no such thing could ever be done or even approximated. Hence, evaluation of language mechanisms tends to be informal. However, as Marc pointed out, one might use things like design patterns [16] in an evaluation, because patterns represent well-known and hard problems in software design at the level of a few classes—which is often the level where language mechanisms for class composition are most relevant.

Finally, we discussed an inversion scenario for the unfolding of software as a vehicle to gain insight into the real nature of class composition and other abstraction mechanisms. Software is unfolded in the following sense: designers and developers create abstractions such as classes, subclasses, type parameterized classes or methods, etc. We may consider inheritance as a short-hand for repeating the declarations inherited from superclasses, and similarly for type parameterization, so the most sophisticated abstractions could be 'unfolded away', leaving us with a simple, flat universe of classes with no inheritance or type parameters, etc. In fact, this would typically yield a correct description of actual objects at run-time and their behavior.

Now imagine that we start from the other end, with a running system of objects and behavior (with no classes or other abstractions defined a priori, as in Self [5]). We could then examine which objects and behaviors are similar, and construct classes and methods to describe them; next we could explore similarities between classes and use them to build inheritance hierarchies, etc.— which is one of the things that Marianne Huchard and others are doing with concept analysis. We would then reconstruct the abstractions from the run-time environment, as opposed to constructing the run-time entities from the abstractions. The latter is an unfolding process, whereas the former is a folding or 'compression' process.

The intriguing insight is that the run-time world can be considered as the primary artifact, with the abstractions as derived entities—just the opposite of typical thinking for class based languages, especially statically typed ones. The very thought that abstractions may be constructed automatically may help to make class composition and other mechanisms more lightweight and less intimidating, and similarly refreshing is the idea that manipulations of a "program" could sometimes take place at the concrete level, with new abstractions arising by subsequent (more or less automatic) analysis of the concrete level.

Of course, this thesis about the wonders of concreteness is immediately followed by an antithesis: abstraction is one of our most powerful tools and hence abstractions should not be reduced to mere implementation details produced by a programming tool. However, abstractions might be more manageable if the top-down unfolding point of view is supplemented with the bottom-up folding point of view.

4.2   Subtyping and Subclassing

The members of this working group were Andrew P. Black, Kim Bruce, DeLesley Hutchins, D. Janakiram, Zoltán Porkoláb, Markus Stumptner and L. Robert Varney. The group focused on the problem of what to do when a programmer finds that it is convenient to subclass an existing class, not to capture a specialization relationship in the domain being modeled, but just to share implementation. It can be argued that this is a bad programming practice, but often the only practical alternative is the wholesale use of copy and paste, which is surely a worse programming practice. William Cook's examination of the Smalltalk Collection Classes [17] shows that the practice is common.

However, this activity can lead to problems. The subtyping relation that does capture the specialization relationship of the domain is at best obscured, and at worst destroyed. For example, in Smalltalk it is obscured: two classes A and B that happen to be defined in completely different parts of the subclass hierarchy, but with sets of methods such that B is a subtype of A, have the property that aB can be substituted for anA. But this property is obscure: it is not expressed explicitly in the program. In Java, the interface construct and the implements keyword let the programmer say explicitly that A and B both implement a common interface, let us call it the "I" interface: this makes the programmer's intention explicit. But Java has its shortcomings too, because Java insists that any subclass is a subtype of its superclass, whether or not this makes sense in the context of the application domain. Moreover, if A was defined by someone else, perhaps someone working for another company, without also stating that it implements the I interface, then when another programmer comes along and tries to define and use aB in place of anA, the program won't compile. In order to substitute aB, not only must A implement I, but all declarations of parameters and variables must use I rather than A.

The goal of the group was to consider this problem and possible solutions. There was agreement that this is fundamentally a problem of language design: a single mechanism (inheritance) is made to play too many roles, with the result that programs are harder to understand. That is, the reason for the use of an inheritance relationship is not explicit in the program text, and the reader must try to infer it.

The problem (outlined above) with Java programs that do not use interfaces could be solved in a backwards-compatible way by a small modification to the language semantics. The idea is to create for each class C an interface with the same name, and to interpret variable and parameter declarations involving C as referring to the interface name rather than to the class name. It would then be possible for a maintenance programmer to define a new class that **implements** C, and instances of this new class could then be used in places that require a C. However, interfaces do have a run-time cost in Java, and this patch would impose that cost on every program. A non-compatible change to Java would involve separating the subtyping (interface) and subclassing hierarchies entirely; this would also make it possible to allow non-subtype-compatible changes in a subclass, such as canceling methods.

An alternative approach is to find another mechanism for code reuse, thus freeing inheritance to be used solely for domain modeling, which several of the participants at the workshop had argued is the primary role of inheritance (see for example papers P3 and P6). The trait concept described in P8 is one candidate for such a mechanism. As currently implemented, traits do not subsume inheritance because they do not allow the declaration of instance variables. However, it seems that an extended trait mechanism without this restriction would provide all of the reuse opportunities offered today by inheritance, as well as others, but without implying any conceptual classification that might not be intended. An implicit or explicit subtyping system could then be used for classification.

4.3   Inheritance Relations Applied to Components

This group consisted of Michel Dao, Marianne Huchard, Ellen Van Paesschen, Antoine Beugnard, Sebastián González, and Tomáš Opluštil. It was established because, although the (mainly academic) research in the field of software architecture and component systems has become mature, not much attention has been devoted to the study of emerged high-level abstractions from the point of view of inheritance relations. This becomes even more important in the context of model transformations (see, e.g., OMG MDA [18]). Therefore the long-term goal of this group is to set up a basis for research on inheritance in architecture description languages (ADLs) and component systems.

The discussion was initiated by Tomáš Opluštil who presented some ongoing research aimed at introducing inheritance in SOFA CDL [19, 20]. This initial discussion resulted in the following list of key long-term goals (of which only the first two were discussed because of time limitations).

- Selecting/defining abstractions in component models and ADLs to which inheritance or specialization can be applied.
- Defining the terms subtyping, specialization and inheritance in the context of components and other higher-level abstractions.
- Proposing purposes for which inheritance should be used in component models and ADLs.
- Proposing corresponding relations in implementation languages (into which inheritance in higher-level abstractions should be mapped).

The main abstractions in component models, which are thus a priori potential candidates for specialization, reuse inheritance or subtyping, are the following: a component is a unit of computation (often both a design-time and run-time entity); an interface is roughly a set of operations; a component type is a set of component interfaces; a connector manages communication between components; an architectural configuration is a set of components and connections. Components have ports or component interfaces, which usually characterize the type of the component. A principle distinction is between client and provided component interfaces which draw required and provided services; additional classifications can be by contingency (optional/mandatory) and cardinality (singleton/collection) as in Fractal [21].

We started with common definitions and uses of subtyping, inheritance and specialization in object-oriented programming and modeling languages, and initiated a discussion about their interpretation in the case of component models.

Subtyping. Static type systems are a way to limit runtime errors in programming languages, mainly preventing inappropriate operations to be called on entities. Subtyping is usually based on the substitutability notion [22]: "a type t_2 conforms to a type t_1 iff any expression of type t_2 can be substituted for (bound to) any variable of type t_1 without any runtime error". Substitutability on classes is ensured by invariant redefinition of attributes and redefinition of methods with covariant (more specific in the subtype) return type and contravariant (more general in the subtype) parameter types. Most of the abstractions listed above that are involved in component systems can be also handled as types, and thus candidates for subtyping. Our attention was primarily focused on interfaces and components. With interfaces, which are usually sets of operation signatures, the same policy that applies to subtyping for classes in class-based OOPLs can apply to interfaces in component systems. For component types (in the Fractal terminology: sets of provided and client component interfaces), substitutability can be understood as the possibility of replacing a component by another without changing the environment (components and bindings) [21]. Errors that we would like to avoid during this substitution may include plugging-binding errors (when a component interface is missing), or invocation of non-existent services and services with bad signatures. Subtyping is usually guided by the idea of providing more services and requiring less services; covariant policy should apply to provided services and a contravariant policy to required services [21, 23]. However, some researchers argue (in as yet unpublished papers) that this notion of subtyping may fail in some special cases, in which a substitution may lead to halting communication in the component system. Therefore alternative approaches to the definitions of subtyping are being introduced; a promising one is based on behavior protocols [24].

Specialization. In object-oriented modeling, class specialization is defined by inclusion of the instance sets (or extensions). Specialization hierarchies should reflect usual domain classifications. When a class C_2 specializes another class C_1, a consequence is that properties of C_1 are inherited by C_2, with possible refinements [22]. The fact that components are intrinsically generalizable elements can be demonstrated by the case of the UML meta-model [25]: metaclass Component is a subclass of Class in UML 2.0 meta-model.

Inheritance. In the object-oriented context, inheritance is a mechanism that allows a class to own (inherit) properties (mainly methods and attributes) of another class. The subclass can specialize, redefine and even cancel the inherited properties. Unlike OOPLs, current proposals for components do not provide much room for inheritance in their design, e.g., in ComponentJ [23] the language designers argue that in the presence of inheritance the result of method invocation (with dynamic binding) is dependent on the class hierarchy, making it difficult to define well-encapsulated pieces of software (which should be independent deployment units). As a result, emphasis is put on aggregation and component sharing rather than on inheritance. However, inheritance is in fact really useful for creating new component definitions by extending or merging existing ones as proposed in Fractal [26] and SOFA [20].

In the case of object-oriented programming and modeling languages, subtyping, inheritance and specialization are unfortunately mixed: inheritance is used to reflect domain specialization for clarity's sake in programs; types are often identified with classes; and subclassing is constrained by type safety [22]. Invariance policy in property redefinition, although too restrictive, is still the usual rule. We can hope that component models will be more careful in their interpretation of such notions: the best choice would be to define these relations independently avoiding all confusion.

We concluded that the adaptation of relations and techniques used in object-oriented languages to the context of component systems provides a lot of room for further research — new, higher-level abstractions, introduced in these systems, can bring on new uses for and give new meanings to the "old" well-explored relations of the object-oriented world.

5   Conclusion

The contents of both the written contributions and the debates described in this document showed that during this workshop we addressed number of interesting topics. Of course we were not able to go into the details of all of them here, but nevertheless feel that this report captures the atmosphere and scope of the workshop. Both modeling and language levels were covered, and the issues of evolution, adaptation and transformation, as well as reusability and type-safety, were given especial emphasis.

The contributions of the participants, and in particular the lively discussion that pervaded the workshop, convince us that workshops where the paper is only the starting point for the exchange of ideas are more profitable than mini-conferences that emphasize presentations of papers. Participants have now enough knowledge on the work of others to think about some collaboration. The working groups which had been set after the three sessions (even though only the subject had been set at this time) already provide some early information on the kind of collaboration that is starting.

A mailing list and a website will be maintained to ensure continuous discussion and visibility even after the end of the workshop.

- **Mailing List:** maspeghi-ecoop2004@i3s.unice.fr
- **Website:** http://www.i3s.unice.fr/maspeghi2004

6   Pointers to Related Work

The reader wishing to delve more deeply into the topic of this workshop might do well to start with the proceedings of the previous workshops dedicated to inheritance [27, 28, 29], to specialization or generalization [30, 31] and to object classification [32, 33]. Several Ph.D theses have also been written on these topics, including references [34, 35, 7, 36, 37]; the books by Gamma [16] and Meyer [38] are also a useful starting point. Papers of particular interest include references [39, 40, 41, 42, 43, 44, 45, 46, 47, 48, 49, 50].

Related Workshops
(workshop nam e, associated conference, num ber of participants and W eb site):

- Maspeghi 2002 - OOIS 2002 - 15 persons.
  http://www.lirmm.fr/~huchard/MASPEGHI/
- Maspeghi 2003 - ASE 2003 - 14 persons.
  http://www.iro.umontreal.ca/~maspeghi/
- Inheritance 2002 - ECOOP 2002 - 27 persons from ten countries (15 were authors or coauthors of an accepted paper).
  http://www.cs.auc.dk/~eernst/inhws/

References

1. Arévalo, G., Astudillo, H., Black, A.P., Ernst, E., Huchard, M., Lahire, P., Sakkinen, M., Valtchev, P., eds.: Proceedings of the 3rd International Workshop on "Mechanisms for Specialization, Generalization and Inheritance" (MASPEGHI'04) at ECOOP'04. University of Nice - Sophia Antipolis, Oslo, Norway (2004)
2. Schrefl, M., Stumptner, M.: Behavior consistent specialization of object life cycles. ACM Transactions on Software Engineering and Methodology **11** (2002) 92–148
3. Conrad, M., French, T.: Exploring the synergies between the object-oriented paradigm and mathematics: a Java led approach. International Journal on Education Sciences and Technology (2004) to appear.
4. Crescenzo, P., Lahire, P.: Using both specialisation and generalisation in a programming language: Why and how? [30] 64–73
5. Ungar, D., Smith, R.B.: Self: The power of simplicity. In: Proceedings of OOPSLA'87. Volume 22(12) of ACM SIGPLAN Notices., Orlando, FL, USA, ACM press (1987) 227–242
6. Agesen, O., Bak, L., Chambers, C., , Chang, B.W., Hölzle, U., Maloney, J., Smith, R.B., Ungar, D., Wolczko, M.: The Self 4.0 Programmer's Reference Manual. Sun Microsystems, Inc., Mountain View, CA (1995)
7. Ernst, E.: gbeta – A Language with Virtual Attributes, Block Structure, and Propagating, Dynamic Inheritance. PhD thesis, DEVISE, Department of Computer Science, University of Aarhus, Aarhus, Denmark (1999)
8. Schaerli, N., Ducasse, S., Niestrasz, O., Black, A.P.: Traits: composable units of behaviour. In: Proceedings of ECOOP'03. LNCS(2743), Darmstadt, Germany, Springer-Verlag (2003) 248–274
9. Ernst, E.: Higher-order hierarchies. In Cardelli, L., ed.: Proceedings of ECOOP'03. LNCS(2743), Darmstadt, Germany, Springer-Verlag (2003) 303–329
10. Torgersen, M.: The expression problem revisited. In Odersky, M., ed.: Proceedings of ECOOP'04. LNCS(3086), Oslo, Norway, Springer-Verlag (2004) 123–143
11. Bracha, G., Cook, W.: Mixin-based inheritance. In: Proceedings of OOPSLA/ECOOP'90. Volume 25(10) of ACM SIGPLAN Notices., Ottawa, Canada, ACM press (1990) 303–311

12. Flatt, M., Krishnamurthi, S., Felleisen, M.: Classes and mixins. In: Conference Record of POPL '98: The 25th ACM SIGPLAN-SIGACT Symposium on Principles of Programming Languages, San Diego, California (1998) 171–183

13. Zólyomi, I., Pórkoláb, Z., Kozsik, T.: An extension to the subtype relationship in C++. In: Proceedings of GPCE'03. LNCS(2830), Erfurt, Germany, Springer-Verlag (2003) 209–227

14. Varney, L.R.: Interface-oriented programming. Technical Report TR-040016, UCLA, Department of computer science (2004)

15. Cook, S.: OOPSLA '87 Panel P2: Varieties of inheritance. In: OOPSLA '87 Addendum To The Proceedings. Volume 23(5) of ACM SIGPLAN Notices., Orlando, FL, USA, ACM Press (1987) 35–40

16. Gamma, E., Helm, R., Johnson, R., Vlissides, J.: Design Patterns – Elements of Reusable Object-Oriented Software. Addison-Wesley, Reading, MA, USA (1995)

17. Cook, W.R.: Interfaces and specifications for the Smalltalk-80 collection classes. In: Proceedings of OOPSLA'92. Volume 27(10) of ACM SIGPLAN Notices., Vancouver, Canada, ACM Press (1992) 1–15

18. Architecture Board ORMSC1: Model Driven Architecture (MDA), document number ormsc/01-07-01. Object Management Group. (2001) http://www.omg.org/docs/ormsc/01-07-01.pdf.

19. Opluštil, T.: Inheritance in SOFA components. Master thesis, Faculty of Informatics, Masaryk University, Brno, Czech Republic (2002)

20. Opluštil, T.: Inheritance in architecture description languages. In J.Šafránková, ed.: Proceedings of the Week of Doctoral Students conference (WDS 2003), Prague, Czech Republic, Charles University, Matfyzpress (2003) 118–123

21. Bruneton, E., Coupaye, T., Stefani, J.B.: The Fractal component model. Specification. Draft, France Telecom R&D (2004) http://fractal.objectweb.org.

22. Ducournau, R.: "Real World" as an argument for covariant specialization in programming and modeling. [30] 3–12

23. Costa Seco, J., Caires, L.: A basic model of typed components. In Bertino, E., ed.: Proceedings of ECOOP'00. LNCS(1850), Cannes - Sophia Antipolis, France, Springer Verlag (2000) 108–128

24. Plášil, F., Višňovský, S.: Behavior protocols for software components. IEEE Transactions on Software Engineering 28 (2002)

25. OMG: Unified Modeling Language (UML) Superstructure - Final Adopted specification. Object Management Group. (2003) Version 2.0.

26. Bruneton, E.: Fractal ADL tutorial 1.2. France Telecom R&D. (2004) http://fractal.objectweb.org.

27. Palsberg, J., Schwartzbach, M.I., eds.: Proceedings of the Workshop "Types, Inheritance and Assignments" at ECOOP'91. DAIMI PB-357, Geneva, Switzerland, Computer Science Department, Aarhus University (1991)

28. Sakkinen, M., ed.: Proceedings of the Workshop "Multiple Inheritance and Multiple Subtyping" at ECOOP'92. Working Paper WP-23, Utrecht, the Netherlands, Department of Computer Science and Information Systems, University of Jyväskylä (1992)

29. Black, A.P., Ernst, E., Grogono, P., Sakkinen, M., eds.: Proceedings of the Workshop "Inheritance" at ECOOP'02. Number 12 in Publications of Information Technology Research Institute. University of Jyväskylä, Málaga, Spain (2002)

30. Bruel, J.M., Bellahsène, Z., eds.: Advances in Object-Oriented Information Systems: OOIS 2002 Workshops. LNCS(2426). Springer Verlag, Montpellier, France (2002)
31. Valtchev, P., Astudillo, H., Huchard, M., eds.: Proceedings of the workshop "Managing Specialization/Generalization Hierarchies" at ASE 2003. DIRO, University of Montreal, Montreal, Quebec, Canada (2003)
32. Huchard, M., Godin, R., Napoli, A., eds.: Proceedings of the workshop "Objects and Classification: a Natural Convergence" at ECOOP'00. Loria, University of Nancy, Sophia-Antipolis, France (2000)
33. Huchard, M., Godin, R., Napoli, A.: Objects and classification. In Malenfant, J., Moisan, S., Moreira, A., eds.: ECOOP'00 Workshop reader. LNCS(1964), Cannes - Sophia Antipolis, France, Springer-Verlag (2000) 123–137
34. Bracha, G.: The Programming Language Jigsaw: Mixins, Modularity and Multiple Inheritance. Ph.D. thesis, Dept. of Computer Science, University of Utah (1992)
35. Cook, W.R.: A Denotational Semantics of Inheritance. PhD thesis, Brown University (1989)
36. Kniesel, G.: Dynamic Object-Based Inheritance with Subtyping. PhD thesis, Computer Science Department III, University of Bonn (2000)
37. Taivalsaari, A.: A Critical View of Inheritance and Reusability in Object-Oriented Programming. PhD thesis, University of Jyväskylä (1993)
38. Meyer, B.: Object-oriented Software Construction. second edn. Prentice Hall, New York, N.Y. (1997)
39. Tip, F., Sweeney, P.F.: Class hierarchy specialization. In: Proceedings of OOPSLA'97. Volume 32(10) of ACM SIGPLAN Notices., Atlanta, Georgia, USA, ACM press (1997) 271–285
40. Ducournau, R., Habib, M., Huchard, M., Mugnier, M.L.: Proposal for a monotonic multiple inheritance linearization. In: Proceedings of OOPSLA'94. Volume 29(10) of ACM SIGPLAN Notices., Portland, Oregon, USA, ACM press (1994) 164–175
41. Godin, R., Mili, H.: Building and maintaining analysis-level class hierarchies using Galois lattices. In: Proceedings OOPSLA'93. Volume 28(10) of ACM SIGPLAN Notices., Washington, DC, USA, ACM press (1993) 394–410
42. Hauck, F.J.: Inheritance modeled with explicit bindings: An approach to typed inheritance. ACM SIGPLAN Notices **28** (1993) 231–239
43. Agesen, O., Palsberg, J., Schwartzbach, M.I.: Type inference of SELF: Analysis of objects with dynamic and multiple inheritance. In Nierstrasz, O., ed.: Proceedings of ECOOP'93. LNCS(707), Kaiserslautern, Germany, Springer-Verlag (1993) 247–267
44. Sakkinen, M.: A critique of the inheritance principles of C++. Computing Systems **5** (1992) 69 – 110
45. Ducournau, R., Habib, M., Huchard, M., Mugnier, M.L.: Monotonic conflict resolution mechanisms for inheritance. In: Proceedings of OOPSLA'92. Volume 27(10) of ACM SIGPLAN Notices., Vancouver, Canada, ACM press (1992) 16–24
46. Szyperski, C.A.: Import is not inheritance - why we need both: Modules and classes. In Madsen, O.L., ed.: Proceedings of ECOOP'92. LNCS(615), Utrecht, The Netherlands, Springer Verlag (1992) 19–32
47. Bracha, G., Lindstrom, G.: Modularity meets inheritance. In: Proceedings of the IEEE Computer Society International Conference on Computer Languages, Washington, DC, IEEE Computer Society (1992) 282–290

48. Cardelli, L.: Structural subtyping and the notion of power type. In: POPL '88. Proceedings of the conference on Principles of programming languages, San Diego, CA, USA, ACM Press (1988) 70–79

49. Cardelli, L., Wegner, P.: On understanding types, data abstraction and polymorphism. ACM Computing Surveys **17** (1985) 480–521

50. Cardelli, L.: A semantics of multiple inheritance. In: Semantics of Data Types, International Symposium Sophia-Antipolis Proceedings. LNCS(173). Springer-Verlag (1984) 51–67

Software Evolution: A Trip Through Reflective, Aspect, and Meta-data Oriented Techniques

Walter Cazzola[1], Shigeru Chiba[2], and Gunter Saake[3]

[1] DICo - Department of Informatics and Communication,
Università degli Studi di Milano,
Milano, Italy
cazzola@dico.unimi.it

[2] Department of Mathematical and Computing Sciences,
Tokyo Institute of Technology,
Tokyo, Japan
chiba@is.titech.ac.jp

[3] Institute für Technische und Betriebliche Informationssysteme,
Otto-von-Guericke-Universität Magdeburg,
Magdeburg, Germany
saake@iti.cs.uni-magdeburg.de

Abstract. Previous workshops related to aspect oriented software development, reflection organized at previous ECOOP conferences (e.g., RMA'00[1].and AOM-MeT'01[2].) and conferences on the same topics (Reflection'01 and AOSD since 2002) have pointed out the growing interest on these topics and their relevance in the software evolution as techniques for code instrumentation. Very similar conclusions can be drawn by reading the contributions to the workshops on unanticipated software evolution (USE 2002 and USE 2003[3].).

Following the example provided by these venues, the RAM-SE (Reflection, AOP and Meta-Data for Software Evolution) workshop has provided an opportunity for researchers with a broad range of interests in reflective techniques and aspect-oriented software development to discuss recent developments of such a techniques in application to the software evolution.

The workshop main goal was to encourage people to present works in progress. These works could cover all the spectrum from theory to practice. To ensure creativity, originality, and audience interests, participants have been selected by the workshop organizers on the basis of 5-page position paper. We hope that the workshop will help them to mature their ideas and to improve the quality of their future publications based on the presented work.

The workshop proceedings are available as research report C-186 of the Department of Mathematical and Computing Sciences of the Tokyo Institute of Technology and freely downlodable from the workshop web site[4].

---

[1] Details at http://www.disi.unige.it/RMA2000.html
[2] Details at http://ecoop2001.inf.elte.hu/workshop/AOMMeT-ws.html
[3] Details at http://www.joint.org/use/
[4] RAM-SE04 Web Site: http://homes.dico.unimi.it/RAM-SE04.html

J. Malenfant and B.M. Østvold (Eds.): ECOOP 2004, LNCS 3344, pp. 118–132, 2004.
© Springer-Verlag Berlin Heidelberg 2004

Workshop Description and Objectives

Software evolution and adaptation is a research area, as also the name states, in continuous evolution, that offers stimulating challenges for both academic and industrial researchers. The evolution of software systems, to face unexpected situations or just for improving their features, relies on software engineering techniques and methodologies. Nowadays a similar approach is not applicable in all situations e.g., for evolving nonstopping systems or systems whose code is not available.

The evolution of software systems, to face unexpected situations or just for improving their features, relies on software engineering techniques and methodologies. Nowadays a similar approach is not applicable in all situations e.g., for evolving nonstopping systems or systems whose code is not available.

Features of reflection such as transparency, separation of concerns, and extensibility seem to be perfect tools to aid the dynamic evolution of running systems. Aspect-oriented programming (AOP in the next) can simplify code instrumentation whereas techniques that rely on meta-data can be used to inspect the system and to extract the necessary data for designing the heuristic that the reflective and aspect-oriented mechanism use for managing the evolution.

We feel the necessity to investigate the benefits brought by the use of these techniques on the evolution of object-oriented software systems. In particular we would determine how these techniques can be integrated together with more traditional approaches to evolve a system and the benefits we get from their use.

The overall goal of this workshop was that of supporting circulation of ideas between these disciplines. Several interactions were expected to take place between reflection, aspect-oriented programming and meta-data for the software evolution, some of which we cannot even foresee. Both the application of reflective or aspect-oriented techniques and concepts to software evolution are likely to support improvement and deeper understanding of these areas. This workshop has represented a good meeting-point for people working in the software evolution area, and an occasion to present reflective, aspect-oriented, and meta-data based solutions to evolutionary problems, and new ideas straddling these areas, to provide a discussion forum, and to allow new collaboration projects to be established. The workshop was a full day meeting. One part of the workshop was devoted to presentation of papers, and another to panels and to the exchange of ideas among participants.

Workshop Topics and Structure

Every contribution that exploits reflective techniques, aspect-oriented programming and/or meta-data to evolve software systems were welcome. Specific topics of interest for the workshop have included, but were not limited to:

- reflective middleware and environments for software evolution;
- adaptative software components;
- feature-oriented adaptation;
- aspect interference and composition for software evolution;
- evolution and adaptability;

- MOF, code annotations and other meta-data facilities for software evolution;
- intercession and introspection;
- software evolution tangling concerns.

To ensure lively discussion at the workshop, the organizing committee has chosen the contributions on the basis of topic similarity that will permit the beginning of new collaborations. To grant an easy dissemination of the proposed ideas and to favorite an ideas interchange among the participants, accepted contributions are freely download-able from the workshop web page:

http://homes.dico.unimi.it/RAM-SE04.html.

The proceedings of the event is also available as research report C-186 of the Dept. of Mathematical and Computing Sciences of the Tokyo Institute of Technology.

The workshop was a full day meeting organized in four sessions. Each session has been characterized by a dominant topic that perfectly describes the presented papers and the related discussions. The four dominant topics were: *reflective middleware for software evolution, software evolution and refactoring, join points and crosscutting concerns for software evolution*, and *parametric aspects and generic aspect languages*. During each session, half time has been devoted to papers presentation, and the rest of the time has been devoted to debate about the on-going works in the area, about relevance of the approaches in the software evolution area and the achieved benefits. The discussion related to each session has been brilliantly lead respectively by Yvonne Coady, Joseph W. Yoder, Günter Kniesel and Hidehiko Masuhara.

The workshop has been very lively, the debates very stimulating, and the high number of participants (see appendix A) testifies the growing interest in the application of reflective, aspect- and meta-data oriented techniques to software evolution.

Important References

To an occasional reader who would like to deepen his(her) knowledge about the topics of this workshop (that is, to learn more about reflection, aspect-oriented programming and software evolution), we suggest to read the following basic contributions:

- Pattie Maes. Concepts and Experiments in Computational Reflection. In *Proceedings of the 2nd Conference on Object-Oriented Programming Systems, Languages, and Applications (OOPSLA'87)*, pages 147–156, Orlando, Florida, USA, October 1987. ACM.
- Gregor Kiczales, John Lamping, Anurag Mendhekar, Chris Maeda, Cristina Videira Lopes, Jean-Marc Loingtier, and John Irwin. Aspect-Oriented Programming. In *11th European Conference on Object Oriented Programming (ECOOP'97)*, LNCS 1241, pages 220–242, Helsinki, Finland, June 1997. Springer-Verlag.
- Keith H. Bennett and Václav T. Rajlich. Software Maintenance And Evolution: A Roadmap. In Anthony Finkelstein, editor, *The Future of Software Engineering*, pages 75–87. ACM Press, 2000.

Whereas, to learn more about the use of reflective or aspect-oriented techniques in the software evolution and maintenance we suggest to look at the following proceedings and books:

- Walter Cazzola, Robert J. Stroud, and Francesco Tisato, editors, *Reflection and Software Engineering*, LNCS 1826. Springer, Heidelberg, Germany, June 2000.
- Akinori Yonezawa and Satoshi Matsuoka, editors. *Proceedings of 3rd International Conference on Metalevel Architectures and Separation of Crosscutting Concerns (Reflection'2001)*, LNCS 2192. Kyoto, Japan, September 2001. Springer.
- The Proceedings of the AOSD Conferences from 2002 to 2004. Available from `http://aosd.net/archive/index.php`.

Besides, to keep up to date with the evolution of the software evolution research area we suggest to consult the following page:

- Program-Transformation.org:

`http://www.program-transformation.org/twiki/bin/view/Transform/SoftwareEvolution`

which collects a lot of useful links related to software evolution (in a general sense).

1   Workshop Overview: Session by Session

In this session of the report we gather together the opinions of the session chairmen (and woman) relatively to the session and the panel they have lead, and their considerations about the future trends.

Session on Reflective Middleware for Software Evolution
Summary by Yvonne Coady (Session Chair, *University of Victoria, Canada*)

There were three papers in the session, all related to reflective middleware for the software evolution.

[2] Reflections on Programming with Grid Toolkits. *Emiliano Tramontana* (Università di Catania, Italy) and *Ian Welch* (Victoria University of Wellington, New Zealand).

Emiliano Tramontana gave the talk.

This paper presents an approach for developing Grid applications. In this approach, developers need not include any code handling toolkit specific concerns nor adaptation for changing conditions of the environment. This proposed solution consists of two aspects. Firstly, applications are developed in a centralised manner and automatically transformed to be distributed into the Grid, where they use a suitable communication primitive. Secondly, an open implementation of Globus is used to enable dynamic changes at run-time of the communication infrastructure and the service container.

Panel session: During the panel session Emiliano was asked if the development of the client and the server side of a Grid system took place all at once or in a coordinated way. His answer was that they are developed separately and the approach proposes to have only a coordinated way to add/remove nonfunctional concerns to/from both sides.

Follow-up questioning then asked whether just the proposed reflective Grid, alone, could satisfy both the need for adapting the application and the middleware. Emiliano's answer was that distribution would still need to be added into the application before its execution could be affected/adapted by the reflective Grid, especially when the application is initially sent for execution to a host that does not provide all the reflective middleware.

[3] Using Aspects to Make Adaptive Object-Models Adaptable. *Ayla Dantas, Paulo Borba* (Federal University of Pernambuco, Brazil) and *Joe Yoder* and *Ralph Johnson* (University of Illinois at Urbana-Champaign, USA).

Paulo Borba gave the talk.

This paper argues that AOP and adaptive object-models (AOM) play complementary roles for structuring adaptive applications. Whereas AOM support flexible dynamic adaptations by representing business rules and entities as data, AOP modularizes the crosscutting adaptation code. In addition to the results presented in the paper, further metrics were presented to quantifiably compare the approaches.

Panel session: The first part of the discussion was about the importance of metrics to provide a meaningful comparison, and the particularly nice job the authors did in the presentation. Follow-up discussion included issues such as the use of generic aspects for implementing adaptation concerns. The general consensus at the end of the discussion was that people thought they would be indeed useful to have reusable adaptation aspects.

[4] RAMSES: a Reflective Middleware for Software Evolution. *Walter Cazzola* (Università di Milano, Italy) and *Ahmed Ghoneim* and *Gunter Saake* (University of Magdeburg, Germany).

Ahmed Ghoneim gave the talk.

This paper presents a middleware for dynamically evolving and validating consistency of software systems against run-time changes. This middleware is based on a reflective architecture that provides objects with the ability to dynamically change their behavior by using design information. The evolution takes place in two steps: first a meta-object (the evolutionary meta-object) plans a possible evolution against the detected external events then another meta-object (the consistency checker meta-object) validates the feasibility of the proposed plan before really evolving the system.

Panel session: The first question involved the use of XMI schemas and their use. XMI is XML Meta Interchange, and this approach extracts XMI schemes from the UML models, and then uses this data at run-time. A second question involved the ability to drive both evolution and consistency. Both the meta-objects in this approach (evolutionary and consistency checker) inherit engine, which includes a set of rules. Script rules are used for modifying the reified XMI for run-time events and check the modified XMI.

Session on Software Evolution and Refactoring
Summary by Joe Yoder (Session Chair, *The Refactory Inc.*)

This session presented four talks on how to handle dynamic aspects and adaptability with AOP. These papers outlined some interesting approaches to adapt to changing requirements which include frameworks for dynamically refactoring separation of concerns and dynamic ways to deal with runtime adaptability.

The outlines of the talks are as follows:

[5] *Ruzanna Chitchyan* (Lancaster University, UK) presented the work on "AOP and Reflection for Dynamic Hyperslices". This paper described a model for dynamic hyperslices which uses a particular aspect-oriented approach - Hyperspaces - for decomposition and reflection as a means for composition of software modules. This model allows for structured, dynamic, incremental change introduction and rollback, thus, supporting run-time evolution yet preserving component modularity. The applicability of the model is illustrated through a schema adaptation scenario.

[6] *Peter Ebraert* (Vrij Universiteit Brussel) presented the work on "A Reflective Approach to Dynamic Software Evolution". The paper outlines a solution that allows systems to remain active while they are evolving. The approach goes out from the principle of separated concerns and has two steps. In the first step, they make sure that the system's evolvable concerns are cleanly separated by proposing aspect mining and static refactorings for separating those concerns. In the second step, they allow every concern to evolve separately. A preliminary reflective framework that allows dynamic evolution of separate concerns is outlined.

[7] *Yvonne Coady* (University of Victoria) presented the work on "OASIS: Organic Aspects for System Infrastructure Software Easing Evolution and Adaptation through Natural Decomposition". The OASIS project explores the potential of aspects to naturally shape crosscutting system concerns as they grow and change. This paper describes ongoing work to modularize evolving concerns within high-performance state-of-the-art systems software, and outlines some of the major challenges that lie ahead within this domain.

[8] *Yoshiki Sato* (Tokyo Institute of Technology) presented the work on "Negligent Class Loaders for Software Evolution". This paper presents a negligent class loader, which can relax the version barrier between class loaders for software evolution. The version barrier is a mechanism that prevents an object of a version of a class from being assigned to a variable of another version of that class. In Java, if a class definition (i.e. class file) is loaded by different class loaders, different versions of the class are created and regarded as distinct types. If two class definitions with the same class name are loaded by different loaders, two versions of the class are created and they can coexist while they are regarded as distinct types.

The following highlight the main questions the presenters and the audience discussed after the presentations:

- How do you ensure consistency when making changes at run-time? Sometimes the model needs to clearly define the adaptability parameters up front, thus managing consistency.
- How do you deal with performance issues while dynamically loading new versions with the class loader? Some well known techniques were discussed such as static code translation, just-in-time hook insertion and modified JVM.

In summary, providing dynamic ways to adapt to changing requirements has some great potential benefits for software developers. Using some well-known reflection techniques in conjunction with AOP can really assist with this by separating what changes from what doesn't and by allowing ways to *refactor* your systems by dynamically applying new weavings for the evolving separation of concerns during run-time. Also, by using AOP to separate adaptable concerns shows promise for assisting with run-time adaptations.

Session on Join Points and Crosscutting Concerns for SW Evolution
Summary by Günter Kniesel (Session Chair, *University of Bonn, Germany*)

This and next session were dedicated to the relation between software evolution and aspect oriented software development (AOSD). This session focused on the influence of join point models, a central concept of AOSD, on evolution and evolvability. The three papers in this session addressed this issue from different perspectives:

[9] *Nicolas Pessemier* (INRIA, France) presented the paper "Components, ADL & AOP: Towards a Common Approach". In his talk he motivated the need for unification and explained the approach taken in the FRACTAL project. FRACTAL integrates the notion of components with ports and port binding from the domain of architecture description languages with the AOSD specific notion of join points.

[10] *Naoyasu Ubayashi* (Kyushu Institute of Technology, Japan) presented the paper "An AOP Implementation Framework for Extending Join Point Models". He argued that current join point models are too rigid and extensible join point models are needed instead to foster unanticipated evolution. Then he introduced a reflective API for defining join points, which gives programmers complete control over join points and the kind of weaving actions to be performed at a specific join point.

[11] *Sonia Pini* (University of Genova, Italy) presented the paper "Evolving Pointcut Definition to Get Software Evolution". She explained the need for a formal model of join points and showed that no satisfactory one is available so far for dynamic join points. Then she introduced the use of UML statechart diagrams as a precise specification of dynamic join points. She showed that evolving the diagram concisely captures evolution scenarios that are hard to express otherwise (in AspectJ, for instance).

In the subsequent discussion the first paper attracted no critical remarks regarding the chosen approach or its utility. The asked questions only requested clarification of technical details of the used join point model.

For the second paper its reliance on a reflective API within an AOP approach triggered a lively discussion. Some attendants argued that such a combination should be avoided since AOP had been motivated in the first place by the desire to provide a simpler abstraction than full reflection. Others pointed out that it may be worthwhile to go "back to the roots" and review "old" design decisions in the light of new experience.

The third paper was received with a mix of positive surprise about the simplicity and elegance of the statechart based join point specification and some skepticism about the compositionality of different specifications and the scalability of the approach.

Session on Parametric Aspects and Generic Aspect Languages
Summary by Hidehiko Masuhara (Session Chair, *University of Tokyo, Japan*)

This session had three talks on AOP languages and frameworks to develop software systems that are more robust to software evolution.

By supporting separation of crosscutting concerns, aspect-oriented programming languages, AspectJ in particular, are known to be useful to develop more reusable programs. For example, Hannemann and Kiczales presented that some of the GoF design patterns can be provided as reusable aspects in AspectJ [12]. However, the experiences also revealed that current AOP languages are not sufficient for providing certain kinds of reusable aspects. The three talks in this session addressed the problem by introducing aspects whose pointcuts, introductions and advices are parameterized. These generic definitions can be tailored to different applications by instantiating some of their parameters. The outlines of the talks are as follows (in the order presented):

[13] *Jordi Alvarez Canal* (Universitat Oberta de Catalunya, Spain) presented the work on "Parametric Aspects: A Proposal", in which parametric aspects can take type parameters, and are useful to define abstract factory patterns in a domain-independent way and simple Enterprise Java Beans.

[14] *Philip Greenwood* (Lancaster University, UK) presented the work on "Dynamic Framed Aspects for Dynamic Software Evolution", in which aspects support dynamic changes in software systems. The approach is based on the Framed Aspects to parameterize the aspects for a specific use.

[15] *Tobias Rho* (University of Bonn, Germany) presented the work on "Evolvable Pattern Implementations need Generic Aspects", which points out that the evolution of design patterns is rarely supported in existing AOP languages. He also introduced the language LogicAJ, an extension of AspectJ in which homogeneously generic aspects are supported. LogicAJ is based on the use of logic meta variables as placeholders for arbitrary program elements, a concept borrowed from logic programming languages.

After the talks, the presenters and the audience discussed the following questions:

– How those proposals are different from each other? While all three talks proposed some form of generic aspects they differ in terms of their primary target, syntax, generality, and so forth. LogicAJ is an attempt to provide general framework to cover various kinds of generic aspects; Parametric Aspects offer simpler syntax; and Framed Aspects are more interested in supporting product lines, rather than supporting reusable design patterns.

– How those proposals support for software evolution? Generally, they all improve modularity of software systems so that independently evolving parts can be separated from others.

– How those proposals ensure the correctness of the generated aspects? Since all those proposals generate base code from generic definitions, it might be possible to generate incorrect code. It would be better if the system could check the safety of a generic aspect and the code that instantiates the aspect into specific context so that incorrect code is never generated[5]. All of the proposals currently check the correctness after they generated base code for specific contexts. LogicAJ aims at checking the correctness before generating aspects by extending its logical framework to static types. Both parametric aspects and framed aspects are willing to offer some means to check before generation as well.

To summarize the session, generic or parametric AOP languages and frameworks are promising means to develop more evolvable and better modularized software systems. At the same time there are also interesting challenges such as supporting rich kind of evolution and statically ensuring correctness.

2   Software Evolution Trends: The Organizers' Opinion

The authors, with this report, would like to go beyond the mere presentation of statistical and generic information related to the workshop and to its course. They try to speculate about the current state of art of the research in the field and to evaluate the role of reflection, AOSD and meta-data in the software evolution.

The Role of Reflection in Software Evolution
Comment by Walter Cazzola (*Università di Milano*)

In [16], *software evolution* is defined as a kind of software maintenance that takes place only when the initial development was successful. The goal consists of adapting the application to the ever-changing, and often in an unexpected way, user requirements and operating environment.

Software evolution, as well as software maintenance, is characterized by its huge cost and slow speed of implementation. Often, software evolution implies a redesign of the whole system, the development of new features and their integration in the existing and/or running systems (this last step often implies a reboot of the system). The redesign and develop steps correspond to an economic effort from the software producer that often does not have an immediate benefit from this extra work whereas the integration step involves also the user of the system.

The chimera of the current and future trends in this discipline is to beat down the cost of evolving a system. The most recognized approach consists of minimizing the impact of the software evolution on the activity of the user and of improving the software adaptability. This statement brings forth the need for a system to manage itself to some extent, to inspect components' interfaces dynamically, to augment its application-specific functionality with additional properties, and so on. To deal with these issues many researchers are developing middleware for supporting the software evolution without affecting the activity or the property of the system that has to be evolved. Few examples of this kind of middleware have been presented also to our workshop, see [3], [7] and [4].

---

[5] Note that it can be checked in some situations as we see in the programming languages with polymorphic types, such as ML.

Reflection is a discipline that is steadily attracting attention within the community of object-oriented researchers and practitioners. From a pragmatic point of view, several reflective techniques and technologies lend themselves to be employed in addressing the software evolution issue. On a more conceptual level, several key reflective principles could play an interesting role as general software design and evolution principles. Even more fundamentally, reflection may provide a cleaner conceptual framework than that underlying the rather 'ad-hoc' solutions embedded in most commercial platforms and technologies, and so on. The transparent nature of reflection makes it well suited to address problems such as evolution of legacy systems, customizable software, product families, and more. The properties of transparency, separation of concerns, and extensibility supported by reflection have largely been recognized as useful for software development and design. These features seem perfect tools to aid the dynamic evolution of running systems providing the basic mechanisms for adapting (i.e., evolving) a system without directly altering or stopping the existing system.

A reflective architecture represents the perfect structure that allows running systems to adapt themselves to unexpected external events, i.e., to consistently evolve. In this kind of reflective architecture, the system running in the base-level should be the one prone to be adapted, whereas software evolution should be the nonfunctional feature realized by the meta-level system. Reflection plays a fundamental role allowing the meta-level system of inspecting and instrumenting the code of the base-level system in a transparent way and independently of the knowledge of such code. This approach, therefore, permits of developing the software evolution as a separate and independent system that could be connected at any time to the system to be adapted without any specific requirement.

In theory, this kind of middleware can provide many benefits (e.g., dynamic patching to critical failures without stopping the system and the consequently the postponement of the system redesigning) but it is not to simple and immediate to realize. To evolve the base-level system and maintain it consistent and stable, the meta-level system must face many problems. The most important are: (1) to determine which events cause the need for evolving the base-level system (2) how to react on events and the related evolutionary actions (3) how to validate the consistency and the stability of the evolved system and eventually how to undo the evolution, (4) to determine which information are need to the evolution and/or are involved by the evolution. Therefore, the future research in reflective middleware for software evolution should face these open issues and many others.

The Role of AOP in Software Evolution
Comment by Shigeru Chiba (*Tokyo Institute of Technology*)

AOP (Aspect Oriented Programming) gives us a new concept called aspects, which improve our ability for modeling and designing software. In traditional OOP (Object Oriented Programming), we must decompose software into a number of objects. A group of objects that have similar functionality is categorized as a class. We have been developing and maintaining software by using a class as a minimum unit of maintenance. However, in practice, there are usually several different means of decomposing software into objects. Developers could take multiple viewpoints for decomposition; every viewpoint would cause different decomposition. A problem is that there is no single best viewpoint for decomposition. Some viewpoints would be good for developing or maintaining some parts of software and others would be good for doing other parts.

AOP enables us to decompose software from various viewpoints – *aspects* – as well as the dominant viewpoint represented by classes. For example, in the AspectJ language, some functionality that must be spread over several classes in a traditional OOP language can be separated into an independent module called an *aspect*. In AOP, such functionality is called a crosscutting concern.

Since AOP enables better modeling and designing of software, it is absolutely useful technology for software evolution. Well modeled and designed software is easy to maintain for evolution. If a crosscutting concern is separated as an independent module, that concern can be maintained without touching other modules. This fact will reduce maintenance costs of software evolution.

An issue actively discussed during the workshop was the maintainability of aspects themselves. Speakers pointed out that the implementation of some aspects heavily depends on other class-based modules and hence those aspects cannot be maintained independently of the other modules. In other words, aspects are in separate files but they must be edited when the classes that the aspects depend on are edited. Such aspects cannot be regarded as a truly separated module. This problem can be avoided by using abstract aspects to a certain degree, but the use of abstract aspects is a limited solution.

A better solution of this problem is to introduce parametric aspects. In fact, one session of this workshop was allocated for discussing this topic. Roughly to say, parametric aspects are generic templates that are used to generate concrete aspects in the given contexts. For example, Rho presented their language called LogicAJ, in which developers can write generic aspects using logic variables. He showed that some design patterns can be implemented as aspects in LogicAJ but the definitions of these aspects can be independent of the definitions of the classes that are woven with the aspects.

Although parametric aspects are powerful language constructs, there is still a question; are there any unique issues or techniques for parametric aspects against parametric classes? For example, the C++ template system is powerful and well-studied. The Java generics system is also. Are parametric aspect systems just straightforward variations of such parametric class systems? If not, what are design issues unique to generics for AOP? In OOP, classes can be regarded as types. Parametric classes have been studied by the researchers of type theory. Is it possible that we apply the results of such study to parametric aspects? If not, is there any theoretical background of parametric aspects?

The Role of Meta-data in Software Evolution
Comment by Gunter Saake (*University of Magdeburg*)

Future software systems should be robust and adaptive to a changing environment and to evolving requirements. This adaptiveness requires a kind of *self-awareness* — a software system has to reason about itself to be able to react on external stimuli requiring a modification.

Current software technology does not allow to build general systems reacting on arbitrary, unforeseen changes which require unanticipated modifications of system structure and behavior. However, for restricted scenarios we can use for example reflection to react on explicit events of the environments with a modified behavior.

A key concept of such software systems are explicit meta-data. Meta-data are used to describe (relevant parts of) system architecture, system objects and behavior in a form which can be processed by a software system. Self-awareness of a system is only possible if the system has a kind of system model of itself and such a system model can be described as meta-data of that system.

This use of meta-data opens some research problems:

- How to represent meta-data? A promising approach is to use standards where appropriate, for example UML notation and XML coding. Are domain-specific languages more appropriate than general frameworks?
- What is the best abstraction level for the system model? It should be detailed enough to represent the implemented system correctly, but abstract enough to have manageable reasoning rules. One solution is to use a design model for reasoning instead of the implementation model. In this case, one has to propagate changes from the design to the implementation each time an adaptation is performed.
- Can meta-data be automatically extracted from source code and documentation? When should the extraction be done? What about continuous extraction versus incremental update of meta-data? How to filter the extracted meta-data? Can all this be done with reasonable performance? Is it possible to performing a kind of meta-data mining process on the running system itself?
- What kind of reasoning is necessary to compute a modification at run-time? A modification has to react on the changed requirements, but system functionality has to be preserved. The reasoning process therefore is driven by a certain goal with some strong constraints on the resulting solution.
- Using extracted meta-data, can we be sure about the consistency of the meta-data w.r.t. the actual system? How to detect discrepancies? How to minimize the amount of extracted information?
- Can we find a general meta-data presentation for different kinds of software systems, or do we need application specific frameworks?
- Is meta-data management done by the system itself, or does the system use services of a meta-data repository? If so, which services are core services for self-adaptive systems?
- Besides the dynamic evolution using reflection, we still have a more static kind of evolution through new releases of the software and so on. These two kinds of evolution have to be synchronized. That is, we need a backpropagation of evolution steps through reflection onto design documents, source code and documentation.

Meta-data for software evolution was not a core topic of the workshop but appears in several presentations notwithstanding that I confide that in the future, meta-data will become more and more important in the software evolution research area. Two presentations make explicit use of meta-data and reflection in their approaches. Cazzola, Ghoneim and Saake [4] propose a reflective middleware, where meta-data based on design models in UML are used for evolution. This meta-data is represented in XMI format. For reflection, two meta-objects play together: the evolutionary object plans evolution steps, and the consistency checker object proves correctness of evolution plans. Ebraert and Tourwé [6] represent the object structure of the system explicit on the meta-level. For evolution, the meta-level evolves and the changes are propagated to the base level.

3   Final Remarks

This workshop main goal was to encourage people to present works in progress in the area of the application of reflective and aspect-oriented techniques applied to software evolution. The workshop was lively and the debates were very stimulating. We hope that the workshop has helped researchers to mature their idea and we encourage the accepted papers to be submitted to the attention of more important venues.

Acknowledgements. We wish to thank Yvonne Coady, Günter Kniesel, Hidehiko Masuhara, and Joseph Yoder both for their interest in the workshop, and for their help during the workshop and in writing part of this report. We wish also to thank all the researchers that have participated to the workshop.

We have also to thank the Department of Informatics and Communication of the University of Milan, the Department of Mathematical and Computing Sciences of the Tokyo institute of Technology and the Institute für Technische und Betriebliche Informationssysteme, Otto-von-Guericke-Universität Magdeburg for their various supports.

A   Workshop Attendee

The success of the workshop is mainly due to the people that have attended it and to their effort to participate to the discussions. The following is the list of the attendees in alphabetical order.

Name	Affiliation	Country	e-mail
Alvarez Canal, Jordi	Universitat Oberta de Catalunya	Spain	jalvarezc@uoc.edu
Borba, Paulo	Federal University of Pernambuco	Brazil	phmb@cin.ufpe.br
Cazzola, Walter	Università degli Studi di Milano	Italy	cazzola@dico.unimi.it
Chiba, Shigeru	Tokyo Institute of Technology	Japan	chiba@is.titech.ac.jp
Chitchyan, Ruzanna	Lancaster University	United Kingdom	r.chitchyan@lancaster.ac.uk
Coady, Yvonne	University of Victoria	Canada	ycoady@cs.uvic.ca
Ebraert, Peter	Vrij Universiteit Brussel	Belgium	pebraert@vub.ac.be
Ghoneim, Ahmed	University of Magdeburg	Germany	ghoneim@iti.cs.uni-magdeburg.de
Greenwood, Phil	Lancaster University	United Kingdom	greenwop@comp.lancs.ac.uk
Kniesel, Günter	University of Bonn	Germany	gk@cs.uni-bonn.de
Masuhara, Hidehiko	University of Tokyo	Japan	masuhara@graco.c.u-tokyo.ac.jp
Monfort, Valérie	MDTVision	France	v-monfort@mdtvision.com
Nyström, Sven-Olof	Uppsala University	Sweden	svenolof@user.it.uu.se
Pessemier, Nicolas	INRIA	France	nicolas.pessemier@lifl.fr
Pini, Sonia	Università degli Studi di Genova	Italy	pini@disi.unige.it
Rho, Tobias	University of Bonn	Germany	rho@cs.uni-bonn.de
Saake, Gunter	University of Magdeburg	Germany	saake@iti.cs.uni-magdeburg.de
Sato, Yoshiki	Tokyo Institute of Technology	Japan	yoshiki@csg.is.titech.ac.jp
Seinturier, Lionel	INRIA	France	lionel.seinturier@lifl.fr
Störzer, Maximilian	Universität Passau	Germany	stoerzer@fmi.uni-passau.de
Tanter, Eric	University of Chile	Chile	etanter@dcc.uchile.cl
Tramontana, Emiliano	Università di Catania	Italy	tramonta@dmi.unict.it
Ubayashi, Naoyasu	Kyushu Institute of Technology	Japan	ubayashi@ai.kyutech.ac.jp
Yahiaoui, Nesrine	Université de Versailles	France	nesrine.yahiaoui@edf.fr
Yoder, Joseph W.	The Refactory Inc.	U.S.A.	joeyoder@joeyoder.com
Yonezawa, Akinori	University of Tokyo	Japan	yonezawa@yl.is.s.u-tokyo.ac.jp

References

1. Cazzola, W., Chiba, S., Saake, G., eds.: Proceedings of the 1st ECOOP Workshop on Reflection, AOP and Meta-Data for Software Evolution (RAM-SE'04). Research Report C-196 of the Dept. of Mathematical and Computing Sciences, Tokyo Institute of Technology. Preprint No. 10/2004 of Fakultät für Informatik, Otto-von-Guericke-Universität Magdeburg (2004)
2. Tramontana, E., Welch, I.: Reflections on Programming with Grid Toolkits. In Cazzola, W., Chiba, S., Saake, G., eds.: Proceedings of ECOOP'2004 Workshop on Reflection, AOP and Meta-Data for Software Evolution (RAM-SE'04), Oslo, Norway (2004) 3–8
3. Dantas, A., Yoder, J.W., Borba, P., Johnson, R.: Using Aspects to Make Adaptive Object-Models Adaptable. In Cazzola, W., Chiba, S., Saake, G., eds.: Proceedings of ECOOP'2004 Workshop on Reflection, AOP and Meta-Data for Software Evolution (RAM-SE'04), Oslo, Norway (2004) 9–19
4. Cazzola, W., Ghoneim, A., Saake, G.: RAMSES: a Reflective Middleware for Software Evolution. In Cazzola, W., Chiba, S., Saake, G., eds.: Proceedings of ECOOP'2004 Workshop on Reflection, AOP and Meta-Data for Software Evolution (RAM-SE'04), Oslo, Norway (2004) 21–26
5. Chitchyan, R., Sommerville, I.: AOP and Reflection for Dynamic Hyperslices. In Cazzola, W., Chiba, S., Saake, G., eds.: Proceedings of ECOOP'2004 Workshop on Reflection, AOP and Meta-Data for Software Evolution (RAM-SE'04), Oslo, Norway (2004) 29–35
6. Ebraert, P., Tourwé, T.: A Reflective Approach to Dynamic Software Evolution. In Cazzola, W., Chiba, S., Saake, G., eds.: Proceedings of ECOOP'2004 Workshop on Reflection, AOP and Meta-Data for Software Evolution (RAM-SE'04), Oslo, Norway (2004) 37–43
7. Gibbs, C., Coady, Y.: OASIS: Organic Aspects for System Infrastructure Software Easing Evolution and Adaptation through Natural Decomposition. In Cazzola, W., Chiba, S., Saake, G., eds.: Proceedings of ECOOP'2004 Workshop on Reflection, AOP and Meta-Data for Software Evolution (RAM-SE'04), Oslo, Norway (2004) 45–52
8. Sato, Y., Chiba, S.: Negligent Class Loaders for Software Evolution. In Cazzola, W., Chiba, S., Saake, G., eds.: Proceedings of ECOOP'2004 Workshop on Reflection, AOP and Meta-Data for Software Evolution (RAM-SE'04), Oslo, Norway (2004) 53–58
9. Pessemier, N., Seinturier, L., Duchien, L.: Components, ADL & AOP: Towards a Common Approach. In Cazzola, W., Chiba, S., Saake, G., eds.: Proceedings of ECOOP'2004 Workshop on Reflection, AOP and Meta-Data for Software Evolution (RAM-SE'04), Oslo, Norway (2004) 61–69
10. Ubayashi, N., Masuhara, H., Tamai, T.: An AOP Implementation Framework for Extending Join Point Models. In Cazzola, W., Chiba, S., Saake, G., eds.: Proceedings of ECOOP'2004 Workshop on Reflection, AOP and Meta-Data for Software Evolution (RAM-SE'04), Oslo, Norway (2004) 71–81
11. Cazzola, W., Pini, S., Ancona, M.: Evolving Pointcut Definition to Get Software Evolution. In Cazzola, W., Chiba, S., Saake, G., eds.: Proceedings of ECOOP'2004 Workshop on Reflection, AOP and Meta-Data for Software Evolution (RAM-SE'04), Oslo, Norway (2004) 83–88
12. Hannemann, J., Kiczales, G.: Design pattern implementation in Java and AspectJ. In: Proceedings of the 17th Annual ACM Conference on Object-Oriented Programming, Systems, Languages, and Applications (OOPSLA'02), ACM Press (2002) 161–173
13. Alvarez Canal, J.: Parametric Aspects: A Proposal. In Cazzola, W., Chiba, S., Saake, G., eds.: Proceedings of ECOOP'2004 Workshop on Reflection, AOP and Meta-Data for Software Evolution (RAM-SE'04), Oslo, Norway (2004) 91–99

14. Greenwood, P., Loughran, N., Blair, L., Rashid, A.: Dynamic Framed Aspects for Dynamic Software Evolution. In Cazzola, W., Chiba, S., Saake, G., eds.: Proceedings of ECOOP'2004 Workshop on Reflection, AOP and Meta-Data for Software Evolution (RAM-SE'04), Oslo, Norway (2004) 101–110
15. Kniesel, G., Rho, T., Hanenberg, S.: Evolvable Pattern Implementations Need Generic Aspects. In Cazzola, W., Chiba, S., Saake, G., eds.: Proceedings of ECOOP'2004 Workshop on Reflection, AOP and Meta-Data for Software Evolution (RAM-SE'04), Oslo, Norway (2004) 111–126
16. Bennett, K.H., Rajlich, V.T.: Software Maintenance and Evolution: a Roadmap. In Finkelstein, A., ed.: The Future of Software Engineering. ACM Press (2000) 75–87

Coordination and Adaptation Techniques for Software Entities*

Carlos Canal[1], Juan Manuel Murillo[2,**], and Pascal Poizat[3]

[1] Universidad de Málaga, ETSI Informática,
Campus de Teatinos, 29071 Málaga, Spain
canal@lcc.uma.es
[2] Universidad de Extremadura, Escuela Politécnica,
Avda. de la Universidad, s/n., 10071 Cáceres, Spain
juanmamu@unex.es
[3] Université d'Évry Val d'Essonne, LaMI,
Tour Évry 2, 523 place des terrasses, 91000 Évry, France
poizat@lami.univ-evry.fr

Abstract. The ability of reusing existing software has always been a major concern of Software Engineering. The reuse and integration of heterogeneous software parts is an issue for current paradigms such as Component-Based Software Development, or Coordination Models and Languages. However, a serious limitation of current approaches is that while they provide convenient ways to describe the typed signatures of software entities, they offer a quite limited support to describe their concurrent behaviour. As a consequence, when a component is going to be reused, one can only be sure that it provides the required interface, but nothing else can be inferred about the behaviour of the component with regard to the interaction protocol required by its environment. To deal with this problem, a new discipline, Software Adaptation, is emerging. Software Adaptation promotes the use of adaptors-specific computational entities guaranteeing that software components will interact in the right way not only at the signature level, but also at the protocol and semantic levels. This paper summarizes the results and conclusions of the First Workshop on Coordination and Adaptation Techniques for Software Entities (WCAT'04).

1   Introduction

In the recent years, the need for more and more complex pieces of software, supporting new services, and for wider application domains, together with advances in the net technology, have promoted the development of distributed systems.

---

* The title of this report should be referenced as "Report from the ECOOP 2004 Workshop on Coordination and Adaptation Techniques for Software Entities".
** This work has been partially supported by CICYT under contract TIC 02-04309-C02-01.

J. Malenfant and B.M. Østvold (Eds.): ECOOP 2004, LNCS 3344, pp. 133–147, 2004.
© Springer-Verlag Berlin Heidelberg 2004

These applications are made up of a collection of interacting entities (either considered as subsystems, objects, components, or —more recently— Web services) that collaborate to provide some functionality.

One of the most complex tasks when designing such applications is to specify the coordinated interaction that occurs among the computational entities. This fact has favored the development of a specific field in Software Engineering devoted to the Coordination of software. Some of the issues addressed by such discipline are:

1. To provide the highest expressive power to specify any coordination pattern. These patterns detail the order in which the tasks developed by each component of the distributed application have to be executed. The state of the global computation determines the set of tasks that can be performed at each instant.
2. To promote reusability, both of the coordinated entities and of the coordination patterns. The coordinated entities could be used in any other application in which their functionality is required, apart from the coordination pattern that directs them. The same holds for the coordination patterns; they could be used in a different application, managing a different collection of entities with different behaviour and different interfaces, but with the same coordination needs.

In fact, the ability of reusing existing pieces of software has always been a major concern of Software Engineering. In particular, the need for the reuse and integration of heterogeneous software parts is at the core of Component-Based Software Development. The paradigm "write once, run forever" is currently supported by several component platforms.

However, a serious limitation of available component platforms (with regard to reusability) is that they do not provide suitable means to describe and reason on the interacting behaviour of component-based systems. Indeed, while these platforms provide convenient ways to describe the typed signatures of software entities via Interface Description Languages (IDLs), they offer a quite limited and low-level support to describe their concurrent behaviour. As a consequence, when a component is going to be reused, one can only be sure that it provides the required interface, but nothing else can be inferred about the behaviour of the component with regard to the interaction protocol required by its environment.

To deal with this problem, a new discipline, Software Adaptation, is emerging. Software Adaptation focuses on the problems related to reusing existing software entities when constructing a new application, and promotes the use of adaptors —specific computational entities for solving these problems. The main goal of software adaptors is to guarantee that software components will interact in the right way not only at the signature level, but also at the protocol and semantic levels. In this sense, Software Adaptation can be considered as a new generation of Coordination Models.

However, Software Adaptation is not restricted to the adaptation of the interaction through coordination models. Other functional and non-functional properties of software systems can be adapted as well, while other topics such as automatic generation of adaptors are under study. With the aim of stating the boundaries and interests of Software Adaptation, the First Workshop on Coordination and Adaptation Techniques for Software Entities (WCAT '04) was held in conjunction with the 18th European Conference on Object-Oriented Programming (Oslo, Norway, 14-18 June, 2004). The topics of interest of the workshop were:

- New coordination models separating the interaction concern;
- Aspect-oriented approaches to software adaptation;
- Coordination and adaptation in concurrent and distributed object-oriented systems;
- Interface and choreography description of Web services;
- Coordination and adaptation middleware;
- Rigorous approaches to software adaptation;
- Identification and specification of interaction requirements;
- Patterns and frameworks for component look-up and adaptation;
- Automatic generation of adaptors;
- Documenting components to enable software composition and adaptation;
- Metrics and prediction models for software adaptation;
- Extra-functional properties in their relation to coordination and adaptation;
- Tools and environments;
- Industrial and experience reports.

The main conclusion of the workshop is that Software Adaptation is an emerging and well-differentiated discipline motivated by the new challenges of Software Engineering on building complex software systems in an efficient way. This paper summarizes the discussions and conclusions from the workshop.

The rest of this paper is organized as follows: Section 2 presents an outline of the contributions submitted, Section 3 summarizes the results of the three discussion groups that worked during the workshop, and Section 4 presents the conclusions of the workshop. Finally, we provide some references to the work on coordination and adaptation being developed by workshop attendants.

2   Summary of the Contributions

According to ECOOP'2004 Workshop Guidelines, we tried to put up a working meeting in which participants not merely presented the technical details of their work, but could instead discuss their points of view, trying to identify which are the main issues, challenges, and their possible solutions in the field of Software Coordination and Adaptation.

For these reasons, in the CfP we asked for short (about five pages long) position papers. We also recommended that papers should contain a section on Open Issues, in which authors indicated the relevant issues that they would like to address during the workshop.

We received twelve submissions, covering a wide range of aspects of coordination and adaptation. In particular, many of them dealt specifically with software adaptation, which was rather encouraging, taking into account that this is the first event specifically addressing this field. As workshop organizers, and acting also as program committee, we reviewed the position papers, and replied to the authors with our impressions, suggesting them to deepen in those aspects that we considered more interesting for the workshop. Due to their quality and interest, we decided to accept all the papers submitted, as a way of ensuring different points of view that would produce more lively discussions. Both the Call for Papers and the final versions of the position papers can be found at the Web page of the workshop:

http://wcat04.unex.es

Fifteen participants, coming from seven different countries, attended the workshop, which started with a short presentation (a five-minutes talk followed by five minutes for questions and comments) of ten of the position papers submitted. Once again, the idea was not to give out academic speeches but to present succinctly the positions, saving time for discussions during the workshop.

The list of participants, together with their affiliation, and the title of the position papers they presented is as follows:

- Marco Autili, marco.autili@di.univaq.it
  University of L'Aquila (Italy)
  Automatic Adaptor Synthesis for Protocol Transformation
- Steffen Becker, becker@informatik.uni-oldenburg.de
  University of Oldenburg (Germany)
  The Impact of Software Component Adaptors on QoS Properties
- Carlos Canal, Workshop Organizer, canal@lcc.uma.es
  University of Málaga (Spain)
  On the Dynamic Adaptation of Component Behaviour
- Antinisca Di Marco, adimarco@di.univaq.it
  University of L'Aquila (Italy)
- Viktoria Firus, firus@informatik.uni-oldenburg.de
  University of Oldenburg (Germany)
- Thomas Heistracher, thomas.heistracher@fh-sbg.ac.at
  Salzburg University of Applied Sciences (Austria)
  Pervasive Service Architecture for a Digital Business Ecosystem
- Tobias Ludwig, toby@gmx.de
  ECOOP'2004 Student Volunteer (Germany)
- Claudius Masuch, claudius.masuch@fh-sbg.ac.at
  Salzburg University of Applied Sciences (Austria)
  Pervasive Service Architecture for a Digital Business Ecosystem
- Juan Manuel Murillo, Workshop Organizer, juanmamu@unex.es
  University of Extremadura (Spain)
  Managing Components Adaptation Using Aspect-Oriented Techniques

- José Luis Pastrana, pastrana@lcc.uma.es
  University of Málaga (Spain)
  Client Oriented Software Developing

- Pascal Poizat, Workshop Organizer, poizat@lami.univ-evry.fr
  Université d'Évry Val d'Essonne (France)
  Formal Methods for Component Description, Coordination and Adaptation

- Sibylle Schupp, schupp@cs.chalmers.se
  Chalmers University of Technology (Sweden)
  How to Use a Library

- Björn Törnqvist, bjorn.tornqvist@bth.se
  Blekinge Institute of Technology (Sweden)
  On Adaptative Aspect-Oriented Coordination for Critical Infrastructures

- Nesrine Yahiaoui, nesrine.yahiaoui@prism.uvsq.fr
  UVSQ Prism (France)
  Classification and Comparison of Dynamic Adaptable Software Platforms

- Jie Yang, jie@cs.uit.no
  University of Tromsø (Norway)

The papers submitted to the workshop may be classified into three categories. The first one corresponds to papers related with Coordination and Adaptation Models. This category includes the works presented by Autili [1], Canal [2], and Heistracher and Masuch [3]. In [1], the authors propose the automatic generation of adaptors to manage the difficulties of building systems from components, in particular when some changes (improvements, evolution, etc.) must be introduced in the composite system. Their approach is based on formal methods. In [2], an approach to deal with component adaptation at runtime is presented. Once again, his proposal is supported by formal methods. Finally, [3] presents an architecture to support the expression of business models addressing the composition of service chains, and its optimization through automatic self-organizing and evolutionary (genetic) algorithms.

The second category is constituted by works focused on Adaptation and Aspect-Oriented Techniques, including the works presented by Murillo [4], Pastrana [5], and Törnqvist [6]. [4] is focused on how adaptation can be considered a crosscutting concern and, consequently, managed with aspect-oriented techniques. In [5], applying the contract metaphor the authors propose the specification of some non-functional requirements aimed over components by means of connectors (adaptors). The work described in [6] presents the future EU integrated power grid as a real case study of coordination and adaptation. The authors propose the use of coordination, aspect-oriented and adaptation techniques to deal with that system.

Finally, the third category corresponds to papers presenting general studies about Coordination and Adaptation, and includes the works presented by Becker [7], Poizat [8], Schupp [9], and Yahiaoui [10]. [7] presents an analysis on the impact that adaptors may have on the Quality of Service (QoS) of adapted components, showing the interdependencies that exist between QoS attributes, and how adaptors can affect such attributes. [8] contains an interesting study about how formal methods can help on designing and composing/adapting CBSE systems. The authors argue for the pragmatic use of formal methods. In [9] the problems of building and using software libraries are highlighted. These problems are similar to those of searching, retrieving, and adapting components from repositories. Finally, [10] analyzes the features shown by platforms allowing dynamic adaptation, and classifies these features in several dimensions.

From the presentation session, a list of open issues that we would like to address was identified and grouped. This helped to make clear which were the participants' interests, and served also to establish some goals for the workshop. Then, participants were divided into three groups (about 4-6 persons each), attending to their interests, each one related to a topic on software coordination and adaptation. The task of each group was to discuss about the assigned topic, to detect problems and its real causes, and to point out solutions. Finally, a plenary session was held, in which each group presented their conclusions to the rest of the participants, followed by some discussion.

3   Summary of the Discussions

As indicated above, after the short presentations a small brainstorming was performed, trying to determine the most common remarks and questions. These issues were classified into three groups of topics:

Problems. This group dealt with which are the different problems that can be solved by adaptation, and how. The main issues were: what does adaptation mean? (i.e. what is to be adapted: functional, or non-functional properties?); static versus dynamic adaptation (i.e. when to adapt/not to adapt?); and what are the relations between adaptation and coordination, maintenance, and aspect-oriented techniques? (the latter related to the adaptation of non-functional properties).

Languages and Processes. This group dealt with the languages and processes that can be used to support coordination and adaptation. The main issues addressed were: which aspects of components to take into account? (either functional, behavioural/protocol, or non-functional properties, such as performance or reliability); how to do it? (e.g. formal methods, contracts, biological metaphors...); what level of detail is needed for describing component interfaces? what are the requirements for connector/adaptor languages? what kind of formalism is required? (and its relation with implementation); is more than one language needed? (for example, using several coordination models, or protocols with value-passing).

Benefits. This group dealt with the benefits that can be expected from the use of coordination and adaptation techniques (apart from solving the adaptation problems). The main issues were: what is the relation between adaptation and quality of service? do adaptation increases the reliability or reusability of components? which measure/assessment mechanisms to use? what about scaling up? and which is the role of tools.

The classification above induced to divide the participants into three different discussion groups. The first group would start by finding out which are the system properties that can be adapted (the what). Then, the means to achieve their adaptation (the how) must be identified, too. Both (what+how) would lead to a definition of adaptation. Finally, this group would compare the concerns of adaptation with those of other related fields, such as aspect-orientation and maintenance. The second group would find out requirements for coordination and adaptation languages in terms of description expressiveness, methods and processes. The third group would discuss on what could be the by-products of coordination and adaptation processes.

3.1   Interest of Adaptation and Coordination

The discussion group was integrated by Steffen Becker, Viktoria Firus, Juan M. Murillo, Nesrine Yahiaoui, and Jie Yang. The aim of the group was to discuss about what adaptation is, the different kinds of adaptation that can be demanded by a system, and the relationships, differences and similarities between adaptation and other fields such as coordination, maintenance and aspect-orientation. The next paragraphs depict the conclusions reached.

The group started discussing about what is software adaptation in a broad sense (and not restricted to the meaning of adaptation underlying in the works being developed by the people in the group). Thus, thinking about what adaptation is, the first emerging question was what kind of properties can be adapted in a software system. The immediate answer was that, of course, several non-functional properties of the system can be adapted. For instance, the interaction constraints of a system can be adapted using coordination models and languages. Indeed, when a coordination model is used for tuning the interaction protocol between two components, these components are being adapted to work altogether. However, adaptation is not restricted to non-functional properties. The functionality of the system can be adapted as well. A system can be adapted to provide new services, or the functionality provided by a piece of software can be adapted for using it in a different system. For example, a component providing the functionality of a list of elements could be adapted for reusing it in a particular system where the functionality of a queue is required. Thus, thinking about adaptation, both functional and non-functional adaptation must be taken into account.

After that, we tried to classify the different ways to proceed with software adaptation (extending the classification presented by Yahiaoui in [10]). The group agreed that a good criteria to classify adaptation is attending to the moment in which the need of adaptation is detected. Thus, three different moments requiring different procedures for adaptation were catalogued:

1. Requirements Adaptation. This kind of adaptation is made when the requirements of a system are extended to meet new properties, or when we

want to reuse a system specification, but it must be adapted to meet the requirements of the new system. Examples of this kind of adaptation are adding a security property to a bank account, or adding an attribute to a table in a database. It could require both functional and non-functional adaptation.

2. Static Adaptation. This is the case in which we want to adapt pieces of software developed independently in order to make them work together. Suppose a Bank_account component providing a get_money service and a Client component requiring a decrement_balance service. As a general characteristic of this kind of adaptation, it can be said that the steps to proceed with the adaptation are known —and have been planned— in advance with respect to the moment in which the adaptation takes place. Although some kind of functional adaptation could be required, usually, static adaptation involves non-functional adaptation.

3. Dynamic Adaptation. Running pieces of software need to be adapted in order to provide some particular service. For example, suppose a mobile phone adapting to the local phone provider of a different company. In comparison with static adaptation, now the components to be adapted are unknown until the moment of the adaptation. Hence, the steps to manage the adaptation are unknown as well. Dynamic adaptation should be limited to non-functional adaptation, if possible[1].

The group also discussed about the procedures to manage adaptation. We agreed that two different procedures can be distinguished:

1. Manual Adaptation. The adaptation steps as well as the adaptors are specified and developed by the people intervening in the software process (designers, architects, programmers, etc). However, the adaptation task may be assisted by software tools. Nevertheless, adaptation must be non-intrusive, that is, it must not require a modification of the component adapted (modifying the adapted component would be more related to maintenance than to adaptation).

2. Automatic Adaptation. All the adaptation steps and the adaptors themselves are automatically generated by a tool. This kind of tool must be able to detect the need for adaptation and whether the required adaptation is possible or not, and will have to determine the steps to manage adaptation, and finally, generate the adaptors.

Anyway, regardless of the adaptation procedure used, the work presented by Becker [7] —focused on how adaptation can affect the QoS attributes— led us

---

[1] Here, it must be understood that the aim of this kind of dynamic adaptation is not to provide new unexpected functionality to a running component. Thus, in the mobile phone example it is considered that, although the operation of contacting a network provider is a functional property, the way in which the provider is contacted is not a part of the functionality (but the way in which the functionality is provided, instead).

to think that it would be good to have procedures to determine whether the adaptation of a component is convenient (instead of building a new component providing the desired functionality).

Having all the above in mind, it is easy to conclude that there exist some relationships between adaptation and other disciplines such us coordination, maintenance and aspect-orientation. However, although such relationships do actually exist, adaptation have connotations that provide it with an own identity.

Coordination models and languages can be used to manage the adaptation of the interaction protocols among components. In particular, exogenous coordination models provide entities —commonly called coordinators— with the aim of forcing the interaction protocols among components. Such coordinators can be considered as adaptors. However, Coordination is not concerned with topics such us how the need of adaptation can be detected, how coordinators can be generated automatically and which is the information needed to achieve it, and, of course, with the adaptation of non-functional properties different from interaction.

Adaptation is close to maintenance as well. Maintenance is concerned with how to deal with system evolution in an easy and efficient way. In particular, adaptation can help maintenance by providing the technical means to deal with changes in the requirements. In some sense, the work by Becker [7] analyzing how adaptation can affect the QoS attributes can be related with maintenance. Nevertheless, maintenance is focused on how software methodologies can face system evolution, and on the methods needed to give support to evolution in the software process, more than on the technical means to adapt an existing system.

Finally, aspect-oriented techniques can be used to adapt non-functional properties of a system. As Murillo presented [4], adding new aspects to an existing software system can have the effect of adapting the system to satisfy new properties. However, apart of this co-lateral effect, Aspect-Oriented Software Development is concerned with how crosscutting concerns can be identified and separated at the different stages of the software life cycle getting out of its scope topics such as automatic adaptation or adaptation of functional properties.

The final conclusion of the group was that adaptation is concerned with how the functional and non-functional properties of an existing software entity (class, object, component, etc.) can be adapted to be used in a software system observing that:

- Adaptation must be non-intrusive.
- The need for adaptation can appear at any stage of the software life-cycle, from requirements specification to system operation stages.
- Software adaptation requires automatic or at least semi-automatic (computationally assisted) procedures.

In practice, some kind of adaptation is being done using tools such as exogenous coordination models or aspect-oriented techniques. However, the new challenges in Software Engineering for building complex software systems in an efficient way do require new techniques, dealing with the detection of adaptation needs, automatic adaptation, functional adaptation, formal methods allowing to reason about adaptation, dynamic adaptation, and automatic adaptation. All these topics are the interest of the emerging discipline of Software Adaptation.

3.2   Languages for Coordination and Adaptation

The discussion group was integrated by Marco Autili, Claudius Masuch, Pascal Poizat, and Björn Törnqvist. The goals of this group was to discuss on the requirements of languages and processes to support adaptation.

The first issue to be discussed was if formal languages were needed. The group recognized then that formal methods have great benefits in any component-based framework (tools for subtyping detection, protocol compliance, ...). The most interesting works on component coordination are now based on formal languages of some form (automata, transition systems, process algebras or MSC). Formal languages are emerging in the more challenging (up to now) challenging application domain for coordination and adaptation techniques, Web services. [8] gives some details on these two points. On adaptation, Autili [1] has very interesting results with MSC. Moreover, the seminal paper on adaptation [11] deals with transition systems. Hence the group accepted that the language should be formal. However, it was also said that the specifications should be executable (which is possible if the language has an operational semantics). This is a mandatory requirement for example to be able to relate component and adaptors specifications with their implementations. This is also needed to be able to have automatic or dynamic adaptation.

Then, the group interested himself on what kind of components are to be adapted. Usually components are black boxes with type-only require/provide interfaces given in an Interface Description Language. It has been recognized both in the ADL and Coordination communities that such interfaces are not sufficient: for example two components may have compatible provide/require interfaces but may fail to interact due to incompatible protocols. Therefore, the group advocated for a Behavioural IDL (BIDL) to describe the components, thus yielding a grey box description of them.

The group rejected the possibility to use white box descriptions of components (i.e. having the whole description of the component in some language, not only its abstract protocol). This would increase the complexity of the adaptation process, which is an important issue in case of dynamic adaptation. Moreover, such interfaces are to be exchanged between components in such adaptation (see for example the Pastrana proposal [5]). Hence they have to be quite small and abstract.

Adaptation has been recognized by the group as composing in some way (depending on the language structuring means) components and adaptors. But this should yield (semantically) a component in order for the adapted component to be reused in place of the first one. Hence adaptation should yield components. Then a question arose: is the adaptation language the same than the components protocol one? Here there are two possibilities.

The first one is to use the same one (a process algebra or any state transition language is the solution). Hence the basic structuring means of the language can be reused (for example parallel composition in process algebras). This is more simple, adaptors can be components too (to be used and reused as components are). This expresses the need for languages in which compositions are components. Moreover, the language could benefit from being compositional. Hence any formal process (verification but also adaptation) could be done on a composition by doing it on its subcomponents (adapting a composed component could be defined as adapting each of its subcomponents). Note that once again abstraction was noted as an important issued here (compositional languages are often the ones with abstraction features).

A second solution is to use a specific language for adaptation (as it can be for coordination using a temporal logic [8] or on adaptation with MSC [1]). This is more expressive as the language has only to have specific hooks on the components protocols but can then extend this. This second solution is much more related to Aspect-Oriented weaving techniques (the adaptation language being used as a description of the joint point).

Then the discussion opened on extensions of the components and/or adaptation language.

A first aspect was some form of state description. The group rejected this for components, or only in a very abstract form (components should be protocol oriented). This is to keep a grey box description of components. However, the interest of states was recognized for adaptors (denoting states of the whole system). In effect, adaptation can depend on a state of the system (Törqvist expressed this on the EU power grid system requirements [6]: different adaptation schemes depending on the power level, etc).

A second aspect was on more expressive communication semantics, mainly queues.

The problem here is that more expressive communication schemes (asynchronous with queues) yield undecidability results. Different queue protocols can be used (for example FIFFO in place of FIFO). However, this question is not so important and adaptation can be more simple at an abstract level (basic synchronous communication) as then lots of tools (such as process algebraic ones) can be used.

Other aspects were then quickly reviewed: non-functional ones. It has been recognized that they are more difficult to be taken into account still keeping in the preceding requirements (formality, abstraction, decidability, tools,...). However, several are interesting such as real time to give boundaries for services or timeouts, probabilities as an information on components for adaptors (again, on the EU power grid case study, possibility for a subsystem of going down), localities. Here a single very expressive language can be used but its verification/adaptation should be difficult. Several languages can also be used (one for each aspect), but then some form of Aspect-Oriented weaving would be needed.

To end the group discussed the use of data. Components may exchange data and may have to be adapted on this. The group decided that data are useful but should be given in a very abstract form in order to make the adaptation possible.

As a conclusion, good candidate languages for adaptation seem to be process algebras (which can be extended for lots of aspects, adaptation in a single formalism) and MSC (should be extended if different aspects, adaptation in MSC and protocols in any state transition language).

3.3   Benefits of Coordination and Adaptation

The discussion group was integrated by Carlos Canal, Thomas Heistracher, José Luis Pastrana, and Sibylle Schupp. Its main goal was to find out which are the benefits that coordination and adaptation techniques may have in software development.

However, it is worth saying that the group also discussed more general questions (e.g. the meaning of coordination and adaptation, their boundaries, etc.) that partly overlapped the goals of the other two groups. Anyway, the group tried to give its particular point of view about these issues, which is with no doubt closely related to each participant's position and experience in the field.

The discussions started considering the value of software adaptation and the need of a discipline devoted to it. The participants agreed that since there are lots of examples of adaptation in our daily life, we have to put it in software, too. Where and when? The group discussed if adaptation could be proactive, or if one must wait till designers find a particular solution for adapting a given component to a given context. The conclusion -however, more a wish list than a state-of-the-art description-, was that it should be proactive, in the dynamic, automatic and self-initiated sense. The group also concluded that this may be better achieved by means of some kind of middleware infrastructure, containing built-in adaptation functions, which could decide when and how to adapt. More precisely, adaptation should be performed at binding time, when a component joins a context, rather than being static (i.e. performed at design time). It should be also as much automated as possible.

The work of Schupp [9] deals with the development of large libraries containing different versions of components performing a single well-defined task (e.g. the Fast Fourier Transform). These libraries are implemented in an object-oriented language, and can be instantiated by parameterization, not only of generic types, but also of higher-order functions. Hence, the technology involved is object-oriented and could be described as pre-component-based. The group took this as a sort of case study, a starting point for discussions, and tried to analyse how the techniques and methods related to the scope of the workshop could help.

First, the group considered if this kind of parameterization could be taken as a form of adaptation. The conclusion was it was not. The use of generics -and also polymorphism- in OO languages provide degrees of freedom to the components developed, which can be customized afterwards. However, these degrees of freedom must be foreseen and carefully defined during design, while adaptation should allow forms of reuse and changes in software characteristics that were not thought of by the original developers of a component. Thus, adaptation is more related to the black-box reuse style of CBSD, than to the white-box reuse typical of the OO paradigm.

One of the problems when using these libraries of components is how to choose the right version. Different users may have different criteria. Hence, the problem of how to describe components characteristics is crucial. The clear benefits are that the components would be more accessible, helping in the scalability of the libraries, and also in the predictability of their behaviour.

Consequently, extended interfaces (containing not only signature specifications, describing not only functional properties) are a strong need, as the only way of scientifically evaluate the software, and take decisions. Anyway, an open issue here is that once we inspect the interfaces and decide which component to use, how could we trust it? That is, how could we ensure it behaves as described? Once again, putting this functionality into the middleware could be a solution.

In particular, the work of Pastrana [5] addresses the specification of extended interfaces for components, following the design by contract metaphor. He made the group reflect on the fact that while the description of functionality has been extensively studied, and one has a sound mathematical background for it (for instance, the use of pre- and post-conditions), much less has been done with non-functional (no-fun!) properties; each of them must be defined individually, and described separately using a specific notation for which a similarly sound foundation should be established. If not, the possibilities for automatic dynamic adaptation, and its benefits will always be very limited.

The group discussed also whether one needs to find the best choice or solution, or just one "good enough". Here, the biological simile present in the work of Heistracher [3] helped the group in considering some kind of dynamic natural selection of components, where different solutions may compete for their existence, and even extinguish. This would help by reducing the number of choices in the future.

Finally, the formal background of the work of Canal [2], related to process algebras for behavioural descriptions, made the group also discuss the role and benefits of formal methods. One of the benefits is that abstraction, hiding the irrelevant details, would help in the selection process, and in component trading in general. However, one has to decide which details are important and which are not, and this decision determines the notation used and also the properties that can be analyzed. Once again, the group arrived to the importance of describing non-functional properties (which notations, and which "algebras" to use here?).

Anyway, we agreed that the benefits of formal methods should be really operational, not only descriptive, which is a lack of many proposals in the field. The importance of tools was also discussed: real solutions should provide real tools!

Other envisioned benefits were reduction of complexity: adaptation techniques try to cope with the complexity of giving a solution; increasing reuse: using more technologies with less time spent in integration; and last, but not at all less important, the value added by these techniques to the software process: allowing more technically advanced developers to compete with solutions based only in man-power.

3.4 Conclusions of the Discussions

After the group discussions, the report from each group was presented and the conclusions were discussed to reach agreement. Summarizing the conclusions of the three groups it can be said that Software Adaptation can be identified as a new discipline with its own topics of interest concerned with how the functional and non-functional properties of an existing software entity (class, object, component, etc.) can be adapted to be used in a software system. The need of adapting a software entity can appear at any stage of the software life-cycle and adaptation techniques for all the stages must be provided. Anyway such techniques must be non-intrusive and based on Behavioural IDLs and formal executable specification languages. Such languages and techniques should support automatic and dynamic adaptation, that is, the adaptation of a component just in the moment in which the component joins the context supported by automatic and transparent procedures.

4 Conclusion of the Workshop

After the presentation of the conclusions of the discussion groups the Closing Session was held. During this session attendants were asked for their general impression about WCAT. We all agreed that the workshop was very interesting and productive. We also discussed about the possibility of having a new edition of WCAT in 2005. Again, all the attendants agreed that it would be good to have a new meeting in one year to mature the discussions about Software Adaptation.

The high quality of the papers submitted to the workshop encouraged us as workshop organizers to put up a special issue where selected technical papers about the works of the groups intervening in the workshop could be presented at length. Currently we are in conversations with an international journal interested in the publication of the special issue.

References

1. Autili, M., Inverardi, P., Tivoli, M.: Automatic adaptor synthesis for protocol transformations. [12] 39–46 Available online at http://wcat04.unex.es.
2. Canal, C.: On the dynamic adaptation of component behaviour. [12] 81–88 Available online at http://wcat04.unex.es.
3. Heistracher, T., Kurz, T., Masuch, C., Ferronato, P., Vidal, M., Corallo, A., Briscoe, G., Dini, P.: Pervasive service architecture for a digital business ecosystem. [12] 71–80 Available online at http://wcat04.unex.es.
4. Eterovic, Y., Murillo, J.M., Palma, K.: Managing component adaptation using aspect oriented techniques. [12] 101–108 Available online at http://wcat04.unex.es.
5. Katrib, M., Pastrana, J.L., Pimentel, E.: Client oriented software developing. [12] 9–16 Available online at http://wcat04.unex.es.
6. Törnqvist, B., Gustavsson, R.: On adaptative aspect-oriented coordination for critical infrastructures. [12] 63–69 Available online at http://wcat04.unex.es.
7. Becker, S., Reussner, R.H.: The impact of software component adaptors on quality of service properties. [12] 25–30 Available online at http://wcat04.unex.es.

8. Poizat, P., Royer, J.C., Salaün, G.:   Formal methods for component description, coordination and adaptation.   [12] 89–100 Available online at http://wcat04.unex.es.
9. Schupp, S.:   How to use a library?   [12] 47–53 Available online at http://wcat04.unex.es.
10. Yahiaoui, N., Traverson, B., Levy, N.: Classification and comparison of adaptable platforms. [12] 55–61 Available online at http://wcat04.unex.es.
11. Yellin, D., Strom, R.: Protocol specifications and component adaptors. ACM Transactions on Programming Languages and Systems **19** (1997) 292–333
12. Canal, C., Murillo, J.M., Poizat, P., eds.: First Workshop on Coordination and Adaptation Techniques for Software Entities (WCAT'04). Held in conjunction with the 18th European Conference on Object-Oriented Programming (ECOOP). Published as a Technical Report of the Universities of Málaga (Spain), Extremadura (Spain) and Évry (France). ISBN 84-688-6782-9. In Canal, C., Murillo, J.M., Poizat, P., eds.: First Workshop on Coordination and Adaptation Techniques for Software Entities (WCAT'04). (2004) Available online at http://wcat04.unex.es.

Model-Driven Development (WMDD 2004)*

Jan Øyvind Aagedal[1,2], Jean Bézivin[3], and Peter F. Linington[4]

[1] SINTEF ICT, Forskningsveien 1, P.O.Box 124 Blindern,
N-0314 Oslo, Norway
[2] Simula Research Laboratory, Martin Linges v 17, Fornebu
P.O.Box 134, N-1325 Lysaker, Norway
jan.aagedal@sintef.no
[3] Atlas Group, INRIA and LINA, University of Nantes,
2, rue de la Houssinière - BP 92208, 44322 Nantes Cedex 3, France
Jean.Bezivin@lina.univ-nantes.fr
[4] University of Kent, Computing Laboratory, Canterbury, Kent CT2 7NF, UK
P.F.Linington@kent.ac.uk

Abstract. The objective of the workshop on model-driven development (WMDD 2004) was to identify and discuss issues related to system modelling and how to transform these models to a level suitable for execution and/or simulation. The workshop contained three sessions for presentation of position papers, and a final session for discussion and drawing conclusions. The topics of the three sessions were transformations, model-driven development aspects, and PIMs for distributed systems, web and B2B.

1 Introduction

Model-driven development is of increasing importance in the object-oriented community. Object technology started out with the simulation and modelling of the real world in the Simula programming language. It is now time to look at which higher level abstraction mechanism is most useful for domain and system modelling, and how to transform these to a level suitable for execution and/or simulation. The goal of this workshop was to attract the community interested in evolving and applying model-driven development, by addressing important issues and solution approaches based on recent experience with the OMG MDA® (Model Driven Architecture) approach, or from other relevant activities. In this context there are a number of interesting issues to be discussed and resolved, in particular around formal models and languages related to model transformations and generative techniques, and in tools and environments related to model simulation, testing and execution. The workshop solicited input from people active in this field, either from researchers, tool developers or from those with

---

* The title of this report should be referenced as "Report from the ECOOP 2004 Workshop on Model-Driven Development (WMDD 2004)".

J. Malenfant and B.M. Østvold (Eds.): ECOOP 2004, LNCS 3344, pp. 148–157, 2004.

practical experience of the model-driven approach. The call for participation contained a detailed list of topics, and is available at the workshop homepage at http://heim.ifi.uio.no/~janoa/wmdd2004. The accepted position papers are also available there.

There were approximately 20 participants at the workshop. There were eight position papers accepted, and one tool demonstration. We organized this workshop into four sessions focusing on different aspects of model-driven development. In the remainder of this paper, we report highlights from each session.

2   Transformations

The first session brought together three position papers that all discussed various aspects of model transformation. The session was chaired by Peter F. Linington.

2.1   Transformations Based on Relations

The first presentation was by David H. Akehurst from the University of Kent, UK. The abstract of his talk is:

> "The Model Driven Architecture (MDA) is an approach to IT systems development fostered by the Object Management Group (OMG). It is based on forming a separation between the specification of a system's essential functionality as a platform independent model (PIM) and the realization of the system using more detailed and specific platform specification (PSM). It is recognized that specifying the mappings or transformations from PIM to PSM is a key enabling aspect of the MDA approach. Currently the OMG's Request for Proposals (RFP) on techniques and facilities to enable transformations is in progress. In this position paper we discuss a technique for specifying transformations that is based on the mathematical foundation of relations. Using these relation specifications we show how the additional definition of some "build" expressions enables the generation of a transformation engine that will map model instances from either side of the specification to the other. This approach has been proved to work on a number of small case studies, using the KMF code generation tools to build transformation engines from specifications."

An issue that was raised during this presentation was how MDA transformations compare with other transformation systems, such as parsers. Akehurst had, without success, tried to model a grammar using the transformation approach. It was argued that some transformations are not suited for the MDA-style of transformation; perhaps we need to classify transformations in a similar way to grammars (LL, LR, LALR, etc.).

2.2   Basic Model Transformation Language MOLA

The next talk was by Audris Kalnins from the University of Latvia in Riga, Latvia. He presented a position paper written by himself and his colleagues Janis Barzdins and Edgars Celms. The abstract of his talk is:

"The paper offers basic elements of a new graphical model transformation language MOLA. The language combines the traditional structured programming with pattern-based transformation rules, the key element being a natural loop construct. The prime goal of MOLA is to provide a natural and highly readable representation of model transformation algorithms."

According to Audris Kalnins, transformation languages should be executable and readable, and the authors believe MOLA, with its graphical syntax, satisfies this. MOLA is based on graph rewriting rules and uses control structures from traditional programming. A question was raised about how to evaluate the usability of such a language. MOLA has been used by several students, but in general it was agreed that we need benchmarks and standard evaluation techniques to be able to determine the usability of a language.

2.3   Transformations in Eclipse

The final presentation in this session was by Catherine Griffin from IBM UK Laboratories, Hursley Park, UK. Her position paper has the following abstract:

"Eclipse is an open platform for tool integration built by an open community of tool providers. The OMG is a member of the eclipse.org consortium, as are IBM, Borland, and other MDA tools vendors. Model transformation is a key technology for MDA. This paper describes the role of transformations in the Eclipse platform and considers the implications of the emerging OMG MOF Queries, Views and Transformations standard (MOF Q/V/T) in this environment."

A point that was noted during this talk was that transformations in Eclipse are regular Java programs, and that QVT must have an option to link to such transformations.

3   Model-Driven Development Aspects

The next session grouped three position papers on different aspects of model-driven development. The session was chaired by Jean Bézivin.

3.1   Model-Driven Development and Non-functional Aspects

The first talk in this session was given by Peter F. Linington from the University of Kent, UK. The initial statements in his position paper are:

"Most of the practical work so far on Model Driven Development has focused on the generation of implementations that manipulate or navigate some form of business model directly. However, the author believes that there are major benefits from the application of these development techniques to the creation of systems with guarantees of less tangible properties than expressed in the explicit steps of the business process.

The assumption here is that main inputs to the construction of a system are in the form of a set of models. The business model is one of these, but others represent supporting policies in areas like security; these policies are likely to be maintained by separate groups of developers from the business processes, and these may operate on a different development cycle, needing to affect significant numbers of business processes."

The importance of considering non-functional aspects in model-driven development was agreed upon, but challenges remain to identify the relevant non-functional properties and how they influence model-driven development. Specifically, one can foresee the generation of performance models alongside regular code-generating transformations, but it is not clear what sort of linkage between the models is needed; in general, non-functional aspects may need many-to-many transformations.

3.2   Model Driven Testing and MDA

The next talk was given by Sergey Olvovsky from IBM Haifa Research Laboratory, Israel. He presented a position paper written by Alan Hartman, Kenneth Nagin and himself. The abstract of the position paper is:

"We describe the AGEDIS project, a European Commission sponsored project for the creation of a methodology and tools for automated model driven test generation and execution for distributed systems. Our emphasis is on the description of the application of model centric methodology to testing, lessons learned over the three year life of the project and the impact of MDA on the future of software testing."

The AGEDIS project has learned many valuable lessons reported in the position paper, and this will be built upon in forthcoming projects such as the new EU-funded Integrated Project MODELWARE, which is to start this autumn. One major issue to explore is the relationship between the design models and the behavioural model built for test purposes. One should expect that these need to be consistent, but research is still necessary to clarify the exact relationships between these two kinds of model.

3.3   UMT - Tool Demonstration

The final talk in this session was given by Jon Oldevik from SINTEF, Norway. He gave a short introduction to the UMT (UML Model Transformation) tool before he gave a demonstration of some of the facilities provided by UMT. UMT is an open source tool available at http://umt-qvt.sourceforge.net/. The tool presentation states:

"UMT-QVT is a tool for model transformation and code generation of UML/XMI models. UMT-QVT provides an environment in which new generators can be plugged in. The tool environment is implemented in Java. Generators are implemented in either XSLT or Java."

The difficulty of exploiting the great variety of features in the many different platforms used was discussed. For instance, the knowledge that one can use the construct "connected by" in Oracle 9i instead of writing your own recursive queries is something that should be incorporated into code generation, but this means that one needs distinct code generators for each combination, considering every version of the platforms.

4   PIMs for Distributed Applications, Web and B2B

This first session after lunch was also the final position paper session. This session was devoted to PIMs for different purposes, namely distributed applications, web and B2B. The session chair was Catherine Griffin. Only two papers were actually presented due to technical reasons.

4.1   Modeled Object's Property-Based Support for Distributed Applications

The first talk in this session was given by Yun Lin from the Norwegian University of Science and Technology, Trondheim, Norway. She presented a position paper written by herself and Darijus Strasunskas. The abstract of this paper is:

"This position paper discusses a vision for methodological support in distributed modeling. The framework has two layers: an ontology layer for representation of basic knowledge about a domain; and a model layer, where models concerning a certain problem within the domain are stored and interchanged. The ontology serves as a knowledge reference point to define various properties of entities and represent dependency between the objects. Ontology and model fragments associated with the concepts from the ontology by sub-class relationship allow the interrelation of different model fragments and assessment of change impact."

The presentation focused on the need for an ontological layer to support traceability between models, and the importance of this layer for model integration.

4.2   Towards a PIM for the Model-Driven Development of Web-Based Systems

The next talk was given by Robert Smith from the University of Kent, UK. He presented a position paper by himself and David H. Shrimpton. Some statements from the position paper are:

"Model driven approaches to the design and realization of software systems are gaining ground. However, some key issues still need to be addressed. Firstly, the MDA specification provides little about the mechanisms for implementing model driven transformations between Platform Independent and Platform Specific Models (PIMs and PSMs). These omissions include: 1) Expressing and implementing transformations between models, including mappings from PIMs to PSMs. 2) Implementing transformations in the form of tool support. To formulate answers to these omissions, the structure and content of any PIMs and PSMs that are used as test cases are very important, since transitional mappings between a single PIM and PSM only provides information on the particular modelling strategy and implementation framework involved. The second issue stems from this problem. The time and effort required to develop a suitable model-driven environment for a specific PIM and PSM pairing may in many cases outweigh the advantages that adopting the approach brings."

The presenter wanted to propose a solution to refute the common assumption that the effort to specify a transformation often outweighs the effort to do the transformation directly. He aimed to do this by introducing patterns of mappings between abstract and concrete specifications. The fact that the introduction of an extra level of indirection solves many problems in computer science was acknowledged in the discussions, but it was still argued that mapping between all possible pairs was not a practical problems since all current tools already deal with this, for instance by having an intermediate layer to bridge to the pairs.

4.3   Applying MDA Approach to B2B Applications: A Road Map

This presentation was not actually given for technical reasons, but some of the ideas were nevertheless discussed at the workshop and are presented on the ATL (ATLAS Transformation Language) web site at www.sciences.univ-nantes.fr/lina/atl. The authors of the position paper are Jean Bézivin, Slimane Hammoudi, Denivaldo Lopes and Frédéric Jouault from France. The abstract of the paper is:

"B2B applications are systems that evolve quickly and they are often developed using different technologies, such as XML/EDI, Distributed Components and Web Services. Many technologies supporting B2B applications exist and others will appear. Recently, the Model-Driven Architecture (MDA) approach has been introduced to support the evolution of systems and the harmonization between different technologies. However, before this becomes a reality, some issues need solutions, such as the creation of mappings between meta-models. In this paper, we provide some insights into the definition of mappings and transformation rules."

5   Discussion Session

Following the three position paper sessions, the final session was a discussion on the workshop topics. This session was chaired by Jan Aagedal.

Although it was late in the day, the debate soon became lively. The discussion was sparked by some rather provocative statements on whether we are reinventing the wheel and just wrapping it in new acronyms and flashy terms to make the old concepts unrecognizable. Given that most of the participants are actively working on advancing the field of MDD, many of the participants felt inclined to defend MDD. For instance, the claim that MDD was merely 4GLs all over again was fiercely refuted by characterizing 4GLs as black-box generators, whereas MDD is more of a white-box approach where the models, meta-models, transformations and transformation specifications are all available to the developers, and they can all be customized to fit a particular domain or business. The 4GLs failed because they soon became tool-specific, and all the investments made in use of one 4GL-tool were hard to build upon when one decided to use another tool or to integrate 4GL-generated applications with new applications made with other tools.

MDD is sometimes also met by arguments that it is not new, because there are already working and well-proven open approaches, for instance SDL in the telecom domain. This position was argued against by characterizing such approaches as domain-specific, being well-suited to some problems, but unsuited to others. For instance, SDL is well-suited to protocol design and state-based systems, but not suited for traditional information systems. In addition, it was claimed that SDL is not widely used due to its complexity and the level of detail needed in the specifications, so SDL should not be mentioned as an undisputed success.

Moreover, it was pointed out that, even if MDD has still not demonstrated its full potential, it is indeed promising and with the continuous increase in complexity and rate of change, one must always be moving towards better tools and techniques just to avoid a decrease in productivity, or, as put by one workshop participant: "one has to keep running to be at the same place".

After this existential start, the debate shifted into a more focussed discussion on various topics taking it as agreed that MDD is indeed a serious research area and is not the emperor's new clothes. Below we summarize the discussions for each of the topics that were touched upon.

5.1   Standardized Abstractions

It is common to mention the analogy with traditional programming languages, compilers and assembly instructions when explaining PIMs, transformations and PSMs. Having this in mind, the question was raised as to whether we should strive to identify and standardize higher level abstractions with standard transformations onto 3GLs, in the same manner as a single construct in a 3GL represents many assembly instructions for each supported instruction set.

Most participants acknowledged that it is not possible to find many abstractions that are both general purpose and on a higher abstraction level, and that can also be mapped unambiguously onto several PSMs. However, it is possible to identify and standardize domain-specific abstractions that can have meaningful transformations. Indeed, much future work is needed to identify and standardize domain-specific concepts organized into distinct conceptual models (domain-specific, best-practise meta-models), together with well-defined transformations into more general-purpose conceptual models.

5.2   Traceability

MDD will not be a reality until models, not code, become the primary artifacts in software development. However, models will become first-class citizens in software development only when there are suitable tools to ensure consistency and traceability between models on different levels of abstraction and from different viewpoints. Nowadays, models in mainstream software development are, at best, used to elaborate design decisions, sort out different concepts, and share ideas. The models are then typically put in the archive when the real system development (by which people generally mean coding) starts.

In MDD, model transformations should preserve information to support bi-directional traceability. The links between model elements in the source and the target models should be established during transformation. If one uses an approach based on relations, this is inherent. To some degree, traceability support is already included in a number of tools, but the majority of general modelling tools do not provide it. We expect, however, that as soon as the QVT standard is in place and supported by tool vendors, bidirectional traceability will be supported.

Consistency is different from, but related to, traceability. Whereas traceability typically relates modelling elements in the source and target models of a transformation, consistency relates modelling elements across viewpoints that make up the set of source models. To check consistency between two modelling elements defined in two different modelling languages requires it to be possible to relate modelling elements across languages and perhaps even across meta-languages. How to represent this is an issue that needs further investigation.

5.3   Domain-Specific Languages

The ability to create and relate domain-specific languages (DSLs) is at the core of MDD. If one follows OMG standards, DSLs should be defined as MOF-compliant meta-models, and they should then be supported by domain-customized modelling tools where both the DSL and its accompanying standardized transformations are available. This means that there is a need for domain experts who are able to identify and specify the crucial concepts that are needed in a domain. These people must be experts both in the domain and in abstraction so that they can do language engineering to create DSLs.

When creating a DSL, some standard language definition concepts are needed. In OMG, one uses MOF. IBM has defined a similar approach in Eclipse termed Ecore, and Microsoft has its own solution, sometimes known as the Microsoft Repository. This means that at least three contenders are available as a basis for the standard mechanism to define DSLs, but they are all evolving, so that there will be new versions; as a result, there may be a problem of diversity. However, most of these approaches are quite similar (in fact, Ecore and MOF 2.0 EMOF are very close, and IBM has indicated that these will be aligned), so even if one chooses a single meta-meta-language initially one participant claimed that, based on practical experience, to shift from one meta-meta-language to another is not a major hurdle. The important fact is not that there are competing meta-meta-languages available, but that all the large players (OMG, IBM, Microsoft and others) share the same basic principles of DSL engineering in software development.

However, it is much more difficult to shift from one DSL to another than to shift meta-meta-language, since many models will have been created with the DSL. But this can also be an advantage. With a plethora of DSLs, organizations may become dependent on just a few DSLs. This may, in fact, be used by large enterprises to freeze their investments. If significant investments are made using a proprietary DSL, it may be that the enterprise can secure its investments by ensuring that they can not easily be made available to others because they are defined in the proprietary DSL.

The final issue that was discussed for DSLs was the fact that some domains have the end users using the DSLs, not programmers or software designers. This is only possible if the DSL is supported by a framework that can interpret or execute DSL statements directly. Such a framework needs to have a great deal of predefined behaviour that the DSL interpreter can use. This means that end user DSLs can only be defined in domains that have much standardized behaviour that the end users can relate to.

5.4   Transformation Specification

Even if the QVT standardization seems to be converging, how to specify transformations is still an issue that needs further investigation. Many of the proposed transformation specification approaches are quite detailed and appeal primarily to transformation experts. Indeed, it was claimed that this is a good thing, because transformation specification should be for experts, just as compiler engineering is for the few compiler engineers. On the other hand, it was claimed by others that this is not always true, and that simple transformations should be simple to specify. Indeed, sometimes transformation specifications are useful to read as documentation; it should thus be possible for more than the few experts to read them.

There was also discussion as to whether one transformation language is sufficient, or whether there is a need for different languages for different types of transformation. No conclusions were reached on this, but some scepticism was expressed as to whether an all-purpose transformation language would meet the requirements in all the different domains.

5.5   Success Criteria for QVT and for MDD

The overall success criterion for MDD is that success will have been achieved when the large vendors supply their tool suites with specialized transformers from PIMs to their tools. For instance, detailed knowledge about Oracle 9i is needed to know that hand-written recursive queries can be replaced by "connect by", and this knowledge could be encoded into a tailored transformation targeting an Oracle PSM.

QVT, as an important piece in MDD, should support reuse of transformations. Moreover, QVT must be ready to compete with Java, since most of the transformations today are written in imperative languages such as Java. It was also claimed that QVT should be like XSLT, but better, meaning that it should be easier to use. Finally, QVT should support traceability, for instance by using relations and specific traceability models.

5.6   Executable Models

One approach to executable models is to create a virtual machine, e.g., a UML virtual machine. If this approach is chosen, one must make sure not to be locked to one version of UML, but instead to support an extensible meta-model.

The final topic for discussion was how executable models fit with MDD. It was argued that executable UML contradicts the basic idea of MDA. Indeed, the basic idea of MDA is to abstract away the differences in middleware technologies and we cannot throw this away by creating a new layer that everyone becomes dependent of. Against this, it was argued that model simulation may be useful, especially simulation of partial models, and for this we need executable models of some kind.

6   Conclusions

The workshop, and in particular the discussion session, showed that there are still many unresolved issues to address before the vision of model-driven development becomes a reality. Before models can be the primary artifacts of system development, both practical issues, such as appropriate tooling, and more fundamental issues, such as the theory of transformation composition, need to have acceptable solutions. However, many researchers are focusing on such topics and they all share the common vision of MDD, and together with continued standardization, the MDD reality seems certain to emerge.

Component-Oriented Programming (WCOP 2004)*

Jan Bosch[1], Clemens Szyperski[2], and Wolfgang Weck[3]

[1] University of Groningen, Department of Computing Science, P.O. Box 800,
9700 AV Groningen, The Netherlands
Jan.Bosch@cs.rug.nl
http://segroup.cs.rug.nl
[2] Microsoft, USA
CSzypers@microsoft.com
http://research.microsoft.com/~cszypers/
[3] Independent Consultant, Switzerland

Abstract. This report covers the ninth Workshop on Component-Oriented Programming (WCOP). WCOP has been affiliated with ECOOP since its inception in 1996. The report summarizes the contributions made by authors of accepted position papers as well as those made by all attendees of the workshop sessions.

1   Introduction

WCOP 2004, held in conjunction with ECOOP 2003 in Darmstadt, Germany, was the ninth workshop in the successful series of workshops on component-oriented programming. The previous workshops were held in conjunction with earlier ECOOP conferences in Linz, Austria; Jyväskylä, Finland; Brussels, Belgium; Lisbon, Portugal; Sophia Antipolis, France; Budapest, Hungary; Malaga, Spain and Darmstadt, Germany The first workshop, in 1996, focused on the principal idea of software components and worked towards definitions of terms. In particular, a high-level definition of what a software component is was formulated. WCOP97 concentrated on compositional aspects, architecture and gluing, substitutability, interface evolution and non-functional requirements. In 1998, the workshop addressed industrial practice and developed a major focus on the issues of adaptation. The next year, the workshop moved on to address issues of structured software architecture and component frameworks, especially in the context of large systems. WCOP 2000 focused on component composition, validation and refinement and the use of component technology in the software industry. The year after, containers, dynamic reconfiguration, conformance and

---

* The title of this report should be referenced as "Report from the ECOOP 2004 Eighth International Workshop on Component-Oriented Programming (WCOP 2004)".

J. Malenfant and B.M. Østvold (Eds.): ECOOP 2004, LNCS 3344, pp. 158–168, 2004.
© Springer-Verlag Berlin Heidelberg 2004

quality attributes were the main focus. WCOP 2002 has an explicit focus on dynamic reconfiguration of component systems, that is, the overlap between COP and dynamic architectures. Last year, the workshop addressed predictable assembly, model-driven architecture and separation of concerns. The 2004 instance of the workshop had a technical and an industrialisation focus. In the technical focus, predicting performance, testing and aspect-oriented software development in the context of component-based software engineering were discussed. In the second focus, issues including the application of CBSE in the context of embedded systems, an analysis of the past, present and future of components and the results of a large, European initiative, CBSENet, were discussed. WCOP 2004 had been announced as follows:

WCOP 2004 seeks position papers on the important field of component-oriented programming (COP). WCOP 2004 is the ninth event in a series of highly successful workshops, which took place in conjunction with every ECOOP since 1996. COP is the natural extension of object-oriented programming to the realm of independently extensible systems. COP aims at producing software components for a component market and for late composition. Composers are third parties, possibly the end users, who are not able or willing to change components. Several component technologies emerged, including CORBA/CCM, COM/COM+, J2EE/EJB, and .NET. There is an increasing appreciation of software architecture for component-based systems and the consequent effects on organizational processes and structures, as well as the software industry in large. WCOP 2004 emphasizes the dynamic composition of component-based systems and component-oriented development processes. Dynamically composable software needs clearly specified and documented contracts, standardized architectures, specifications of functional properties and quality attributes, and mechanisms for dynamic discovery and binding. A typical example is web services. A service is a running instance that has specific quality attributes, while a component needs to be first deployed, installed, loaded, and instantiated. Comparing service and component composition models is interesting and a proposed workshop focus. Flexible development processes (such as agile ones) and component-based development support each other in that the use of existing components can reduce the development effort. Positions on development processes relating to the use of components are welcome. Finally, we also solicit reports on practical experience with component-oriented software, where the emphasis is on interesting lessons learned.

COP aims at producing software components for a component market and for late composition. Composers are third parties, possibly the end users, who are not able or willing to change components. This requires standards to allow independently created components to interoperate, and specifications that put the composer into the position to decide what can be composed under which conditions. On these grounds, WCOP'96 led to the following definition: A component is a unit of composition with contractually specified interfaces and explicit context dependencies only. Components can be deployed independently and are subject to composition by third parties.

Often discussed in the context of COP are quality attributes (a.k.a. system qualities). A key problem that results from the dual nature of components between technology and markets are the non-technical aspects of components, including marketing, distribution, selection, licensing, and so on. While it is already hard to establish functional properties under free composition of components, non-functional and non-technical aspects tend to emerge from composition and are thus even harder to control. In the context of specific architectures, it remains an open question what can be said about the quality attributes of systems composed according to the architecture's constraints. As in previous years, we could identify a trend away from the specifics of individual components and towards the issues associated with composition and integration of components in systems. While the call asked for position papers on the relationship to web-services and services in general, we did not receive papers on that subject. An emphasis on anchoring methods in specifications and architecture was noticeable, going beyond the focus on run-time mechanisms in the previous year. Ten papers by authors were accepted for presentation at the workshop and publication in the workshop proceedings; for one paper the authors withdrew the paper from the workshop; for one paper no presenter showed up at the workshop. About 25 participants from around the world participated in the workshop. The workshop was organized into four morning sessions with presentations, one afternoon breakout session with three focus groups, and one final afternoon session gathering reports from the breakout session and discussing future direction.

2   Presentations

This section summarizes briefly the contributions of the nine presenters, as grouped into four sessions, i.e. analysis, performance, direction of CBSE and application of CBSE.

2.1   Analysis

The first paper, presented by Thomas Cottenier, discusses the use of aspect-oriented programming (AOP) techniques for non-invasive component adaptation at load-time, compose-time and runtime. The paper starts from the observation that existing approaches to AOP operate at the code level, rather than at the component level, destroy the locality of runtime control flow and break component encapsulation. These issues complicate the predictability and certification of component-based systems exploiting aspects. The paper proceeds with identifying that different types of aspects are used in different phases of the lifecycle, e.g. resource management aspects at deployment time, adapter aspects at composition time and dynamic adaptation aspects at run-time. The authors propose the use of an aspect-sensitive component profile that provides expressiveness for semantic contracts, temporal properties, quality attributes and access control contracts. This component profile is than used in an MDA-style form of aspect weaving to obtain the desired component and system behaviour. Judith Stafford presented the second paper. This paper starts with the observation that software development is compositional in nature, but that most analysis approaches assume complete system. Consequently, the system needs to be flattened, which is expensive and may be infeasible if external, e.g. COTS, components are present do not allow access to their internals. To achieve compositional analysis, each component in a system should be accompanied with an analytic asset. Once these assets are available, compositional analysis can be performed by analyzing input-output pathways and the specific configuration of the components in the system. The paper raises, as open issues, the selection of analysis algorithms, the representation of analytical assets and packaging of these assets.

2.2   Performance

Viktoria Firus presented the first paper in the performance session. This paper discusses the notion of parametric performance contracts for components and the compositionality of these contracts. The initial observation in the paper is that early evaluation of software architectures is important as the design decisions taken during the architecture design phase have a large impact on performance. The evaluation can be used to select the best design decision. The authors identify three dimensions that are of importance for quality predicting models, i.e. validity, compositionality and parametricity. Parametricity refers to the need for prediction models to reflect the context dependencies of a component. The authors then proceed to define parametric performance contracts. The approach taken models the performance of a component service by a distribution which itself depends on the performance distribution of the external services called. Then an overview of existing work was given. The discussion following the paper presentation focused on the difficulty of providing accurate performance predictions, especially since many performance issues result from resource contention rather than execution. An alternative approach was presented by Trevor Parsons. The authors present a framework for automatically detecting and assessing performance anti-patterns in component-based systems using run-time analysis. The authors start by highlighting the importance of performance in the context of component-based systems. Problems of performance analysis in these systems results from the large amounts of data, the lack of support for achieving solutions and the lack of bottleneck identification. The authors attack the problem by identifying performance anti-patterns. These patterns are identified by proposed framework. The framework consists of three main parts, i.e. monitoring, detection and assessment and visualization. The authors employ data mining algorithms to deal with the large amounts of data generated during monitoring. During the discussion, the main topic was that the approach seems promising, but needs to be employed in practice before its applicability can be determined.

2.3   Direction of CBSE

Different from the first two sessions that were very technical, the third session was of a more conceptual nature, evaluating the notion of component-based software engineering (CBSE). The first paper, presented by Jean-Guy Schneider, discusses an assessment of the past, present and future of CBSE. The authors analyze the achievements of the CBSE community using six factors, i.e. functionality (what is/does a software component?), interaction (how do we compose components?), quality (what results in a composition of components?), management (how to publish and retrieve existing components?), evolution and tools (what support is needed for application development?) and methodology (how to use CBSE, e.g. process and development models). The conclusion of the authors is that much has been achieved, but that especially the methodology, quality and management factors require more research before these can be considered solved. The discussion around the paper centred on the question whether progress actually had been made in the CBSE community or not! The second paper is this session, presented by Stefano de Panfilis, discusses the results of the CBSEnet network of excellence and open issues and concerns of CBSE. CBSEnet, as a project, has resulted in several valuable outcomes, including a classification model, a landscape document and a portal. The landscape document presents concepts and process issues, business concerns, product related topics, issues surrounding COTS components, domain specific concerns of component systems, e.g. business information systems, geographical information systems and embedded systems, and related paradigms, such as service-oriented computing and model driven engineering. The presenter stresses the importance of realizing that CBSE is not a goal in itself, but a means to improve productivity, quality and time-to-market.

2.4   Application of CBSE

The first paper in the final session, presented by Jasminka Matevska-Meyer, addressed the description of software architectures for supporting component deployment and dynamic reconfiguration. The authors define the requirements that an architecture description language (ADL) should satisfy, i.e. expressiveness for supporting dynamic configuration, runtime component behaviour description, timing constraints, runtime dependencies and composition features for describing subsystems. Subsequently, existing ADLs were evaluated against these requirements, leading to the conclusion that no ADL supported all requirements sufficiently. As an initial step towards a solution, the authors presented a meta-model and a reconfiguration manager. The authors identified a number of open issues, including a concrete ADL syntax for their approach, the need for a resource mapping view and a prototype implementation. The final paper was presented by Ivica Crnkovic and addressed the use of software components in the context of embedded systems. The presenter started by explaining the developments in the embedded industry, especially the automotive industry, where the demands on software have changed from basic to complex functions, causing multiple functions to share sensors, networks, processing nodes and actuators. The challenge is to offer an open but dependable platform for automotive applications, i.e. to balance flexibility and predictability. The presenter proceeded to distinguish between large and small embedded systems, focusing on the latter type. The main conclusion from the presentation was that component technology for embedded systems needs to focus on pre-deployment composition, the particularities of the run-time environment, fine-grained components, white-box reuse and source-code level component exchange. Concluding, component-technologies are becoming feasible for embedded systems, but require adaptation to the context of embedded systems.

3   Break-Out Sessions

In the afternoon the workshop participants were organized in break-out sessions addressing three specific topics, i.e. compositional reasoning on quality attributes, runtime re-configuration and re-deployment and, metaphorically, "The Big Picture". Each group had a nominated scribe who, as named in the subsection titles below, contributed the session summaries.

Compositional Reasoning on Quality Attributes by Ralf Reussner

This break-out group was concerned with the question how to predict or guarantee quality attributes of a component based system given the quality attributes of inner components and the architecture of their interconnection. This discussion started by listing and classifying the quality attributes the participants were interested in. A classification and a comprehensive overview on quality attributes is given in the ISO 9126 standard. Quality attributes of particular interest were: availability / reliability, performance (throughput, reaction time, response time) and resource consumption (memory, cache, etc.). We agreed to consider "scalability" a meta-quality attribute, as it describes changes of a quality attribute by varying resources, such as the response time of a clustered database application depending on a changing number of processors. Quality attributes can be classified according to the kind of statements one wants to derive from them. (a) predictions are of concern for quantitatively measured quality attributes, such as reliability or performance. (b) Guarantees are made by non-quantitative attributes, such as correctness, safety or security. (c) Monotonic or preservation statements are of concern if quality attributes can be measured in a discrete ordered scale (such as "low, medium, good"). As a special case, this scale includes all quantitatively measured attributes. Generally, quality attributes can be classified according their kind of metric: stochastic / deterministic and discrete / continuous. That is, the correlation among attributes depends at least also on the system's architecture (in the example, determining the presence or absence of redundancy). One factor of the complexity of reasoning on quality attributes are their interdependencies. A change of a system usually affects more than one quality attribute. For example, improving security by adding encrypted communication channels will most likely affect performance due to the computation costs for encryption and decryption. Remarkably, a pair of attributes is not always positively or negatively correlated. For example, adding replicated computing resources to increase performance may also increase reliability due to an increased fault-tolerance. However, exactly the inverse relationship also exists: by adding on a load-balancer and increasing network-traffic the replication of computing resources improves performance but lowers the reliability of the overall system. An important issue is to understand, that basically all quality attributes of a component are not constant properties of the component itself, but are highly dependent on the component context. Basically, the quality attributes depend on three groups of influence factors:

- The usage profile of the component: The way a component's services are used (the frequency, the parameters, etc) depend on the component's context. However, it is clear that the quality exhibited depend on this usage profile. For reliability, this is true by definition, as software reliability is defined as a function of the profile. However, the performance of a component service will also frequently depend significantly on the arguments provided for service parameters. (A download of 10 KB will be considerably faster than a download of 20 MB.)
- The use-relationship to other components: A component service most often makes use of several other external services. As a consequence, the quality of a service also depends on the qualities of external services. An highly unreliable external service will also influence the reliability of services building upon it.
- The deployed-on-relationship: Each component is deployed on resources, such as processing nodes, network connections or other resources. Obviously, the performance of the deployment hardware, the middleware, virtual machines, and the like influences reliability and performance of a component heavily.

Resource contention, leading to discontinuous quality behaviour, can happen via the use-relationship and the deployed-on-relationship. Any compositional reasoning has to take both relationships into account. The composition of quality attribute values can be either symmetric or asymmetric. Asymmetric composition of quality attribute values happens, if a component "inherits" the quality of another component. For example, an insecure component used within a secured environment (such as a sandbox) will become "secure". Symmetric composition of quality attribute occurs when the quality of an outer component can be computed by a commutative function of the inner components. The composition itself can be performed by many composition-operators. In principle, each architectural pattern or style defines a composition operator. However, one could ask for the minimal set of basic composition operators. Any composition operator should be expressible as a finite combination of basic composition operators. Some candidates for such basic composition operators can be (motivated by operators of process algebras): parallel, sequential, alternative, refinement, extension. Finally, we listed different calculi and their use for prediction models: Queuing Models (performance), Petri-Nets (concurrency), Finite State Machines (protocols), Markov-Models (reliability), Process Algebras (protocol), symbolic (logic) representations (memory, performance), timed-logics (time, liveness). The following participants participated in the break-out group: Steffen Becker, Thomas Cottenier, Viktoria Firius, Trevor Parsons, Ralf Reussner, Sibylle Schupp and Richard Torkar.

Runtime Re-configuration and Re-deployment by Jasminka Matevska-Meyer

The main concern of this break-out group was the definition of the scope of runtime re-configuration and re-deployment and the main issues to enable them.

First we compared the common goals of our projects and thus identified the topics of interest. This helped us to distinguish re-configuration from re-engineering approaches. Re-configuration is the process of (a) changing, (b) re-building and (c) re-deploying a system. It is thus a subset of re-engineering processes, including techniques to perform the necessary changes to the system while maintaining its consistency. The process of reconfiguration can include the identification of change requests (e.g. context dependencies), but it mainly focuses on processing those change requests. Hence, it only ensures the technical consistency of the system. Questions concerning the sense of the reconfiguration are to be answered by re-engineering approaches. Runtime re-configuration takes place at system runtime. The affected sub-system should be changed, re-build and re-deployed at system runtime. Runtime re-deployment should also include consistency checks of the system. It can be seen as an extension of hot deployment and dynamic reloading including consistency checks. We consider "rich" components (with information on services, connections, composition properties, hence more than mere executable code). The main problem here is the application at runtime. To successfully perform a runtime re-configuration we need much more information about the running system than its structural dependencies. We need an appropriate architecture description including (1) structural view (describing the hierarchical system structure and enabling its composition), (2) dynamic view (description of the system's runtime behaviour, particularly concerning the use dependencies among instances of components) and (3) resource mapping view. A well defined mapping between the views including relationships between description and implementation (reflection) is essential to identify and isolate the affected sub-system. Furthermore, we need techniques for checking consistency like monitoring, simulation, model checking etc. For identifying necessary changes we need an additional definition of environmental (contextual) dependencies. It becomes clear that enabling runtime re-configuration while maintaining the consistency of the system is a very complex problem. So, a legitimate question about the sense of those approaches arises. There are a variety of systems which are characterised through high availability (e.g. mission critical systems) and have to be changed at runtime. Performance aspects, like load balancing (horizontal and vertical) or resource driven adaptation (foraging) could also trigger a runtime reconfiguration. Finally, our group briefly proposed our concrete approaches concerning runtime re-configuration of component-based systems: (1) architecture-based (PIRMA) considering runtime dependency graphs, (2) resource-contract driven (CoDAMoS) as a context driven adaptation of mobile services and (3) Programming driven (XParts) treating dynamic distributable Java components. The following participants participated in the break-out group: Anders Gravdal, Jasminka Matevska-Meyer, Peter Rigole, Ulf Schreier and Bart de Win.

The Big Picture by Jean-Guy Schneider

In the following, we will summarize the results of the discussion of the breakout group on "the Big Picture". The main motivation of this breakout group was to step back from current trends and set component-based Software Engineering

(CBSE) into a bigger picture. In this context, we discussed various issues related to CBSE from a broader perspective and tried to come up with some directions towards which the discipline might be heading. As a starting point, we discussed the question where we could apply a component-based approach for software development. It was argued by one group member that CBSE is very time consuming, requires dual application development, and considerable knowledge in the respective application domain is essential. Furthermore, a group of experts is needed to apply CBSE successfully ("For most normal people CBSE is way too hard!"). In this context it was also mentioned that the existence of reusable components is not only a precondition for CBSE, but also a sign of a maturing domain. Hence, we concluded that CBSE can only be applied in mature domains where reusable components already exist. But what are the problems of finding reusable components and composing them in such a domain? It was stated that component repositories are not the issue, but skills in social dialogs are: talking to people to find out whether a component you need is available seems to be a much more promising approach than searching in a repository. Dedicated component repositories are not easy to set up and use as it is difficult to come up with suitable ontologies to classify components. Furthermore, ad-hoc search strategies are often more successful ("Why worry about UDDI, one can use Google"). What about composing components? It was argued that the real complexity is not in interfacing with existing components, but the real problem lies in the semantics of the data. Hence, we concluded that component models should focus (more) on standardizing component connections ("Standards are the key to setting up a component market at all"). So what is the situation with web services? One group member pointed out that web services are basically a trick by commercial vendors to make both developers and end users select their respective platforms, but, as such, are nothing else than components offering their services on the web. Hence, we came to the agreement that "web service" is probably not such a good term and should be replaced by something like "e-Service". There was also some consensus that the people in the discipline are working too much on the solution domain (components, component models, composition environments etc.), but not enough in the problem domain (what kind of problems are suitable for CBSE). However, we acknowledged that CBSE has solved many technical issues - other areas have been addressed, but not yet solved. Does CBSE cover all aspects of Software Engineering? This turned out to be quite a difficult question to answer. After some discussion it was suggested that CBSE covers some of the traditional SE life-cycle activities, but it does a rather poor job when it comes down to requirements engineering. However, we failed to clearly identify which aspects are covered well and which ones poorly (or not at all). Hence, this is a topic where further investigations are needed. Finally, we addressed the question whether CBSE is just hype and will disappear in five years or is it here to stay. Not surprisingly (and probably due to a certain bias within the group), we agreed that CBSE is here to say and will not disappear in the near future. Unfortunately, we did not have the time to talk about many more issues that were raised during the lively discussion. Summing up what we were able to talk about, we came to the conclusions that

- it is the market, legal issues, and standardization, but not technology which will govern the success of CBSE,
- CBSE works well for product lines and in-house development, but not on the open market, and
- specialized people are needed to cope with the technology/complexity to develop applications using component-based Software Engineering approaches.

The following people participated in this breakout group (in alphabetical order): Ivica Crnkovic, Bernhard Groene, Stefano De Panfilis, Jean-Guy Schneider, David Thomas, and Hoang Truong.

4   Final Words

As organizers, we look back on yet another highly successful workshop on component-oriented programming. We are especially pleased with the constantly evolving range of topics addressed in the workshops, the enthusiasm of the attendees, the quality of the contributions and the continuing large attendance of more than 25 and often as many as 40 persons. We would like to thank all participants of and contributors to the ninth international workshop on component-oriented programming. In particular, we would like to thank the scribes of the break-out groups.

5   Accepted Papers

The full papers and additional information and material can be found on the workshop's Web site (http://research.microsoft.com/cszypers/events/WCOP2004/). This site also has the details for the Microsoft Research technical report that gathers the papers and this report. The following list of accepted papers is sorted by the name of the presenting author.

1. Ivica Crnkovic (Mlardalen University, Sweden). "Component-based approach for embedded systems"
2. Thomas Cottenier, Tzilla Elrad (Illinois IT, USA). "Validation of context-dependent aspect-oriented adaptations to components"
3. Jasminka Matevska-Meyer, Wilhelm Hasselbring and Ralf H. Reussner (University of Oldenburg, Germany). "Software architecture description supporting component deployment and system runtime reconfiguration"
4. Stefano De Panfilis (Engineering Ingegneria Informatica S.p.A., Italy) and Arne J. Berre (SINTEF, Norway). "Open issues and concerns on component-based software engineering"
5. Trevor Parsons (Dublin City U, Ireland) and John Murphy (University College Dublin, Ireland). "A framework for automatically detecting and assessing performance antipatterns in component based systems using run-time analysis"

6. Ralf H. Reussner, Viktoria Firus and Steffen Becker (University of Oldenburg, Germany). "Parametric performance contracts for software components and their compositionality"
7. Jean-Guy Schneider and Jun Han (Swinburne University of Technology, Australia). "Components - the past, the present, and the future"
8. Judith A. Stafford (Tufts University, USA) and John D. McGregor Clemson University, USA). "Top-down analysis for bottom-up development"
9. Amir Zeid, Michael Messiha and Sami Youssef (American University Cairo, Egypt). "Applicability of component-based development in high-performance systems"

10th Workshop on Mobile Object Systems*

Ciarán Bryce[1] and Crzegorz Czajkowski[2]

[1] Object Systems Group,
University of Geneva, Switzerland
Ciaran.Bryce@unige.ch
[2] Sun Microsystem Laboratories,
Mountain View, California, USA
Grzegorz.Czajkowski@sun.com

Introduction

The ECOOP Workshop on Mobile Object Systems is now in its 10th year. Over the years, the workshop has dealt with topics related to the movement of code and data between application platforms, security, operating system support, application quality of service, and programming language paradigms. In many cases, the workshop has been a forum to discuss traditional object-oriented issues, since mobility influences such a broad spectrum of topics.

To celebrate the 10th anniversary of the workshop, we decided to accept papers dealing with all aspects of mobility. Eight presentations in total were made at the workshop, and some time was allocated to discussion of each. The tone of the discussions was informal. The workshop took place on Monday, June 14th, 2004, in Oslo University, just prior to the main ECOOP conference.

The Talks

The presentations made at the workshop were the following:

- Portable CPU Accounting in Java by Jarle Hulaas and Walter Binder.
- Reducing the Overhead of Portable CPU Accounting in Java by Jarle Hulaas and Walter Binder.
- An Environment for Decentralized Adapted Services: A Blueprint by Rüdiger Kapitza, Franz J. Hauck and Hans Reiser.
- An Extensible Directory Service for Efficient Service Integration by Walter Binder, Ion Constantinescu and Boi Faltings.
- Mobile Code, Systems Biology and Metamorphic Programming by Christian Tschudin.
- Perspectives on Mobile Code by Eric Jul.

---

* The title of this report should be referenced as "Report from the ECOOP 2004 10th Workshop on Mobile Object Systems".

J. Malenfant and B.M. Østvold (Eds.): ECOOP 2004, LNCS 3344, pp. 169–176, 2004.

- Proactive Resource Manipulation for Agile Computing by Niranjan Suri, Marco Carvalho and Jeffrey M. Bradshaw.
- A Security Model for Autonomous Computing Systems by Ciarán Bryce.

Jarle Hulaas from EPFL in Switzerland kicked-off the workshop by presenting joint work with Walter Binder entitled Portable CPU Accounting in Java for the first part of the talk, and Reducing the Overhead of Portable CPU Accounting in Java for the second part. Following an approach entirely based on portable bytecode transformation schemes, in order to allow ubiquitous support for CPU accounting, the presented research has yielded several significant improvements to J-RAF, a previous effort on portable CPU accounting in Java.

Accounting and controlling the resource consumption of applications and individual software components is crucial in server environments that host components on behalf of various clients, in order to protect the host from malicious or badly programmed code. Java and the Java Virtual Machine (JVM) are being increasingly used as the programming language and deployment platform for such servers (Java 2 Enterprise Edition, Servlets, Java Server Pages, Enterprise Java Beans). Moreover, accounting and limiting the resource consumption of applications is a prerequisite to prevent denial-of-service (DoS) attacks in mobile object systems, for which Java is the predominant programming language. However, currently the Java language and standard Java runtime systems lack mechanisms for resource management that could be used to limit the resource consumption of hosted components or to charge the clients for the resource consumption of their deployed components.

Prevailing approaches to providing resource control in Java-based platforms rely on a modified JVM, on native code libraries, or on program transformations. Resource control based on program transformations at the bytecode level offers an important advantage over the other approaches, because it is independent of a particular JVM and underlying operating system. It works with standard Java runtime systems and may be integrated into existing server and mobile object environments. Furthermore, this approach enables resource control within embedded systems based on modern Java processors, which provide a JVM implemented in hardware that cannot be easily modified.

CPU accounting in the initial version of J-RAF relied on a high-priority scheduling thread that executed periodically in order to aggregate the CPU consumption of individual threads and to adjust the running threads' priorities according to given scheduling policies. This approach hampered the claim that J-RAF enabled fully portable resource management in Java, because the scheduling of threads within the JVM is not well specified and the semantics of thread priorities in Java is not precisely defined. Hence, while some JVMs seem to provide preemptive scheduling ensuring that a thread with high-priority will execute whenever it is ready to run, other JVMs do not respect thread priorities at all. Therefore, scheduling code written for environments using J-RAF may not exhibit the same behaviour when executed on different JVM implementations.

To overcome this limitation, the new version J-RAF2 (the Java Resource Accounting Framework, Second Edition) comes with a new scheme for CPU accounting. In J-RAF2 each thread accounts for its own CPU consumption, taking the number of executed JVM bytecode instructions as platform-independent measurement unit. Periodically, each thread aggregates the collected information concerning its CPU consumption within an account that is shared by all threads of a software component and executes scheduling code that may take actions in order to prevent the threads of a component from exceeding their granted CPU quota. In this way, the CPU accounting scheme of J-RAF2 does not rely on a dedicated scheduling thread, but the scheduling task is distributed among all threads in the system. Hence, the new approach does not rely on the underlying scheduling of the JVM.

During the second part of his presentation, Jarle Hulaas covered different optimization schemes, the goal of which is to lower the additional execution time needed by code transformed by the J-RAF2 tool. Such optimization techniques essentially consist in trying to minimize the number of inserted bytecode instructions, or adding the CPU account as last argument in all method profiles, including the JDK. In the end, the measurements showed an overhead dropping from 300% (for older JVMs) or 40% (for the most recent JVMs from Sun and IBM) down to around 27%. With certain approximation schemes designed to further reduce the amount of inserted accounting instructions, but at the expense of a loss of precision, the overhead would even be as low as 20%.

Rüdiger Kapitza then presented joint work with Franz J. Hauck and Hans Reiser from the Universities of Ulm and Erlangen, entitled An Environment for Decentralized Adapted Services: A Blueprint

This talk described the design and implementation of an infrastructure for service provision that ranges from the traditional client-server to a peer-to-peer approach. This infrastructure is based on the Fragmented Object model. In effect, nodes can negotiate their entry into a service group. The aim of the system is to combine the advantages of both client-server and peer-to-peer.

In the last few years peer-to-peer systems have been one of the most evolving research areas. Apart form the great public demand, the use of peer resources is a major reason for this. In pure peer-to-peer systems, every peer has almost equal responsibilities and provides resources for the whole system. This concept has certain drawbacks in the context of a high number of nodes participating only for short periods of time or peers which try to attack the system. In these cases the overall system performance and service quality degrades or the system may even collapse. In contrast, traditional client-server applications can cope with these problems quite smoothly but offer no possibility to exploit client-side resources.

To fill the gap between the traditional client-sever model and a peer-to-peer based approach, the authors propose a model entitled Decentralised Adaptive Services. This concept enables the usage of client-side resources in a controlled, secure fashion and provides services in a scalable, fault-tolerant manner. Decentralised adaptive services consist of a fragmented object which is spread over a dynamic set of peers. Each part of the object might be replicated in the scope of the peer set for fault tolerance or load balancing reasons. Furthermore each part of the service is mobile and can migrate on demand of the service within the scope of the peer set. Thus a decentralised, adaptive service can be seen as a distributed mobile agent. The peer set dynamically expands or shrinks depending on the participating peers. In this way, decentralised adaptive services are comparable to peer-to-peer systems. In contrast to peer-to-peer systems, where each new peer does not have to support the system. First a peer has to signal the willingness to support the service and provide information about the offered resources. Second the decentralised adaptive service has to decide if the offering is accepted and in what way the provided resources can be used in the context of the service. In fact a decentralised adaptive service can dynamically change the internal service model from a client-sever scenario where client-side resources are simply not used to a peer-to-peer based approach by accepting only peers which offer resources and give each peer the same responsibilities for service provision.

The aim of the Environment for Decentralised Adaptive Services (EDAS) is to provide the basic concepts and mechanisms for the development and the operation of decentralised adaptive services. This includes mechanisms for group membership, resource monitoring and management, mobility, and mechanisms for the use of resources of partially trusted or untrustworthy peers.

Walter Binder presented joint work with Ion Constantinescu and Boi Faltings from EPFL, Switzerland entitled An Extensible Directory Service for Efficient Service Integration. The talk presented two techniques for improving the quality of service of an Internet directory service. The first is the addition of sessions, the goal of which is to ensure that an interacting client sees the same view of the directory despite changes that might occur in the services registered. The second modification is a framework for the deployment of ranking functions in the form of mobile code. The code is verified on deployment to ensure safety. An API for these extensions was also presented.

In a future service-oriented Internet, service discovery, integration, and orchestration will be major building blocks. One particularly important issue is the efficient interaction between directory services and service composition engines. In previous work, the authors designed special index structures for the efficient discovery of services based on their input/output behaviour. Each service is characterized by the set of its required input parameters (name and type) and the set of the output parameters provided by the service. The indexing technique is based on the Generalised Search Tree (GiST), proposed as a unifying framework by Hellerstein. Moreover, the authors have also developed service composition algorithms that incrementally retrieve service descriptions from a directory service during the service integration process. The composition problem is specified by a set of available inputs and a set of required outputs. The service integration algorithm creates a workflow that describes the sequence of service invocation and the passing of parameters in order to obtain the required results.

The authors present two recent extensions to their directory, service integration sessions and user-defined ranking functions. The session concept provides a consistent long-term view of the directory data which is necessary to solve complex service integration problems. It is implemented in a way to support a large number of concurrent sessions. Custom ranking-functions allow to execute user-defined application-specific heuristics directly within the directory, close to the data, in order to transfer the best results for a query first. As a consequence, the tranfer of a large number of unnecessary results can be avoided, thus saving network bandwidth. As different service integration algorithms require different ranking heuristics (e.g., forward chaining, backward chaining, etc.) it is important to have a flexible way to dynamically install new ranking functions inside the directory. As custom ranking functions may be abused for attacks, the directory imposes severe restrictions on the code of these functions.

Christian Tschudin from the University of Basel in Switzerland presented M obile C ode, System s B iology and M etam orphic P rogram m ing. The talk discussed some commonalities between computer science and life sciences. Christian Tschudin argued that the lack of acceptance of mobile code is mainly due to the poor general understanding we have of large systems, and that this weakness also is hampering advances in life sciences. Suggestions are made to build methodologies that might benefit both sciences.

The interpretation offered is that mobile code, if one wants to focus on its failure so far, hit the systems wall right from the beginning. Only its very restricted forms (Applets, update deployment) have been successful, while the fully autonomous versions of mobile code were rejected, not so much because of the psychological problem of losing control, but because of the inablity of its proponents to predict the resulting behavior at the system level. Both sides, computer science and system biology, lack engineering know-how about the assembly of mobile code fragments and molecular pathways.

A first avenue presented by the speaker is to cut a slice through the design space such that at least some form of processing can be engineered and tailored for specific requirements. Taking the hypothetical task of creating an artificial cell from scratch, this would mean to first come up with basic building blocks, transistor like, and to build a hierarchy of complexity abstractions up to the point where one can program such a cell. The analogy in the networking area would be the GRID where the next service level is achieved by adding a coordination layer to an existing infrastructure. A basic belief and hope of this approach is that all additional levels of complexity can still be mastered, even for molecular or for otherwise massive computing systems.

The other approach is basically bottom up and is a propagation of the methods found in molecular biology: It consists in turning the basic exploratory instruments into a generative tool by combinatorial means and blind mutation. Translated into computer science this means that one explores the design space in a methodological way instead of cutting out a slice. By generating and evaluating a huge number of program candidates, new solutions can be extracted from the program space that an engineer would never dream of. This second approach is specifically promising for mobile code.

The Fraglet system starts with a simple and executable model that blends code and data: Whether some mobile item is named a data packet or a mobile code fragment becomes a (human) interpretation which is irrelevant. Writing

Fraglet code resembles very much the programming with monadified functions a la metamorphic computing and is tedious at best (for humans). Although it is conceivable to use Fraglets as a target for a BioAmbient compiler, one sees a more attractive use in exploring algorithmic solutions outside the range induced or imposed by a modeling environment. The belief in this case is that search strategies for exploring program space can remain simple while producing high quality results in reasonable time.

In conclusion, complex (man made) systems are a recent challenge both in computer science and biology. The author argues that advances in mobile code research will be linked to progress in this area. There is a natural affinity between mobile code and the corresponding level of autonomous molecules that has become visible in the research literature and that was anticipated in the metaphorical speech of early mobile code research. In another ten years we will better understand their relationship.

Eric Jul from the University of Copenhagen then gave an invited talk on object mobility. The talk compared issues and challenges facing mobile object system designers today, with those faced by the Emerald system designers over 20 years ago. Interestingly, there are close similarities, despite the fact that Emerald was initially designed for a local area network of machines and current object systems aim for the Internet or pervasive computing environments.

One of the issues that all application designers face is when to migrate an object. Moving an object A can also require moving objects that closely communicate with A, since otherwise, the advantage of migrating A is offset by the overheads of the resulting communication between A and these objects. The Emerald system dealt with this issue using the **attach** command, which allowed the application to specify the set of objects to move with an object. Another mobility issue that designers still face is to locate objects. In Emerald, the fix command allowed an application to bind an object to a specific machine, so that mobility can be controlled to a certain extent.

So what are the new challenges for object mobility today? Perhaps the answer lies in how mobility will be exploited in emerging applications, notably in the pervasive computing domain.

Afterwards, **Niranjan Suri** and **Marco Carvalho** from the Institute for Human and Machine Cognition (USA) and Lancaster University (UK) presented joint work with Jeffrey M. Bradshaw entitled Proactive Resource Manipulation for Agile Computing.

This talk's subject deals with the exploitation and active manipulation of any available computing resources in order to get a job done. Resource manipulation may even include physical displacement of the computer. The approach also generalizes a number of domains, including peer-to-peer, active networking and mobile agents.

Exploitation of a resource discovery involves assigning a task to the node that contains the resource. The request to use the resource is handled by the middleware operating on the node. One of the key concepts in the approach is the use of mobile code in order to provide complete flexibility in how the resource is used. For example, suppose node A contains spare CPU capacity that the agile computing middleware plans to exploit in order to carry out a computation. In order to use that capacity, the middleware will dispatch code that embeds the computation to node A, which in turn will instantiate and execute the code. Similarly, in order to use a node's excess storage capacity, code that is capable of receiving, holding, and serving data would be dispatched. In the same way, in order to use network bandwidth, code that is responsible for relaying data would be dispatched. Mobile code plays a key enabling role in the realization of agile computing without which the system could not be opportunistic. If a new, previously unexpected node with resources is discovered in the military settings we have been investigating, the probability that this node already contains the code necessary to service the request at hand is minimal. Dynamically pushing code allows any resource that is discovered to be put to use as needed.

Policies play an important role in regulating the autonomous behavior of agile computing middleware. If we look at agile computings role as "exploiting the wiggle room" through taking advantage of underutilized system resources, the role of policy is to define and bound the wiggle room so that people are comfortable with allowing their resources to be manipulated and used by the agile computing middleware. The middleware relies on the existence of policies previously defined by humans that constrain the manipulation of resources. For example, policies may be used to govern the movement of the robotic platforms. Policies are defined in the KAoS framework and may range from basic constraints (a ground robot may not venture into water) to safety constraints (a robot must stay a minimum of three feet away from a human) to operational constraints (a robot must not be positioned in the middle of a road and thereby blocking traffic). Policies may also govern various aspects of information feeds (e.g., latency, resolution, access control) from sensor resources. At a more abstract level of consideration, policies may also constrain the adjustment of autonomy itself in an agile computing context.

The FlexFeed middleware realizes the goal of agile computing for distributed sensor networks. FlexFeed addresses several challenges including providing efficient sensor data feeds, hierarchical distribution of data, and policy enforcement. FlexFeed relies on a coordinator that computes resource utilization costs in order to determine the best possible data distribution approach.

Ciarán Bryce from the University of Geneva then presented A Security M odel for Autonom ous System s. This talk described results from the European project entitled SECURE (IST-2001-32486), a collaboration between the Trinity College Dublin, the University of Cambridge (U.K.), the University of Strathcylde (U.K.), the University of Aarhus (Denmark) and the University of Geneva (Switzerland).

The goal of the SECURE project is to develop a trust-based security model for autonomous systems. Given the very large number of entities in these systems, a model of security was designed that is closer to the way that humans establish trust than to traditional computer models. The heart of the SECURE project is the development of a computational model of trust that provides the formal basis for reasoning about trust and for the deployment of verifiable security policies. The trust model alone is not sufficient to allow us to deliver a feasible security mechanism for the global computing infrastructure. It is equally important that we understand how trust is formed, evolves and is exploited in a system, i.e., the trust lifecycle; how security policy can be expressed in terms of trust and access control implemented to reflect policy; and how algorithms for trust management can be implemented feasibly for a range of different applications. Further activities address these issues based on an understanding of trust derived from the formal model but also contributing to the understanding of trust as a feasible basis for making security decisions to be embodied in the model.

The result has been the development of a software framework encompassing algorithms for trust management including algorithms to handle trust formation, trust evolution and trust propagation. The framework was used in the development of a SPAM filter application that classifies mail messages as SPAM based on the trust established in the message sender, either via observation of his behaviour or from recommendations received for him. This application is being used to help us to evaluate the SECURE approach. More information about SECURE can be found at the web site:

`http://secure.dsg.cs.tcd.ie.`

Conclusions

The consensus at the end of the workshop was that the workshop was a success, and that the theme of object mobility is present in applications, in some form or another.

One of the issues discussed at the end of the day was whether the workshop series should continue to be held in the context of the ECOOP conference. On the one hand, the number of attendees has been falling over the years as the vision of objects roaming the Internet becomes less attractive. Research into mobility has shown that security is still a major challenge and that programming abstractions for building mobile object applications are missing.

It was suggested that the pervasive computing field might be closer to the mobile object domain today than is standard object-orientation. Many of the issues that are treated in mobile objects occur in pervasive computing. In the former, mobility occurs through objects and threads changing their site of execution. In the later, mobility occurs by physically carrying the device – and its objects and threads – from one network environment to another. A key suggestion in the future is to involve people from the pervasive computing domain in the workshop series.

All papers and presentations of this year's workshop and of all previous editions are available at our website:

`http://cui.unige.ch/~ecoopws`

Fifth International Workshop on Object-Oriented Reengineering*

Roel Wuyts[1], Stéphane Ducasse[2], Serge Demeyer[3], and Kim Mens[4]

[1] Université Libre de Bruxelles, Brussels, Belgium
roel.wuyts@ulb.ac.be,
http://homepages.ulb.ac.be/~rowuyts/
[2] University of Bern, Bern, Switzerland
ducasse@iam.unibe.ch,
http://www.iam.unibe.ch/~ducasse/
[3] University of Antwerp, Antwerp, Belgium
http://win-www.uia.ac.be/u/sdemey/
[4] Université catholique de Louvain, Louvain-la-Neuve, Belgium
kim.mens@info.ucl.ac.be,
http://www.info.ucl.ac.be/ingidocs/people/km/research/KimResearch.html

Abstract. This paper reports on the results of the *Fifth International Workshop on Object-Oriented Reengineering* in Oslo on June 15, 2004. It enumerates the presentations made, classifies the contributions and lists the main results of the discussions held at the workshop. As such it provides the context for future workshops around this topic.

1 Objectives of the Workshop

The workshop on Object-Oriented Reengineering was co-located with the 18th European Conference on Object-Oriented Programming, and took place at Oslo (Norway) on June 15, 2004. There were 13 participants, most of which contributed with a position paper that was reviewed and revised before the workshop.

The workshop gathered people working on solutions to reengineer object-oriented legacy systems, a vital matter in today's software industry. We claim that software evolution and reengineering is a key issue of software engineering, be it object-oriented or not. This shift of importance is starting to be noticed in research and industrial efforts.

The workshop builds upon the following important related achievements:

1. a series of workshops on Object-Oriented Software Evolution and on
2. Object-Oriented Software Re-engineering held at OOPSLA'96, ECOOP'97, ESEC'97 [1], ECOOP'98 [2], ECOOP'99 [3], WSR1999, WSR2000, WSR2001, ECOOP'2003 [4] and ETAPS2003.

---

* The title of this report should be referenced as "Report from the ECOOP 2004 Fifth International Workshop on Object-Oriented Reengineering".

J. Malenfant and B.M. Østvold (Eds.): ECOOP 2004, LNCS 3344, pp. 177–186, 2004.

3. The work done in the FAMOOS project (Framework-based Approach for Mastering Object-Oriented Software Evolution), carried out within the ESPRIT IV framework.

4. The Scientific Research Network on Foundations of Software Evolution funded by the Fund for Scientific Research — Flanders, Belgium[1] and the related Scientific Network "Research Links to Explore and Advance Software Evolution (RELEASE)" funded by the European Science Foundation Scientific Network[2].

2   Contributions

Eight papers were accepted in the workshop. This section gives an overview of the contributions (in no particular order)[3].

Opportunities and Challenges in Deriving Metric Impacts from Refactoring Postconditions by Bart DuBois (bart.dubois@ua.ac.be).

Refactoring transforming the source-code of an object-oriented program without changing its external observable behaviour is a restructuring process aimed at resolving evolution obstacles. Currently however, the efficiency of the refactor process in terms of quality improvements remains unclear. Such quality improvement can be expressed in terms of an impact on Object-Oriented metrics. The formalization of these metrics is based on the same constructs as refactoring postconditions. Therefore, using a uniform formalism, we can analytically derive how refactorings affect OO metrics. The result of these derivations are conditional impact descriptions, which specify under which conditions a refactoring improves or degrades a specific OO metric.

Based on these conditional impact descriptions, refactoring guidelines can be composed which focus time-investment only in those refactoring opportunities that will improve known indicators for specific quality indicators. Such qualitative feedback helps to steer the refactoring process, which is essential to make refactoring a technique for supporting maintenance. More empirical research will verify the practical usefulness of these guidelines from an external quality perspective.

Logic and Trace-Based Object-Oriented Application Testing by Stéphane Ducasse (ducasse@iam.unibe.ch), Michael Freidig and Roel Wuyts (homepages.ulb.ac.be/~rowuyts/).)

Due to the size and the extreme complexity of legacy systems, it is nearly impossible to write from scratch tests before refactoring them. In addition object-oriented legacy systems present specific requirements to test them. Indeed late-

---

[1] http://prog.vub.ac.be/FFSE/network.html

[2] http://labmol.di.fc.ul.pt/projects/
release/

[3] The full papers can be found on the workshop's website:
http://kilana.unibe.ch:9090/WOOR

binding allow subclasses to change fundamental aspects of the superclass code and in particular call flows. Moreover Object-oriented programming promotes a distribution of the responsibilities to multiple entities leading to complex scenario to be tested. In such a context one of the few trustable source of information is the execution of the application itself. Traditional forward engineering approaches such as unit testing do not really provide adequate solution to this problem. Therefore there is a need for a more expressive way of testing the execution of object-oriented applications. We propose to represent the trace of object-oriented applications as logic facts and express tests over the trace. This way complex sequences of message exchanges, sequence matching, or expression of negative information are expressed in compact form. We validated our approach by implementing the prototype tool TestLog, which uses MethodWrappers [5] to reify an execution trace, and reasons on this using Soul [6], a logic programming language that can directly reason over Smalltalk objects, and can execute Smalltalk code. We used TestLog to test the Moose reengineering environment [7] and a meta-interpreter.

Visualizing and Characterizing the Evolution of Class Hierarchies by Tudor Girba (girba@iam.unibe.ch) and Michele Lanza (lanza@iam.unibe.ch).

Analyzing historical information can show how a software system evolved into its current state, but it can also show which parts of the system are more evolution prone. Yet, historical analysis implies processing a vast amount of information which makes the interpretation difficult. To address this issue, we introduce the notion of history of source code artifacts as a first class entity and define measurements which summarize the evolution of such entities. We then use these measurements to define polymetric views [8] for visualizing the effect of time on class hierarchies [9]. We show the application of our approach on one large open source case study and show how we can classify the class hierarchies based on their history.

Analyzing Large Event Traces with the Help of a Coupling Metrics by Andy Zaidman (Andy.Zaidman@ua.ac.be) and Serge Demeyer.

Gaining understanding of a large-scale industrial program is often a daunting task. In this context dynamic analysis has proven it's usefulness for gaining insight in object-oriented software. However, collecting and analyzing the event trace of large-scale industrial applications remains a difficult task. In this paper we present a heuristic that identifies interesting starting points for further exploratory program understanding. The technique we propose is based on a dynamic coupling metric, that measures interaction between runtime objects.

Reverse Engineering Aspectual Views Using Formal Concept Analysis by Kim Mens (kim.mens@info.ucl.ac.be) and Tom Tourwé (Tom.Tourwe@cwi.nl).

In this position paper, we report on an initial experiment using the technique of formal concept analysis for reverse engineering aspectual views from object-oriented source code. An aspectual view is a set of source code entities, such as class hierarchies, classes and methods, that are structurally related in some way, and often crosscut a particular application. Initially, we follow a lightweight approach, where we only consider the names of classes and methods. This simplistic technique already results in the discovery of interesting and meaningful aspectual views, leaving us con- fident that more complex approaches will perform even better, and should be studied in the future.

Automatic Renovation of Java Programs Using ReRAGs — Examples and Ideas by Torbjörn Ekman (torbjorn@cs.lth.se) and Görel Hedin (gorel@cs.lth.se).

When a language evolves and new features are added, it is usually desirable to renovate existing programs to make use of the new features. Some new features could make old programs illegal, and make renovation necessary. Other new features may allow old idioms to be replaced by clearer code. The evolution need not always concern the language as such. It could as well concern the evolution of standard frameworks, for example by adding new operations that should be used in favor over others that are deprecated.

This paper outlines how these kinds of problems can be handled using Rewritable Reference Attributed Grammars (ReRAGs), an object-oriented translation technique that we have recently developed [10]. In ReRAGs, a program is represented as an object-oriented abstract syntax tree (AST). Computations on the AST, e.g., to support name analysis, type checking, etc., are easy to express in ReRAGs, and can be used by conditional rewrite rules that can transfrom the AST to a suitable new form.

In the evolution of the Java programming language from 1.4 to 1.5, a number of new language constructs are added, allowing many programs to be simplified. This paper uses the new for-loop construct, that allows many iterations to be expressed in a simpler way, as a running example illustrate a renovation technique based on ReRAGs.

Constructing a Project Model and a Metadata Model for Experience Extraction by Hei-Chia Wang (hcwang@mail.ncku.edu.tw).

This paper proposes a project model and an experience metadata model to remember project experiences for software re-engineering. The experiences could be any product in the process of a project, such as plan documents, UML diagrams, and source code. In a software project, many phases and activities will be gone through and many artefacts will be generated. Properly organizing these resources for reuse can facilitate software re-engineering. However, in the past, the metadata schema for describing experience has not been defined and this made the resources difficult to store in a unified format for public searching and reusing.

The paper proposes a way of keeping all related project experiences in an experience web to solve this problem. The experience stored in this repository can then be retrieved and reused. Once an experience is reused, a feedback will be given as a new experience and the relation will be linked. Consequently, an experience web can be established for later users. The user can therefore get different views from previous works.

Towards an Aspectual Analysis of Legacy Systems by Bedir Tekinerdogan (B.Tekinerdogan@ewi.utwente.nl).

Aspect-Oriented software development provides explicit mechanisms for coping with concerns that crosscut many components and are tangled within individual components. Current AOSD approaches have primarily focused on coping with crosscutting concerns in software systems that are developed from scratch. In this paper we will investigate the applicability of AOSD to the evolution of legacy information systems. Various approaches have been already proposed to enhance LIS, however, these approaches have not explicitly considered crosscutting concerns and/or AOP techniques. We provide a categorization of legacy systems and give some early results in identifying and specifying aspects in legacy systems.

We also had two researchers that provided us with a position statement instead of a full paper:

1. *Jonne Itkonen's Position Statement.* Jonne's interest in object-oriented reengineering comes from the software evolution side. It is interesting to see how the software develops over time, what kind of structures, patterns and anti-patterns emerge, when and why. Not only should this data and knowledge be used as input for reengineering practices, but to validate the choices made on forward engineering. He would like to see this to help to design better tools for software developers. Tools, that can be used in a way that Charles Rich and Richard C. Waters explained in their article "Programmer's Apprentice". That is, tools, that report gently to the developer the suspicious structures that have have lurked into the code, possibly suggesting alternative designs, possibly even learning from the choices made.

    We are confirming the discovered methods and metrics, and tools written, by applying them to an in-house developed study enrolment and management system called Korppi. It is a web-based system written mostly in Java, and it has been in development since 2001. As many different projects have written, developed and changed it over the years, it's code has started to show some unwanted features. This is why it gives as a pretty good example of the so called "real world code" to reengineer. The Korppi development team has also been a valuable asset when evaluating the design of the tools, and the applicability of the tools to real world software development situations.

2. *Isabel Michiels's Position Statement.* In the context of the ARRIBA research project, we are exploring techniques and tools that can support the integration of large-scale software entities that have not necessarily been designed to coexist. As a basis for these techniques, we are doing research about code mining, i.e. the extraction of knowledge out of large-scale, poorly or non documented software applications. Therefore we create abstract representations of these systems, and then use a logical engine for reasoning about and extracting knowledge out of the systems .Recently, we started exploring

the use of aspect technology as instrumentation mechanism to explore and register the behavior of legacy systems in order to understand what these systems do and how their components relate to one another. By now we established a mapping of COBOL code to an XML representation of that code, and we are able to go back from that XML representation to COBOL. And we are using a declarative language as a medium to express aspects and pointcuts to instrument the XML representation of the COBOL code.

All this material was available to the participants of the workshop, and they were asked to familiarize themselves with each others' positions and research before the start of the workshop. This eased the discussions.

3   Presentations

The morning session was devoted to selected presentations, subdivided in groups. The presentations were chosen by the organisers because they had a higher potential for generating issues that would stimulate the discussions.

To structure the morning presentations we decided to group the submitted papers in three topics. Note that other groups could have been chosen, but these choices distributed the presentations quite evenly.

- Topic 1: Metrics. Several papers used metrics to attempt to characterize evolution or aid with refactoring.
    - Visualizing and Characterizing the Evolution of Class Hierarchies uses metrics obtained from the version information of a system to visualize evolution of a system.
    - Analyzing large event traces with the help of a coupling metrics introduces a metric that is useful to quickly get evolution information on large event traces.
    - Opportunities and challenges in deriving metric impacts from refactoring postconditions wants to derive the impact from a refactoring on source code by studying its pre- and postconditions, and as such determining whether it is useful to apply it.
- Topic 2: Program understanding. Since systems to be reengineering are typically unknown, some submissions discussed techniques to aid with program understanding.
    - Reverse Engineering Aspectual Views using Formal Concept Analysis discusses how the mathematical technique of formal concept analysis could be used to understand an existing system.
    - Logic and Trace-based Object-Oriented Application Testing uses logic queries on the execution trace to help express and test on patterns found in the execution of the software.
- Topic 3: Various. Last but not least we were left with two papers that we could not fit into meaningful groups because they differed from the other submissions and each other.

- Automatic renovation of Java programs using ReRAGs shows how a rewriting system can be used to help code evolve, for example from one version of a language to another one.
- Constructing a Project Model and a Metadata Model for Experience Extraction proposed a meta model to capture and use experience.

4   Discussion

The afternoon session was entirely devoted to discussions. A common decision was made to discuss about the following 5 topics in a single group:

Transformations. The participants identified that there clearly is a need for a more structured approach to transforming code. A lot of the participants were interested in refactorings in this context, and identified the need for pre- and postconditions of refactorings to become explicit. If this were the case, refactorings could be compared across tools (or even across languages, up to a certain extent), and they could be kept track of as semantic entities (which would help the analysis of evolution histories). The participants doubted that is was realistic to formalize the transformations themselves. As a result from a comparison between the ReRag rewrite system presented in the morning session, and Soul (a logic meta-programming language that allows one to reason on Smalltalk and Java code) an overview of Soul was presented by R. Wuyts. Soul has, both as advantage and disadvantage, that it is a logic programming language, meaning that users need to be able to write logic programs, while ReRags uses Java (which results in slightly larger programs, but in the same language). Both approaches stress the fact that they are declarative as a key asset. When discussing unit tests, and their relation to code, the participants decided that it would be beneficial to co-evolve unit tests and code.

Dynamic Analysis. Several techniques exploit dynamic information (typically gathered from code instrumentation) to analyse systems. The lack of a common interchange format was perceived as problematic by some participants, since it meant that different existing tools were not interoperable.

Abdelwahab Hamou-lhadj mentioned that he was working on CTF, a common dynamic information common exchange trace format, which resulted in a lot of discussion, especially regarding the meta information used to represent the dynamic information and the comparisons with other models. Important is that the model allows annotations of events (and hence that it is open), that it has built-in compression by representing the trace as an acyclic graph, and that it is streaming. As a result, participants agreed that CTF could be very interesting, but that more work needs to be invested to determine to see whether their current approaches could be expressable in the format. For example one participant needs to explictly keep the state of objects, which is currently not supported by CTF (it reifies objects by their identifier only).

Visualization. Since in a lot of cases large data sets needs to be represented somehow, visualizing is an important topic that needed to be discussed. A first question raised was why not many approaches use 3D visualization approaches, add sound (some research plays back programs, allowing a trained developer to recognize bugs audibly), or employ multiple monitors. The general feeling was that m ore research in hum an-com puter interaction is necessary to m eaning-fully use such advanced visualization techniques. In the absence of this research, current tools that use such techniques should take care to stay functional. A second question raised was why even simple visualization technology is not used more often in the context of reengineering. The participants indicated that vi-sualoverload (resulting in too m uch scrolling) and the lack of properly integrated tools ham pered the broader usage of visualization.

Meta Modeling. A fourth topic that was discussed extensively focussed on meta modeling, and first of all on the requirements for a meta model for reengi-neering. First of all it is important to note that for space reasons alone a meta model representation is preferred over an abstract syntax tree (AST)-based model. Experience by several independent partners also agreed on the fact that a comm on language independentA ST representation is extrem ely com plicated to obtain. Next a number of advantages and disadvantages of three existing m eta-m odels were discussed: D M M , G X L and TA .

- DMM: is a model for representing the static part for different system and program artefacts. It does not capture the history. But, as mentioned by Ducasse, this is an orthogonal issue. While DMM is used widely, the absence of an API means that tool support is lacking.
- GXL: an XML-based model for storing source code as a graph. It has the disadvantage that it is extremely verbose and not very readable, but the advantage that it is standardized. But it also lacks support by tools (as put by one participant: there is a difference between talking and doing).
- TA (tupple attributes): a nicer model, but not used a lot.

Last but not least S. Ducasse noted that languages that languages that sup-port introspection make it easier to write tools to extract meta models. However most of them (with Smalltalk and CLOS as notable exception) forget to add access and invocations of ▪elds and m ethods. As a result one cannot ask 'who references this particular item', and these rules have to be coded by individual rules (which, depending on the scoping rules of the language, can become very difficult and error-prone).

Tools and Techniques. This topic was concerned with what experience do people have with tools and techniques useful to support object-oriented software engineering. A decision was made to add a webpage to the website for the work-shop to let people list the tools they m ake or use. Following tools will certainly be listed: MOOSE (a language-independent reengineering environment that sup-ports program visualization and has support for evolution analysis), SourceNav-igator (a stable tool to parse C++ and Java, and was recommended by some participants), RERags (a rewrite tool for Java), Soul (a logic meta-programming language that supports Smalltalk and Java).

5   Conclusion

The workshop brought together researchers working on object-oriented reengineering. Apart from lots of experiences and information that was exchanged on the workshop, the following bigger questions were raised:

- pre- and postconditions of refactorings need to become explicit.
- support is need to co-evolve unit tests and code.
- the CTF (Common Trace Format) model to interchange execution traces is interesting but needs more work.
- more research in human-computer interaction is necessary to meaningfully use all kinds of advanced visualization techniques.
- visual overload (resulting in too much scrolling) and the lack of properly integrated tools hamper the acceptance of visualization techniques.
- a common language independent AST representation is extremely complicated to obtain.

Tackling these problems will certainly result in interesting discussions to be held at the following workshop that is being planned.

About the Organizers

Prof. Stéphane Ducasse, from the University of Berne, is a member of the Software Composition Group headed by Prof. Oscar Nierstrasz.

Prof. Serge Demeyer is leading a research group investigating the theme of "Software Reengineering" (LORE - Lab On REengineering). They are the authors of the book "Object-Oriented Reengineering Patterns" published by Morgan Kaufman [11].

Prof. Kim Mens is one of the originators of the "reuse contract" technique for automatically detecting conflicts in evolving software [12] and is currently interested in the problem of "co-evolution" between source code and earlier life-cycle software artifacts [13].

Prof. Roel Wuyts bootstrapped research in co-evolution of design and implementation with the declarative meta-programming language Soul [14]. He focusses now on language symbiosis, program composition and programming language support for unanticipated evolution.

References

1. Demeyer, S., Gall, H., eds.: Proceedings of the ESEC/FSE Workshop on Object-Oriented Re-engineering. TUV-1841-97-10. Technical University of Vienna — Information Systems Institute — Distributed Systems Group (1997)

2. Stéphane, D., Weisbrod, J.: Report of the ecoop'98 workshop on experiences in object-oriented re-engineering (1998)
3. Ducasse, S., Ciupke, O., eds.: Proceedings of the ECOOP'99 Workshop on Experiences in Object-Oriented Re-Engineering, Forschungszentrum Informatik, Karlsruhe, Germany (1999) FZI 2-6-6/99.
4. Demeyer, S., Ducasse, S., Mens, K., Trifu, A., Vasa, R.: Report of the ecoop'03 workshop on object-oriented reengineering (2003)
5. Brant, J., Foote, B., Johnson, R., Roberts, D.: Wrappers to the Rescue. In: Proceedings ECOOP '98. Volume 1445 of LNCS., Springer-Verlag (1998) 396–417
6. Wuyts, R.: Declarative reasoning about the structure object-oriented systems. In: Proceedings of the TOOLS USA '98 Conference, IEEE Computer Society Press (1998) 112–124
7. Ducasse, S., Gîrba, T., Lanza, M.: Moose: a collaborative and extensible reengineering environment. In: Reengineering Environments. to be filled (2004)
8. Lanza, M., Ducasse, S.: Polymetric views — a lightweight visual approach to reverse engineering. IEEE Transactions on Software Engineering **29** (2003) 782–795
9. Gîrba, T., Ducasse, S., Lanza, M.: Yesterday's weather: Guiding early reverse engineering efforts by summarizing the evolution of changes. In: Proceedings of ICSM 2004 (International Conference on Software Maintenance). (2004)
10. Ekman, T., Hedin, G.: Rewritable Reference Attributed Grammars. In: Proceedings of ECOOP 2004. Volume 3086 of Lecture Notes in Computer Science., Springer-Verlag (2004)
11. Demeyer, S., Ducasse, S., Nierstrasz, O.: Object-Oriented Reengineering Patterns. Morgan Kaufmann (2002)
12. Lucas, C.: Documenting Reuse and Evolution with Reuse Contracts. PhD thesis, Programming Technology Lab, Vrije Universiteit Brussel, Brussels, Belgium (1997)
13. D'Hondt, T., De Volder, K., Mens, K., Wuyts, R.: Co-evolution of object-oriented software design and implementation. In: Proceedings of the international symposium on Software Architectures and Component Technology 2000. (2000)
14. Wuyts, R.: A Logic Meta-Programming Approach to Support the Co-Evolution of Object-Oriented Design and Implementation. PhD thesis, Vrije Universiteit Brussel (2001)

Evolution and Reuse of Language Specifications for DSLs (ERLS)*

Thomas Cleenewerck[1,**], Krzysztof Czarnecki[2],
Jörg Striegnitz[3], and Markus Völter

[1] PROG, Vrije Universiteit Brussel, Belgium
[2] University of Waterloo, Canada
[3] Research Centre Juelich, Germany

Abstract. This report summarizes the results of the workshop on evolution and reuse for language specifications for DSLs. The focus of the workshop was twofold: exploration of the current research activities concerning reuse and evolution of language specifications and discussion of the identification, extraction, and composition of reusable parts of DSL specifications. The workshop combined presentations with focused discussions on these emergent topics: reusable assets, role of object-orientation, conflicts among reused assets, and the quest for a DSL test-case example to facilitate and guide future discussions.

1   Introduction

With the advent of rewrite rule systems, template transformation languages and attribute grammars, the development of compilers for domain-specific languages has been greatly facilitated. Despite these technologies compiler development is usually started from scratch, i.e. the grammar and the semantic specifications are completely written starting from nothing. Unfortunately the cost of adapting an existing DSL implementation or the implementation of another similar DSL often boils down to the same amount of work. Naturally, given the already existing implementation of a DSL, this cost is too high.

The aim of this workshop was to bring researchers together and provide a forum to discuss the issues in DSL development and evolution with the particular focus on identifying, extracting, and composing reusable parts of DSL specifications. We specially concentrated on, but not limited the workshop to the use of object oriented techniques and concepts like encapsulation and inheritance to make DSLs more reusable.

Since this was the first workshop of its kind, the focus of the workshop included a wide range of topics concerning evolution and reusability to explore

---

* The title of this report should be referenced as "Report from the ECOOP 2004 Workshop on Evolution and Reuse of Language Specifications for DSLs (ERLS)".
** Edited by.

J. Malenfant and B.M. Østvold (Eds.): ECOOP 2004, LNCS 3344, pp. 187–201, 2004.

current research activities. The topics of interest include but were not limited to:

- Implementation technologies and paradigms: transformation systems, meta-programming, interpreters
- Reusable assets ranging from individual transformations to patterns
- Reusability techniques: customization, configuration, adaptation, encapsulation, compositions and inheritance

Of course not all of the above suggested topics could be discussed. The following discussion topics are the topics that emerged during the workshop in the afternoon: reusable assets, role of object-orientation, conflicts among reused assets, and the quest for a DSL test-case example to facilitate and guide future discussions.

The workshop report consists of summaries of the contributions in section 2 and reports of the discussions and the results of the topics 3. Table 1 lists all the participants and their affiliation. The position papers are available at the workshop website (http://prog.vub.ac.be/~thomas/ERLS/).

Table 1. List of workshop participants

Name	Affiliation	E-mail Address
Thomas Cleenewerck	*Vrije Universiteit Brussels, Belgium*	tcleenew@vub.ac.be
Krzysztof Czarnecki	*University of Waterloo, Canada*	czarnecki@acm.org
Jörg Striegnitz	*Research Centre Juelich, Germany*	J.Striegnitz@fz-juelich.de
Markus Völter	*none*	voelter@acm.org
DeLesley Hutchins	*University of Edinburgh, UK*	d.s.hutchins@sms.ed.ac.uk
Barrett R. Bryant	*University of Alabama at Birmingham, USA*	bryant@cis.uab.edu
Pieter Van Gorp	*Universiteit Antwerpen, Belgium*	Pieter.VanGorp@ua.ac.be
Simon Dobson	*Trinity College, Dublin IE*	simon.dobson@cs.tcd.ie
Sofie Goderis	*Vrije Universiteit Brussels, Belgium*	sgoderis@vub.ac.be
Torbjörn Ekman	*Lund University, Sweden*	torbjorn.ekman@cs.lth.se
Görel Hedin	*Lund University, Sweden*	gorel@cs.lth.se

2   Contributions

The contributions are ordered as follows: two cases, a formalization and two implementations. We start off with two contributions where a domain is presented and for DSLs where there is a great potential for reuse and evolution and the conflicts that may arise during reuse. The two domains are respectively user interfaces and middleware patterns. The implementation of the former is based on logic rules and the implementation of the latter by a transformation system with various extensions. The next contribution investigates and attempts to formalize object oriented approaches using descriptive logics for capturing transformational knowledge. The following two contributions each incorporated reuse in their transformation system, respectively ReRags and TLG.

2.1   The Write Once, Deploy N MDA Case Study Combining Performance Tuning with Vendor Independence (Pieter Van Gorp)

Summary. In this paper, we presented a complex middleware pattern as a realistic case study for model-driven development. From this case study we derived concepts of a transformation language that would allow us to generate such patterns towards different application servers. The language supports the specialization of common transformations, the separation of concerns, and evolution conflict resolution. For the latter feature we applied the familiar concept of design by contract. Following this principle, code generation can be integrated with architectural consistency rule checking: consistency constraints can be considered as the postconditions of transformation rules. Failed postconditions trigger a reconciliation unit that can be considered as the body of a transformation rule. Reconciliation units can often be generated from declarative OCL postconditions. For new components, reconciliation will result in code generation. Evolution conflicts in existing software require reconciliation units that correct the inconsistencies without regenerating other items. For this purpose, such units can analyze source and target models by navigating traceability models that maintain a persistent link between these two. Since conflict resolution logic cannot always be generated by the transformation engine, transformation specifiers need language support to implement it manually. By carefully inheriting from common superclasses in the design of metamodels for PIMs and PSMs, one can specify consistency constraints across abstraction layers in a very concise manner. At a low level of abstraction, imperative code templates can be integrated with the model (to model) refinement process.

2.2   A Declarative DSL Approach to UI Specification - Making UI's Programming Language Independent (S. Goderis, D. Deridder)

Summary. A large number of researchers are trying to find innovative ways to tackle the problem of separation of concerns. In our research we focus on the concern of User Interfaces and application interactions because these are seldom separated from each other. A clean separation would nevertheless facilitate UI development and evolution. Figure 1 depicts this idea of separating the UI from its underlying application. One should keep in mind that both interact externally with each other and internally with themselves. When separating concerns it will therefore be important to focus on factoring out these interactions since they are the main cause for the code entanglement. In our work we focus on the interactions between the UI and the application (figure 1 number 3), and within the UI itself (figure 1 number 2), as well on the different layers of abstraction within the GUI box (figure 1 number 1).

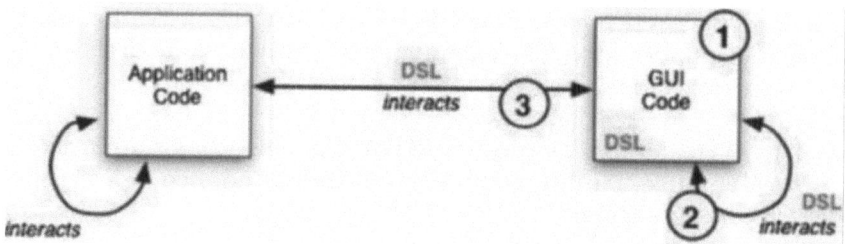

Fig. 1. Separating GUI and Application Interactions

Once the separation between UI and application is achieved, different examples can be thought of where separation is beneficial. For instance, deploying the UI to another platform without having to rebuild completely, or adapting the interface to different kinds of users.

In order to solve this problem we will express high level UI components (i.e. the GUI components in figure 1 (1 and 2)) by means of declarative meta-programming. This denotes that a user interface is described declaratively by means of rules and facts and later on is composed through a problem solver. Different concerns, as well as different UI abstraction layers, will lead to different sets of rules. The problem solver will combine all of these in order to get to the user interface that is wished for. Consequently we provide a declarative user interface framework as a domain specific language to program user interface concerns and their interactions with the application code.

As shown in figure 1 we can consider the declarative specifications for the User Interface and the interactions as being a DSL, namely for the domain of User Interfaces.

Relation to the Workshop. We have encountered several issues related with DSL's for which the workshop could provide us with new insights.

Inheritance. Reusing existing rule-bases can be done by parameterizing one rule-base by another one. We need to investigate how to ensure inheritance between different UI sets, or how to make them dependent on each other. This is also related to evolution issues.

Customization and Configuration. We want to generate the UI based on the declarative rules and facts. Nevertheless we should not restrict ourselves to static User Interfaces since a lot of the UI power is currently left unattended because of this staticness. It should be possible to customize a User Interface dynamically. For instance, when someone resizes a window, another layout strategy might have to be applied. These layout strategies should be applied to the user interface dynamically, without need for recompiling the static UI.

Another issue related to this topic is putting constraints between the different UI building blocks [1, 2]. For instance, how to specify that a certain component should be placed above another one (and what to do if conflicts arise)?

Evolving and Adapting. It is not clear which abstractions will be needed. It is not possible to anticipate all possible abstract UI components, as this will depend on the developers' point of view as well. Furthermore a certain abstraction might play a role in different UI framework parts, and it is not always clear where to draw the line. We acknowledge that it will never be possible to completely separate the UI from the application (since they have to interact at some point in time). But also on the level of the application interactivity layer it is not clear where to stop making abstractions.

Once the basic entities are defined, they are composed into more complex and abstract entities. A user will want to use these higher level entities without having to care about lower level entity descriptions. This implies that users will consider the high level entities as black boxes without knowing what the low level entities actually look like. Therefore two high level entities may contradict each other without the user knowing it.

2.3   Knowledge Representation in Domain Specific Languages (D. Hutchins)

Summary. Most domain-specific languages are layered on top of an existing general-purpose language, such as C or Java. As a result, it is convenient to think of individual DSLs (or DSL fragments) as program transformation systems; they translate domain-specific constructs into a base language.

Transformation systems can be difficult to use because they operate on abstract syntax trees, and do not have any real understanding of the *meaning* of the code they modify. Two different transformations may conflict if they alter the code base in incompatible ways. I argue that capturing the semantic meaning of domain-specific concepts is the real challenge of developing reusable DSLs.

A domain-specific language encodes knowledge about the problem domain. Instead of encoding knowledge by translating domain-specific concepts into C or Java, I propose to define such concepts directly, using a dedicated knowledge-representation language. Under this model, a DSL or DSL fragment is represented as an ontology of concepts and relations between concepts. Combining two different DSLs together is a matter of merging the two ontologies.

Description logics (DLs) are a knowledge representation system that is currently used by the artificial intelligence community. DLs as they are ordinarily defined are essentially a type system – they can describe the interface of objects, but they cannot be used to implement the behavior of objects. This limitation prevents them from being used to implement DSLs.

In this paper, I introduce the Sym calculus, which is a formal object calculus that extends descriptions logics into a full-fledged programming language. This language not only supports standard functions, classes, and generics, but it can be used to implement virtual types, mixins, features, components, and aspects. Sym achieves this flexibility because it is based on a knowledge representation system, and can thus handle the semantics of terms at a much more abstract level than mainstream OO languages.

Relation to the Workshop. The focus of this workshop was using object-oriented techniques to make DSLs more reusable. Most proposals discussed ways of using OO constructs to implement program transformation systems.

It is well known that one way to implement a grammar is to define each non-terminal as a class. If a non-terminal has more than one definition then it can be defined as an abstract base class, with each variation as a concrete subclass. The grammar thus becomes a class hierarchy. This is a particularly attractive mechanism for implementing more advanced systems, such as attribute grammars, because the class hierarchy can be used to annotate the abstract syntax tree with additional information beyond that what's present in the raw syntax.

The advantage of using classes to represent non-terminals is that each node in the abstract syntax tree has a type and a well-defined interface. This means that the AST can be queried and manipulated via method calls, just like any other OO data structure.

This is essentially the philosophy that I have taken with the Sym calculus. My approach is to ignore the question of syntax altogether, and focus on developing more flexible ways of defining and manipulating complex object structures.

Concepts in Sym are defined much like OO classes, but they may be related to other classes via type equations. Type equations are evaluated at compile-time. This means that Sym can be used as an "extensible compiler" architecture for implementing DSLs. If an abstract syntax tree is constructed at compile time (via an external parser), then information will propagate through the tree at compile-time. Unlike the OO method-call mechanism, there is no run-time penalty to using domain-specific constructs.

2.4   Reusable Language Specification Modules in JastAdd II (T. Ekman, G. Hedin)

Summary. This paper discusses how to build domain specific languages (DSL) on top of a general purpose language (GPL) using our language implementation tool JastAdd II. The specification formalism in JastAdd II is based on Rewritable Reference Attributed Grammars (ReRAGs) [3], that combines object-oriented abstract grammars, static aspect-oriented programming, reference attributed grammars, and conditional rewriting.

The technique is illustrated by evolving a matrix framework into new language constructs that are added on top of Java. The GPL, in this case Java, is extended at both the syntactic level and the semantic level. The semantic extensions affect name analysis as well as type analysis. The code generation finally transforms the extensions into the base language by using a matrix computations framework. The extension is done in a modular way and re-uses large part of the static semantic analysis from the base grammar.

Relation to the Workshop. The DSL approach used in the paper is based on the JastAdd II tool, a combined attribute grammar and transformation system. The paper focuses on how to express DSL extensions and GPLs in a modular fashion and how to compose new languages from these individual parts. The same technique can be used to customize an exisiting language.

The specification formalism in JastAdd II allows modular specification and provides several synergistic mechanisms for separation of concerns, e.g. inheritance for model modularisation, static AOP for cross-cutting concerns, rewrites that allow computations to be expressed on the most suitable model, and declarative formalism to allow transparent composition of attributes and rewrites. This enables the DSL and GPL specifications to be expressed separately in modular fashion and combined in a transparent way.

2.5   Object-Oriented Language Specifications: Current Status and Future Trends (M. Mernik, X. Wu, B. R. Bryant)

Summary. The challenge in domain-specific language definition is to support modularity and abstraction in a manner that supports reusability and extensibility [4]. The language designer wants to include new language features incrementally as the programming language evolves. Ideally, a language designer would like to build a language simply by reusing different language definition modules (language components), such as modules for expressions, declarations, etc. These reusable components should be straightforwardly extendible to reflect language design changes.

Our position statement is that the use of object-oriented techniques and concepts, like encapsulation and inheritance, improves language specification languages to a much greater extent towards their modularity, reusability and extensibility than any other technique. In this paper two of our latest approaches are briefly described. In the LISA approach the attribute grammar as a whole is subject to inheritance employing "Attribute grammar = Class" paradigm. We call this multiple attribute grammar inheritance. With our approach, the language designer is able to add new features (syntax constructs and/or semantics) to the language in a simple manner by extending lexical, syntax and semantic specifications. In the second approach, we combine Object-Oriented Two-Level Grammar [5] specifications with Java to implement domain-specific languages. We specify the lexical, syntax and abstract (domain-independent) semantics rules by TLG specification and implement the concrete semantics by user-supplied Java classes. We also apply several object-oriented design patterns (interpreter pattern, composite pattern, chain of responsibility pattern) to help improve the modularity and abstraction level of TLG specification to enhance the reusability of formal specifications in language implementation.

Relation to the Workshop. Object orientation plays an important role in the design of language specifications for DSLs. This paper is a position paper that describes the evolution of object-oriented language specifications. It explores the current status of applying modular formal specification in language definitions and introduces several modern language specification approaches, such as object-oriented attribute grammar [6], intentional programming [7], two-level grammar [8], action semantics [9], JTS[10], JJForester [11], etc. Current shortcomings and future trends of language specification language are also introduced at the end of this paper.

We conclude in the paper that the use of object-oriented techniques and concepts, like encapsulation and inheritance, improves language specification languages to a much greater extent towards their modularity, reusability and extensibility than any other technique. To illustrate this, our two latest object-oriented approaches are introduced in the paper. The attribute grammars we used in LISA system have been modeled as objects, which is similar to Jast-Add II introduced by Ekman and Hedin. Likewise the two level grammars in our second approach are also modeled and designed after objects. We go even further and state that many object oriented design patterns are in fact useful for the implementation of a TLG-based compiler generation system. Our two approaches have been proven successful in developing various domain-specific languages (e.g. SODL, COOL, AspectCOOL, PLM, PAM, Matrix language). Our experience with these non-trivial examples shows that object-oriented specification languages are very useful in managing the complexity, reusability and extensibility of language definitions. Specifications become much easier to read, maintain and to modify.

3   Discussions

3.1   Reuse

Reuse of DSL specifications is hard, because of their domain dependent nature. Lifting part of these specifications to general language constructs and generally applicable semantics is therefore not easy. We compiled a non-exhaustive list of general constructs and semantics that are most likely to be found in many DSL implementations:

Value Construction. The computation of new values and new AST nodes.

Value Propagation and Distribution. The propagation of new values throughout the tree and the distribution of the values to the AST nodes that require these values. Various propagation schemes like tree traversals, xpaths, attribute inheritance and synthesis, etc., already exist.

Name Resolution and Binding. In the grammar names are merely a syntactic entity represented by some kind of an identifier or hierarchical identifier. Because the actual semantic meaning of names is often context dependent, a name resolution or analysis process must resolve their semantic meaning.

Type Analysis. Statically typing (whether it is explicit or implicit in the DSL language) is a cornerstone to insure the correctness of a program written in a DSL. In order to infer type correctness type analysis is required which (1) connects the use sites to the declaration sites and (2) checks the operations in the use sites against the operation supported by the type.

Construction of Typed Nodes According to a Pattern. The type of an AST node plays in many transformation systems a crucial role because it is one of the quantifiers to select certain transformations and computations on the tree. However, the exact type can often only be determined after some analysis of the tree. Therefore during transformation, the obtained information is used to construct new AST nodes of a more appropriate type.

Resolving Non-local Results of One-to-Many Transformations. One-to-many transformations exert an influence in the form of non-local AST nodes on various parts of the parse tree. Appropriate mechanisms are needed to deal with such non-local nodes.

Null-Value Elimination. Structural mismatches between the source and target language break the fundamental in-place substitution principle of many transformation systems because certain source AST nodes cannot be substituted by the produced new AST nodes after their transformation. When this is the case, null-values or empty subtrees must be removed from the tree.

The items in this list are closely related to implementation, compiler and language infrastructure. How broad or narrow the notion of infrastructural mechanism can be interpreted was a point of discussion. Some argued that DSL editors, etc., were also part of this infrastructure, while others rather narrowed this notion to implementation mechanisms. An item that is particularly difficult to categorize are semantic validators. If the semantics of a language is described via a transformation to another language, then semantic validators would not be considered as infrastructure. When the semantics of a DSL is expressed with some kind of formalism, validators based on that formalism would be considered as infrastructure. Currently the reuse of language modules is largely investigated in context of evolving a DSL to another version. Out of the discussions we strongly believe that there is a lot reuse potential for language modules belonging the same domain. More research and field expertise is needed to further broaden and increase reuse for the development of DSLs. The exploration of reuse among researchers that are often not familiar with the domain proved to be very difficult. Concrete cases of reuse could help us understand the required mechanisms and the current difficulties better. Since reuse is rather at its early stages, these cases are currently not available.

3.2 Role of Object Orientation

Object orientation plays an important role in the design of todays transformation systems. The introduction of OO techniques and concepts in transformation systems facilitates the development of new languages, increases the modularity of the components and allows more reuse. Let us discuss each of the techniques and concepts borrowed and used of OO in the design of a transformation system.

The notion of an object as an encapsulated entity with state and behavior gets applied to language modules (either BNF rules, rewrite rules, linglets, templates or attributes depending on the kind of transformation system). Language modules become configurable entities containing data and behavior. In Delesley, language entities are concepts modeled after objects with fields and functions. The attribute grammars discussed by Ekman and Bryant have been modeled as objects where productions correspond to classes and attributes to methods.

Likewise the two level grammars discussed in Bryant are also modeled and designed after objects. Finally VanGorp points out that template transformation languages like xDoclets -used to implement his model to code transformations- are encapsulated entities containing datamembers and functions. Inheritance is the mechanism object orientation offers for code reuse and code specialization. In class based languages subclasses can override and inherit behavior and data, respectively specialize and reuse existing code. Inheritance has been successfully adopted towards language modules of DSLs. In the JastAdd II transformation system described in the paper of Ekman, name analysis and typing for a matrix extension to Java is introduced with a minimal amount of effort hereby reusing existing name analysis and specializing typing rules. VanGorp argues that there is a lot of potential for an inheritance mechanism to reduce the code base containing the model to model and model to code transformations of MDA for distributed enterprise Java applications. Bryant goes even further and shows that many object oriented design patterns are in fact useful for the implementation of a TLG-based transformation system.

Besides inheritance as a reuse mechanism there are other mechanisms as well. Goderis is exploring how to achieve reuse in the context of logic programming by specializing certain rules or providing extra alternatives. This way existing rules are reused and new behavior is accented for.

Because of this encapsulation, DSL designers can now pay more attention to modularity, in terms of the relationship of the language components with the rest of the compiler. Modularity is important because it is one of the corner stones for reusability. In other words, encapsulation brought us a step closer to our goal.

3.3   Conflicts

The reuse of language constructs and semantics can be hampered by conflicts and information dependencies that occur when two or more of those reusable elements are combined. The definition of a conflict was a point of much debate in the workshop. From the debate the following preliminary definition of a conflict can be summarized as follows: a conflict is a non-trivial resolution of two language components, which have a mutual interest. An interest of a language component can be every part of the language on which the component depends:

Constrains. The conditions under which a component may be executed.
Requirements. The conditions which a component relies on when executing.
Inputs. The information or structures the component needs to performs its task.
Outputs. The information or structures the component produces and/or changes of a conflict categorization of conflicts.

In target-driven transformation systems the conflicts are resolved manually in the modules that produce the targets. These modules actually deal with several concerns at the same time. The transformations are in this regard not well modularized from a separation of concerns viewpoint. Source-driven transformation systems tried to unhook most of the different concerns and put them in separate modules. As a result of this separation of concerns, the conflicts that were manually tackled must now be tackled by the transformation systems itself. There exist various schemes to cope with conflicts. The most common approach is to define an order by scheduling the two language components to achieve the desired combined result. The prerequisite for this schema is that there must exists some correct partial order in which the language modules must be executed. But for language modules which both create the same entity with a different content, ordering is not sufficient and more invasive composition mechanisms are needed like the ones supported in LTS (Linglet Transformation System). Additionally the constraints and requirements of language modules could also be more taken into account. The semantics of a DSL is often specified by its translation to another language. Although this is a formal semantics, it is hard to derive any properties form such a description. Up till now, one could consider typing as the most widely spread implementation of this idea. A richer mechanism like operational semantics, descriptive logic, f-logic, ontology semantics, etc., would certainly help to detect and even resolve conflicts. Despite most of these formalisms being around for quite some time, very few DSL designers seem to revert to them. There are several reasons for that but the main reason is that it is for most DSLs (like for example specification languages) quite unclear what we would like to describe. Krzysztof suggested the use of state charts as an alternative mechanism. Although it doesn't capture the full semantics, there are interesting properties that can be calculated out of a start chart. In an offline discussion Bryant and Cleenewerck argued that a more suitable and specific semantic formalism is needed. Some of the attendees pointed out that a lot of those conflict resolution schemes can be found in other research tracks like aspects, hyperspaces, subject oriented programming, etc. The ideas and mechanisms of these schemes probably could contribute to the existing transformation systems.

3.4   DSL Test-Case Example

The discussions were often broken off or stalled because of the absence of a single shared test-case DSL. The problems mentioned were initially very abstract because we didn't want to delve to deep in a particular problem domain and implementation approach. Soon we realized that such statements are no help for anybody. Not every participant had the same background making it impossible to understand the statement. In order to concretize some of the statements, the statements were rephrased with more problem domain information. Although this helped a bit, since most of the participants were not familiar with problem domain itself, the general problem domain knowledge was difficult to grasp. Moreover, in a single afternoon there is not enough time to discuss the problem domain, the general concepts and the ideas behind the domain-specific statement. So after such an attempt it was up to the other participants to recognize the abstract statement in their problem domains. Not seldom due to the absence of such recognition of ideas and statements there was only a poor response. It became rapidly clear that a shared test-case DSL would greatly ease the discussions.

In response to that need we tried first to get a more solid grip on the true nature of a domain-specific language. In Ekman and Bryant a DSL is an set of syntactical and semantical extensions to a general purpose language. In DeLesley a DSL is described with a set of concepts and rules described using logics. The DSLs of VanGorp are meta-models which are refinements (model to model transformations) and model to code transformations. In Goderis a DSL is a logic program querying facts to produce an effect. Clearly there is no strict definition of what a DSL is. We found that DSLs can be classified according to number of axes:

Language Axis. The language axis refers to the relationship between GPL (general programming language) and DSLs. DSLs range from GPL programs, to extensions of GPLs all the way to an entirely new language.

Structural Axis. The structural axis refers the amount of flexibility and mechanisms to compose a program. In GPL a program is a complex composition of fine-grained language constructs. Any construct can almost be composed with any other construct. The more domain-specific a DSL is, the more the composition of language constructs is restricted. At the far-end of this spectrum we find the specification languages, which constitute merely of the assigning of values to properties. Domain-specifity is thus more a matter of a degree. Because of this wide range of DSLs we may need to revert to a set of smaller DSL examples instead of searching after the holy grail in programming languages.

As a first attempt to reach a shared test-case DSL we distilled and reformulated our research questions to a set of requirements to which such a common DSL should adhere to.

A Declarative DSL Approach to UI Specification. The three most important and distinguishing research questions in the context of a declarative DSL approach to UI specifications are:

- How to make keywords dependent on each other
- Which keywords should be provided and which keywords can be extended. And how to allow a developer to extend keywords.
- How to ensure a developer does not violate the meaning of a certain keyword when extending it such that contradictions are avoided.

From these research questions we can compile the following list of requirements to which a test-case DSL should adhere to:

- Dependencies among keywords
- Open variability's in the language which must be provided and/or extended.
- Conflicting and non-conflicting constraints caused by simple use of the existing keywords or by the extensions of them.

Knowledge Representation in Domain Specific Languages. There are various DSL implementation techniques with very different capabilities. A formal comparison of these techniques would reveal how knowledge is captured and made executable. From that comparison, properties on the kind of information that can be handled can be derived and used to establish a hierarchy of DSL techniques and DSLs, much like the regular-language, context-free language, and Turing machine hierarchy in complexity theory.

For example: Small-step operational semantics is a classical way of formally defining programming languages. Small-step semantics is based on the process of term *reduction*. Each term is reduced to a simpler term, until it becomes a *normal form* which cannot be further reduced. Reduction has two nice properties:

(1) Reductions only make use of local information. Reducing a term only affects that particular term; it does not affect any surrounding terms. Assuming that the reduction rules are confluent, reductions can be applied in any order.

(2) User-defined reductions can be supported within a language by means of partial evaluation. If an expression only references constants, then it can be evaluated (i.e. reduced) at compile-time. This mechanism is completely transparent and requires very little in the way of compiler support; it's what the Sym calculus uses to handle type equations.

Full transformation systems which use rewrite rules are considerably more powerful than partial evaluation. A rewrite rule can affect any number of terms in any way. Rewrite rules are also especially prone to clashes and conflicts, which makes them difficult to use and debug.

The important question here is, in the context of common DSL test-case, what kinds of DSLs require the full power of a rewriting transformation system, and what kinds can be implemented with simpler processes.

Reusable Language Specification Modules in JastAdd II. Our paper deals with the approach where a GPL is extended with a DSL, and where the DSL extensions are expressible in the base language. The DSL is transformed into the GPL either through direct translation to GPL code or through calls to a framework. This situation is useful when the generated code is to verbose to hand code or to complicated to write by hand and therefore needs additional semantic checks. The DSL high-level representation may also simplify domain specific optimizations.

Some questions that form the basis for our work include:

Composition. How can we express the language specifications to enable transparent composition of separate GPL and DSL specificiations?

Separation of Concerns. How can we achive good separation of concerns in the language specifications? We would like to separate the logical phases in the compiler such as name binding, type analysis, and code generation while at the same time allowing language constructs to be expressed in a modular fashion.

GPL API. How do we model a suitable API to the GPL that the DSL can use to reuse existing components such as name binding and type analysis? Can the DSL also contribute to these components, e.g. add new scopes to the name binding module?

A suitable test-case DSL for this research must require a tight integration with the target language (in this case the GPL) compilation phases, e.g. name binding, type analysis, etc., on the one hand, but remaining modular with respect to the target language and other extension module on the other hand.

Object-Oriented Language Specifications: Current Status and Future Trends. As already mentioned, the use of object-oriented techniques and concepts greatly improves language specification languages towards better modularity, reusability and extensibility. To achieve modularity, extensibility and reusability to the full extent these techniques need to be combined with aspect-oriented techniques since semantic aspects also crosscut many language components. Moreover, special algorithms have to be invented (e.g. forwarding) to improve modularity of underlying formal methods. Another shortcoming of current approaches is lack of scalability since they do not fully support grammatical operators such as described in [12]. The ideal solution where the language designer can freely combine language components based on different formal methods is less likely to appear in forthcoming years.

In order to experiment or validate further research in this direction a test-case DSL is required which is more like a family of DSLs or a DSL production line constructed out of a set of different language components.

4   Conclusion

Summarizing what was said in each discussion topic, we conclude that :

- There is a lot of potential for reuse in (1) languages that must be customized to support different sub-domains by means of language extensions and in (2) languages that evolve overtime to keep up with changes in their associated domains. Reusable language specifications for various domains are still rather rare and tend to be more related to language implementation mechanism then to language features.
- Object orientation plays an important role in the design of todays transformation systems. The introduction of OO techniques and concepts in transformation systems facilitates the development of new languages, increases the modularity of the components and allows more reuse.
- The reuse of language constructs and semantics can be hampered by conflicts and information dependencies that occur when two or more of those reusable elements are combined. A richer mechanism like operational semantics, descriptive logic, f-logic, ontology semantics, etc., but customizable and more suitable for DSLs would certainly help to detect and even resolve conflicts. Also the ideas and mechanisms of conflict resolution schemes available in aspects, hyperspaces, subject oriented programming, etc. probably could contribute to the existing transformation systems.
- The discussions were often broken off or stalled because of the absence of a single shared test-case DSL. As a first attempt to reach a shared test-case DSL we distilled and reformulated our research questions to a set of requirements to which such a common DSL should adhere to.

References

1. Epstein, E., Lalonde, W.: A smalltalk window system based on constraints. In: Proceedings of OOPSLA88, ACMPress (1988)
2. Freeman-Benson, B.: Constraint technologie for user-interface construction in ThingLabII. In: Proceedings of OOPSLA89, ACMPress (1989)
3. Ekman, T., Hedin, G.: Rewritable Reference Attributed Grammars. In: Proceedings of ECOOP 2004. Volume 3086 of Lecture Notes in Computer Science., Springer-Verlag (2004)
4. M. Mernik, J. Heering, T.S.: When and how to develop domain-specific languages. Technical Report Technical Report, SEN-E0309, CWI (2003)
5. Bryant, B., Lee, B.S.: Two-level grammar as an object-oriented requirements specification language. In: Proceedings of the 35th Annual Hawaii International Conference on System Sciences (HICSS'02)-Volume 9, IEEE Computer Society (2002) 280
6. Paakki, J.: Attribute grammar paradigms a high-level methodology in language implementation. ACM Comput. Surv. **27** (1995) 196–255
7. de Moor, O.: Intentional programming. (2001)
8. van Wijngaarden, A.: Revised report on the algorithmic language ALGOL 68. Acta Inf. **5** (1974) 1–236
9. Doh, K.G., Mosses, P.D.: Composing programming languages by combining action-semantics modules. Sci. Comput. Program. **47** (2003) 3–36
10. Batory, D., Lofaso, B., Smaragdakis, Y.: JTS: tools for implementing domain-specific languages. In: Proceedings Fifth International Conference on Software Reuse, Victoria, BC, Canada, IEEE (1998) 143–153
11. Kuipers, T., Visser, J.: Object-oriented tree traversal with jjforester. In van den Brand, M., Parigot, D., eds.: Electronic Notes in Theoretical Computer Science. Volume 44., Elsevier (2001)
12. Wile, D.: Integrating syntaxes and their associated semantics. Technical Report Technical Report, USC/Information Science Institute (1999)

Programming Languages and Operating Systems*

Olaf Spinczyk[1], Michael Schoettner[2], and Andreas Gal[3]

[1] University of Erlangen-Nuremberg, Germany
Olaf.Spinczyk@informatik.uni-erlangen.de
[2] University of Ulm, Germany
schoettner@informatik.uni-ulm.de
[3] University of California, Irvine, USA
gal@uci.edu

Abstract. This report gives an overview over the First ECOOP Workshop on Programming Languages and Operating Systems (PLOS 2004). It explains the motivation for the workshop and gives a summary of the workshop contributions and discussions during the workshop.

1   Introduction and Overview

The ECOOP Workshop on Programming Languages and Operating Systems (PLOS) has its root in the ECOOP workshop series on Object-Orientation and Operating Systems (OOOSWS), which started in conjunction with ECOOP'97. Over the past years the number of participants of OOOSWS has grown constantly and many high quality papers have been presented at this workshop, some of which were later published at relevant conferences and journals. For 2004, the workshop organizers decided to give the workshop a more interactive format and a stronger focus on the special tension and nearly historic relationship between programming languages and operating systems. To underline this change in focus, a new workshop title was chosen as well.

The PLOS workshop aims to bring together researchers and developers from the programming languages (PL) and the operating systems (OS) domain. It provides a platform for discussing new visions, challenges, experiences, problems, and solutions arising from the application of advanced programming and software engineering concepts to operating systems construction.

The 2004 PLOS workshop was a very successful event and was attended by 23 participants (11 presenters, 1 invited speaker, 2 organizers, and 9 other ECOOP attendees) from 11 different countries. The papers presented at the workshop as well as the presentations by the working groups formed during the workshop are available from the workshop web site at **http://www.betriebssysteme.org/plos**.

The remaining parts of this report are organized as follows. Section 2 describes the motivation for organizing a workshop on this particular combination of topics. This is followed by a section on the requirements on workshop contributions, the reviewing

---

* The title of this report should be referenced as "Report from the ECOOP 2004 Workshop on Programming Languages and Operating Systems".

J. Malenfant and B.M. Østvold (Eds.): ECOOP 2004, LNCS 3344, pp. 202–213, 2004.

process, and the workshop format. Section 3 briefly summarizes the presentations given at the workshop. A major part of the workshop was dedicated to group work and discussions. The results of this work are presented in section 5. The report concludes with some final remarks in section 6 and tables containing the list the workshop participants and program committee members.

2   Motivation

Developing operating systems (OSs) is a highly complex task. OS programmers often have to deal with millions of lines of code and common OS issues like concurrency, performance optimization, real-time, deadlocks, and configurability make their work even harder.

Today, the historic language C—created in the early seventies—is still predominantly used to implement OS. Only in a few cases have OS implementors switched to more advanced languages like C++ or Java. Developing a new kernel and device drivers from scratch is often rendered impossible by the sheer size and complexity of operating systems. Thus, research is often limited to extend or modify existing systems. Widely deployed general purpose OSs like Linux and the Windows OS family continue to be developed using very conservative methods and languages. Modern software engineering concepts and languages, which are well-known and proven in other domains, are not adopted for the sake of performance optimization and backward compatibility. However, the arousing discussion about security and reliability of OSs especially with respect to internet attacks is an example that shows the drawbacks of the traditional development approach and a demands for new ideas.

In this workshop we wanted to address this problem from the programming language perspective and bring together researchers from both domains. The aim was to facilitate a lively discussion about novel approaches in OS construction based on language concepts in general. Examples are object-orientation, type safety, language support for OS verification, testing/debugging, separation of concerns by aspect-oriented programming, and domain-specific languages.

3   Requested Contributions and Workshop Format

Prospective participants were asked to submit a position paper or experience report of 4 pages maximum. Suggested topics included, but were not limited to:

- object-oriented OSs, type-safe languages for OS
- separation of concerns in OS code, AOSD and OS
- domain-specific languages for OS development
- language support for OS verification, testing, and debugging, static configuration, dynamic reconfiguration, and specialization

Each submitted paper was evaluated by at least two reviewers. All reviewers are destinguished members of the community and have an excellent international reputation. The names of the program committee members are listed at the end of this report.

Only authors of accepted papers were invited to the workshop to present their work. For each presentation a 15 minutes slot was scheduled. All authors were asked to give only a brief summary of their paper during the workshop (5-10 minutes). To make the workshop highly interactive accepted papers were posted on the workshop website ahead of the venue and participants were expected to familiarize themselves with the content of the other contributions. In particular, participants should prepare questions, comments and a list of suggested improvements for the authors.

Table 1. PLOS 2004 Workshop Program

9.00 - 9.05	Welcome and introduction
9.05 - 09.35	Keynote: *"Domain Specific Languages : A Safe and Efficient Approach for Developing OSes"*, Gilles Muller
09.35 - 09.45	Discussion
09.45 - 10.30	Session 1: Languages *"Modularity for the Bossa process-scheduling language"*, Julia L. Lawall, Anne-Françoise Le Meur, and Gilles Muller *"APPLE: Advanced Procedural Programming Language Elements"*, Christian Heinlein *"Implementing high-performance in-kernel network services with WYKIWYG"*, Sapan Bhatia and Charles Consel
10.30 - 11.00	Coffee break
11.00 - 12.30	Session 2: Operating Systems and Security *"On Objectifying Untyped Memory in Java Operating Systems"*, Christian Wawersich, Meik Felser, and Jürgen Kleinöder *"Managing Code Complexity in a Portable Microkernel"*, Uwe Dannowski *"Flexible Bindings for Type-Safe Embedded Operating Systems"*, Damien Deville, Christophe Rippert, and Gilles Grimaud *"Generic Trigger Variables and Event Flow Wrappers in Reflex"*, Karsten Walther, Reinhard Hemmerling, and Jörg Nolte *"Executing Legacy Applications on a Java Operating System"*, Andreas Gal, Christian Probst, and Michael Franz *"Adding protection to the object model as the basis for secure operating systems"*, Darío Álvarez, María Ángeles Díaz Fondón, Iván Suárez Rodríguez, Fernando Álvarez García, and Lourdes Tajes Martínez
12.30 - 13.30	Lunch
13.30 - 14.00	Session 3: Aspects in Operating Systems *"On Adaptable Aspect-Oriented Operating Systems"*, Daniel Lohmann, Wasif Gilani, and Olaf Spinczyk *"RADAR: Really low level Aspects for Dynamic Analysis and Reasoning"*, Owen Stampflee, Celina Gibbs, and Yvonne Coady
14.00 - 15.00	Discussion groups: Questions
15.00 - 15.30	Coffee break
15.30 - 16.15	Discussion groups: Answers
16.15 - 17.00	Presentation and discussion of the workshop results

4   Presentations

The workshop started with an invited talk by Gilles Muller from École des Mines de Nates, France. He is the vice chair of the ACM Special Interest Group on Operating Systems (SIGOPS) and, thus, represents European research on operating systems in the international community.

The presentations of the position papers were grouped in three sessions. The complete workshop program is shown in table 1.

In the following the talks and discussions during the presentation sessions are briefly summarized.

4.1   Invited Talk

In his talk Gilles motivated the interest of using domain-specific languages (DSLs) for operating system development. Domain-specific languages are languages that are restricted to express a family of applications. They offer a high level of abstraction over the considered domain. The advantages are that programming is easier, faster, and more concise. Also domain-specific languages enable strict constraints to be enforced and specific properties to be determined. Therefore, domain-specific languages permit to increase software quality and the productivity level.

To present this approach Gilles described his work on Bossa, a framework and a DSL for the development of scheduling policies. Bossa provides high-level abstractions that are specific to the domain of scheduling. These constructs simplify the task of specifying a new scheduling policy and facilitate the static verification of critical safety properties. Bossa has been prototyped in Linux and can transparently replace the 2.4 kernel. Its overhead is negligeable on standard applications such as compilation, web servers and multimedia players. Overall, Gilles and his team found that Bossa simplifies scheduler development to the point that kernel expertise is not required to add a new scheduler to an existing kernel. As such Bossa is used to teach scheduling in several French Universities.

Gilles finished his presentation with an impressing demonstration of a running Bossa/Linux system. With a Bossa scheduler he was able show a video stream while compiling the Linux kernel. The same experiment, but with using the standard Linux scheduler, led to unacceptable quality of the video.

4.2   Languages

The first session of the workshop was dedicated to programming languages design for or used in operating system development and implementation. Julia Lawall gave the first presentation on *Modularity for the Bossa process-scheduling language*. Bossa is a framework for implementing complex scheduling policies in standard "off-the-shelf" operating systems. Most existing operating systems use a general purpose language to implement the scheduler proper. In contrast, the Bossa framework provides a domain-specific language (DSL) that eases the specification of scheduling policies. Even more importantly, because Bossa is a DSL, it allows to verify certain key properties of the scheduler specification and implementation. For example, schedulers written in Bossa are automatically checked for complete coverage, i.e. the Bossa compiler ensures that appropriate handler code exists for all states of the scheduler. After a brief introduction of Bossa, the talk quickly focused on the idea of modular schedulers. The speaker showed how complex schedulers such as Round-Robin (RR) can be composed from simple scheduler modules (in this particular example Block, Interrupted, Fork, FIFO-Timeslice, FIFOYield, and RRPriority). At the language level this was achieved by adding a new module construct to the Bossa language. The talk concluded with an assessment of the modular Bossa language by re-engineering the Linux scheduler from existing Bossa modules. For this, only a single Linux scheduler-specific module had to be written. The remaining aspects of the Linux scheduler could be covered by re-using five existing Bossa scheduling modules.

The next talk was given by Christian Heinlein. He reported on *Advanced Procedural Programming Language Elements* (APPLE). The talk started of with a critique of existing programming languages such as AspectJ. The speaker felt that they were too complex, making them both, hard to learn and hard to apply them in practice. He went on and pointed out the simplicity of procedural programming languages in comparison to today's object-oriented/aspect-oriented languages. Given this observation, the speaker suggested to go back to the starting point of procedural programming languages and extend them into a different direction in order to create advanced procedural languages which are significantly simpler than aspect-oriented languages while offering comparable expressiveness and flexibility. In particular, the speaker proposed replacing simple, statically bound procedures with arbitrarily overridable dynamic procedures, which are roughly comparable to around advice in AOP. With some additional syntactic sugar, this would cover the whole range of dynamic dispatch strategies usually found in object-oriented languages. Similarly, replacing simple record types having a fixed set of fields with modularly extensible open types and attributes would cover classes and interfaces, field declarations in classes and aspects, multiple inheritance and subtype polymorphism, plus inter-type parent declarations and advice based on get and set pointcuts. The speaker then walked the audience through some example code written in "Advanced C", an advanced procedural programming language. The talk concluded with a discussion how Advanced C could be used in Operating System development. The speaker pointed out that operating systems, like software systems in general, evolve over time and that this kind of evolution is not well supported by existing programming languages. When using conventional programming languages, the introduction of each new concept typically requires modifications to numerous existing functions in addition to implementing new functions. Using open types and dynamic functions instead offers at least the chance to be able to implement new functionality in a truly modular way by grouping new functions and necessary redefinitions of existing functions together in a single new unit of code.

The final talk in the Languages section was given by Sepan Bhatia on *Implementing High-performance In-kernel Network Services With WYKIWYG*. In his talk the speaker introduced the design philosophy and underlying principles of WYKIWYG, a language to implement high performance in-kernel network services. A WYKIWYG compiler, unlike compilers for traditional languages, is empowered with the knowledge of underlying OS mechanisms such as task management, memory management, the device I/O interface etc. It generates code which is especially optimized for these mechanisms, and can even go as far as modifying or extending them in a controlled manner. The speaker went on and discussed several optimizations that the WYKIWYG compiler is able to perform because it has access to domain specific knowledge. For example, superpages are used for memory allocations whenever possible for improved TLB utilization. The WYKIWYG compiler also optimizes in-kernel servers by removing the overhead usually associated with thread management by collapsing them into language-level constructs. Finally, the WYKIWYG compiler removes the overhead of going throw an socket interface by generating code that directly communicates with the OS scheduler, instead of using high-level abstractions such as signals or system calls.

4.3   Operating Systems and Security

The second – and longest – session of the workshop focused on operating systems and security. The first talk on *Objectifying Untyped Memory in Java Operating Systems* was given by Christian Wawersich. He presented an approach to access memory-mapped registers directly from Java. For this, the authors use memory objects to describe the layout of a memory region. Instead of composing memory objects from primitive types, which would limit the approach to the few primitive types specified by the JVM, but would not work for unsigned registers or different byte orders, the authors compose memory objects from predefined Java classes. Each such Java class represents a certain register size and endianess. Using classes to describe the layout of memory-mapped register regions allows to precalculate the offset for each register inside the memory area. The authors use an extended Java virtual machine that recognizes get and set operations on memory objects and replaces them with machine instructions to faciliate the memory access. This eliminates the overhead that is usually incurred for method calls. The talk concluded with a performance evaluation of memory objects in the JX operating system. The speaker pointed out that while memory objects offer a significant performance improvement over direct memory access using native Java methods, their greatest benefit is a more robust driver design. Driver developers often wrap the memory objects into task-oriented classes that provides methods for structured access to memory. These methods just delegate the calls to a memory object. This kind of abstraction layer can be replaced by memory-mapped objects and therefore improve the performance.

The next talk in the OS and security section was held by Uwe Dannowski. He argued that increasing code complexity can become a serious issue even in a software project as small as a microkernel. He reported on how the authors address this problem in the L4Ka::Pistachio microkernel. Pistachio consists of multiple configuration dimensions and code fragments are assigned to the appropriate dimensions. The kernel build system combines code fragments for the specific configuration. While this approach avoids the run-time costs of a full-blown object-oriented design, it does not avoid code duplication. To address the code duplication problem, the authors model the code selection with class hierarchies using multiple inheritance and polymorphism. However, the run-time overhead of virtual functions results in a serious performance hit for the time-critical kernel functionality. To address this latter problem, the authors apply class flattening to completely eliminate the overhead of virtual function calls. The idea of class flattening is to create a flat class from a whole class hierarchy by moving members of base classes into the most derived class while maintaining semantic equivalence as far as possible. The authors evaluation shows that a kernel with flattened class hierarchies performs as fast as one without class hierarchies. The speaker concluded that, thus, advanced object-oriented programming techniques need no longer be avoided in performance-focused microkernels.

Damien Deville gave the next talk on *Flexible Bindings for Type-Safe Embedded Operating Systems*. He presented the binding model implemented in Camille, an extensible operating system for resource-limited devices. Modern embedded systems need on the one hand to fully exploit the limited hardware on which they run and on the other hand to dynamically adapt themselves to changes in their runtime environment. Camille is an exokernel which supports static customization of components and dynamic loading of system extensions. Dynamic kernel and application adaptation is implemented by an inter-component communication model. This model is based on flexible bindings which permit to fully customize the way components interact with each others. Bindings can be static, virtual or compiled to guarantee performances of inter-component communications. The speaker argued that using this model it is possible to build a flexible operating system without sacrificing runtime performances, even for devices as constrained as smart cards. He first presented the architecture of the Camille exokernel and the intermediate language Facade into which applications and system components are translated to ease type verification and then described the component model implemented in Camille and the inter-component communication scheme based on embedded binding factories. The talk concluded with an outlook on future work, which will focus on the extraction of selected properties such as the worst case execution time of real-time tasks from generated code.

The next talk by Andreas Gal dealt with *Executing Legacy Applications on a Java Operating System*. The speaker argued that the lack of backward-compatibility of Java operating systems is one of the main reasons for their lack of acceptance in the commercial marketplace. Traditional Java operating systems are design to execute Java programs – and Java programs only. They struggle to support established application programming interfaces such as POSIX or Win32 as these are founded on the idea of direct execution of native machine code. Instead of using the host processor to execute legacy applications which would eliminate most of the security and portability benefits of using a type-safe language for the OS implementation in the first place, the authors propose using a virtual processor implemented on top of the virtual machine infrastructure to execute legacy applications. The speaker explained that the virtual processor translates the machine code into Java bytecode, which is then executed by the Java virtual machine. Because many modern virtual machines employ just-in-time (JIT) compilation, this means that frequently execute machine code fragment will be translated to host machine code and execute at full machine speed. The talk concluded with a discussion of potential future work, which includes porting the prototype system to the Microsoft .NET architecture. The speaker argued that the .NET VM has better capabilities regarding dynamic code generation, which should help to overcome certain performance systems in the current implementation.

Dario Alvarez gave the last talk in this section on *Adding protection to the object model as the basis for secure operating systems*. He pointed out that Operating environments (such as operating systems) are increasingly being built with object-oriented languages, for with virtual-machine runtime environments implementing the object model of the language. He argued that adding protection to the traditional properties of the object model (the ability to protect a method call from an object to another object) can be of great advantage for building secure operating systems, using the protection property of the object model as the access-control mechanism of the system. Using well-known capabilities model as protection mechanism, the authors have implemented this approach in their experimental system Oviedo3 as well as the Microsoft .NET virtual machine (SSCLI). The speaker concluded his talk with a performance evaluation of both implementations and reported that in both cases the performance overhead was neglible.

4.4   Aspects in Operating Systems

The last paper session of the workshop covered novel ideas which exploit aspect-oriented programming for the design and implementation of operating systems.

The first talk was given by Daniel Lohmann. With his work on *Adaptable Aspect-Oriented Operating Systems* Daniel aims to provide OS support for emerging computer science areas like Pervasive Computing, Sensor Networks, Smart Devices, etc. An important common property of these areas is that many very small (mobile) devices are interacting in large networks. To cope with the strict resource limitations in this domain operating systems have to be structured as a software product-line, which is configurable at compile time and reconfigurable at run time. Aspect-Orientation has shown to be useful for the design and implementation of software product-lines. However, dynamically reconfigurable product-lines based on an aspect-oriented implementation are widely unexplored. From the technical perspective dynamic aspect weaving would be indespensible, but naturally dynamic weaving is much more expensive (in the sense of consumed resources) than loading or unloading of ordinary modules. Therefore, the talk concentrated on a bunch of techniqes which could help to make dynamic aspect weaving affordable in areas with strict resource constraints. For example, the speaker presented Server-Side Weaving (delegation of the weaving/reconfiguration to a remote server) and Application-Specific Weaver Tailoring (using *a priori* knowledge to restrict the set of potentially affected points in the code). The message of Daniel's talk was "Do as much as possible statically". This means that a lot of static knowledge exists even in a dynamically reconfigurable system. The development tools have to aid the developers to exploit their knowledge in order to build more efficient system system software.

Yvonne Coady gave the last talk of the workshop. Her paper on *RADAR: Really low-level Aspects for Dynamic Analysis and Reasoning* made the case for using aspects for dynamic analysis in OS code. The authors are convinced that an effective tool for reasoning about run-time behavior of systems software must provide selective analysis of *uninstrumented* code. Lengthy instrumentation cycles stand as a deterrent to developers who could otherwise benefit from performing customized analysis in aid of comprehension. Yvonne outlined current useful techniques for dynamic analysis of OS kernels. Especially with AspectC++, Arachne, and TinyC AOP languages and tools are maturing to a state where a really useful dynamic OS analysis tool like RADAR could be implemented and would have a chance to be accepted by OS developers.

5   Group Work

The afternoon sessions of the workshop were allocated for collaborative work in discussion groups. We formed three groups, namely the AOP experts, the type-safe and secure operating system experts, and the DSL experts. During the first discussion session each group had to prepare a list of hard questions for each of the other expert groups. In the second discussion session these questions had to be answered by the experts. The workshop closed with a panel where a speaker of each group presented the answers and all other participants had the opportunity to comment them.

The following sections show some of the questions and answers from the workshop. The whole list can be downloaded from the workshop web site.

5.1   Questions for the "AOP Experts"

1. *What is the real use of AOP in an OS?*
   First of all, there are the same goals as with other applications, i.e. better modularization and separation of concerns. However, there are also many specific OS concerns, which typically crosscut the whole implementation. Examples are the concerns which are usually associated with global OS policies like synchronization (coarse-grained vs. fine-grained) or protection (e.g. single-user vs. multi-user). Another important difference between an OS and normal software systems is that many OS are statically or even dynamically (re-)configurable. If the implementation of a crosscutting concern is well modularized it can be configured fairly easy.

2. *What problem does AOP address that can not be solved with a more traditional programming language technique?*
   AOP addresses *Crosscutting Concerns*. A traditional implementation of such concern leads to *Code Tangling*, and thus reusability, configurability, and maintainability problems.

3. *Is profiling the killer application for dynamic AOP. Are there others?*
   No, profiling is not *the* killer application. There are others. The dynamic weaving techniques have a lot in common with techniques for dynamic loading of modules. Everybody agrees that dynamically loadable modules are a good thing. What is their killer application?

4. *How feasible is dynamic weaving in static languages (performance impact)?*
   Doing something dynamically is always expensive. The idea is to do it only if you really need it. The rule of thumb should always be: "do as much statically as possible".

5. *How difficult is it to understand and teach AOP?*
   Our experience is that teaching AOP is not difficult at all if the studend has already been involved in a bigger development project where crosscutting concerns were a real problem. Experienced software developers understand AOP very quickly. In general, it is easier to teach AOP than OO.

6. *What compiler optimizations are potentially harmful for joinpoints in a dynamic AOP environment?*
   There are a lot. Basically everything that removes symbol information. For example, function inlining might hide a function from the dynamic weaver. A programmer would be unable to define advice for the execution of this function.
7. *Are static/dynamic optimization an aspect?*
   Some could be implemented as one, if they are crosscutting, e.g. caching.

5.2   Questions for the "Type-Safe and Secure Operating System Experts"

1. *Why use a language designed for applications for OS development when it is obviously not made for that?*
   To build an OS a language only needs few domain specific features (e.g. machine access operations). An OS is a very complex application and needs similar high level abstractions. Problems found in OS are similar to those found in applications like Database Servers, Web Servers, Transaction Systems. Thus, we don't see a reason for a special OS programming language.
2. *Why spend money on type-safe OS methodology instead of educating OS developers?*
   Even good programmers have a bad day and make mistakes. These mistakes are very expensive as debugging is a very time intensive labour. Tools and Methodology scale better than (educated) developers. Common errors are eliminated. Writing OS still requires educated developers. Good guys with good tools is the best combination.
3. *Killer question: How to convince the OS community and the industry that this is the way to go?*
   One has to start with domains where the problems addressed by type-safe languages are particularly grave. Another convincing argument is that type-safe languages allows to employ cheaper programmers
4. *What are the implementation and the runtime benefits of type-safe languages in OS development?*
   The implementation benefits from static type-checking. It helps catching implementation errors at compile time. Static type checking is also beneficial at runtime. For example, if the arguments of system call are strongly typed, runtime checks on these arguments can be reduced to a minimum. Type-safe languages can further be used to replace classic isolation mechanisms like MMU-based address space separation. As a result inter-process communication can be implemented highly-efficient.
5. *What is a Java OS?*
   A JavaOS is an OS that is written for the JVM machine model. It can be written in Java (Source Language), but it doesn't have to.

5.3   Questions for the "DSL Experts"

1. *Why not strip away features from existing general-purpose languages (GPLs) that hinder analysis (for example require bounded loops)?*

This is a good way to design a comprehensible syntax. However, in a DSL you often want to express things that are not natural to express in a GPL.

2. *When we have DSLed everything, how do all these DSLs integrate?*
   In the context of an OS, there would be a DSL per service. Interaction and integration are solved by service composition.

3. *How different are DSLs for different domains?*
   They are as different as declarative and imperative languages.

4. *Real world domains have the tendency to change. How do you find a language for a changing domain?*
   A well-defined domain will not change very often. We try to isolate fundamental points of the domain, not implementation details. In a well-designed language, language abstractions should mirror future evolution.

5. *Can a DSL be Turing-complete?*
   No, a Turing-complete language is a general-purpose language. However, there some DSLs which have been "badly influenced" and eventually became Turing-complete.

6. Why use DSLs and not code analysis?
   There are some things that are impossible to analyze in a GPL (e.g. termination). Analysis of DSL code only has to consider specific program patterns, that could be implemented in many different ways with a GPL.

7. *Is it always implicit that a DSL is also about verification as well?*
   Yes, DSLs help us to verify the program. At the same time, they make the life of the programmer easier. Verification is the difference between a DSL and a scripting language.

6   Final Remarks

During the months leading up to the PLOS workshop, the organizers decided to make PLOS significantly more interactive than the previous OOOSWS workshop series. To a certain extent this has been a gamble as many workshops in both fields, operating systems and programming languages, are more focused on paper presentation than actual discussion. Considering the record number of attendees, the interesting discussions resulting from the group presentations, and the feedback we got, it seems that the new format of PLOS was well received by the attendees. A quick poll at the end of the workshop indicated that there is significant interest to continue with the PLOS workshop in conjunction with future ECOOPs.

>From a distant perspective programming languages and operating systems are only small sub-disciplines of computer science. Thus, it might have been a surprise for some participants how different we speak, how different we get our motivation, and how different our solutions are. This diversity is good, but from time to time we should come together and share our latest ideas. This is essential for a research community to come up with mature solutions at the well-established conferences. We are convinced that some of the ideas presented at this PLOS workshop will follow this pattern.

Finally we would like to thank the program committee members for their reviewing work, all authors for sharing their novel ideas, and all attendees for their participation.

List of Participants

Name	Affiliation
1. Darío Álvarez	University of Oviedo, Spain
2. Rafik Amir	Amerikan Univerity, Cairo, Egypt
3. Safan Bhatia	Univesity of Bordeaux, France
4. Bartosz Blimke	University of Wroclaw, Poland
5. Gilad Bracha	Sun Microsystems
6. Yvonne Coady	University of Victoria, Canada
7. Uwe Dannowski	University of Karlsruhe, Germany
8. Damien Deville	University of Lille, France
9. Frode v. Fjeld	University of Tromso, Norway
10. Andreas Gal	University of California, Irvine, USA
11. Wasif Gilani	University of Erlangen-Nuremberg, Germany
12. Christian Heinlein	University of Ulm, Germany
13. Arushi Kawamoto	Technical University of Denmark
14. Julia Lawall	DIKU, University of Copenhagen, Denmark
15. Daniel Lohmann	University of Erlangen-Nuremberg, Germany
16. Gilles Muller	École des Mines de Nantes, France
17. Sven-Olof Nyström	Uppsala University, Sweden
18. Christophe Rippert	Inria Lille, France
19. Aline Senart	Trinity College, Dublin, Ireland
20. Olaf Spinczyk	University of Erlangen-Nuremberg, Germany
21. Robert Strandh	University of Bordeaux, France
22. Karsten Walther	BTU Cottbus, Germany
23. Christian Wawersich	University of Erlangen-Nuremberg, Germany

Program Committee Members

Name	Affiliation
1. Michael Schoettner (chair)	University of Ulm, Germany
2. Michael Franz	University of California, Irvine, USA
3. Michael Golm	Siemens AG, Corporate Technology
4. Jürg Gutknecht	ETH Zürich, Switzerland
5. Julia Lawall	DIKU, University of Copenhagen, Denmark
6. Gilles Muller	École des Mines de Nantes, France
7. Wolfgang Schröder-Preikschat	University of Erlangen-Nuremberg, Germany
8. Peter Schulthess	University of Ulm, Germany

Author Index

Lecture Notes in Computer Science

For information about Vols. 1–3253

please contact your bookseller or Springer